QUEST FOR A
PHILOSOPHICAL JESUS

QUEST FOR A PHILOSOPHICAL JESUS

CHRISTIANITY AND PHILOSOPHY IN ROUSSEAU, KANT, HEGEL, AND SCHELLING

Vincent A. McCarthy

MERCER

ISBN 0-86554-210-4

Quest for a Philosophical Jesus
Copyright © 1986
Mercer University Press, Macon, Georgia 31207

Library of Congress Cataloging-in-Publication Data
McCarthy, Vincent A., 1947–
    Quest for a philosophical Jesus.

    Bibliography: p. 225.
    Includes index.
    1. Christianity—Philosophy—History—18th century.
2. Christianity—Philosophy—History—19th century.
3. Jesus Christ—History of doctrines—18th century.
4. Jesus Christ—History of doctrines—19th century.
5. Rousseau, Jean-Jacques, 1712-1778—Views on Christianity.
6. Schelling, Friedrich Wilhelm Joseph von, 1775-1854—Views on Christianity.
7. Kant, Immanuel, 1724-1804—Views on Christianity.
8. Hegel, Georg Wilhelm Friedrich, 1770-1831—Views on Christianity.
I. Title.
BR100.M33   1986   209′.2′2   86-2521
ISBN 0-86554-210-4 (alk. paper)

CONTENTS

ACKNOWLEDGMENTS

This study began as the outcome of an NEH Summer Seminar for College Teachers conducted by Professor Hans W. Frei of the Department of Religious Studies, Yale University.

A major portion of the research and writing was made possible by fellowship grants from the Alexander von Humboldt Foundation of West Germany and from the American Council of Learned Societies.

The Philosophisches Seminar of the University of Tübingen, and Professor Klaus Hartmann in particular, provided a stimulating research environment and experience that was also personally enriching and that I shall always cherish.

Additional support was provided by the U.S.-German Fulbright Commission, Central Connecticut State University, and by the CCSU Research Foundation.

To these many patrons of scholarship and to the many helpful individuals behind the organizational names, I express my very sincere appreciation and gratitude and the hope that they shall not be disappointed in the work that they have enabled.

Vincent A. McCarthy
West Hartford, Connecticut
August 1985

PREFACE

The intellectual climate of the eighteenth and nineteenth centuries that set troubled theologians in quest of the historical Jesus was shaped not only by the work of Hermann Samuel Reimarus but also by the searing philosophical questioning of the Enlightenment and the initial responses from philosophers of the post-Enlightenment. Thus, if the title of this essentially historical study evokes a famous theological work of the early twentieth century, that is as it should be, for the two movements are intimately connected.[1]

For Enlightenment thinkers had intellectually dared all and had soon come to examine religion, to scrutinize Christianity in particular and in the process to attack many of its cherished teachings. In the wake of Reimarus's *Fragments*[2] and then of the writings of Lessing, Diderot, Voltaire and others, not only the Old Testament's God but also the New Testament's Son of God had become stumbling blocks for reasonable men, impediments and embarrassments that, they suggested, needed to be cleared from the intellectual roadway.

The momentum of Enlightenment philosophical questions and doubts combined with post-Enlightenment answers and set into motion the theological search, yet at the same time philosophy so influenced it that the theological search was not always a reaction but frequently a continuation of a philosophical quest that had preceded it.

In the chapters that follow, the philosophical quest and four principal inquiries are investigated. The works examined are more than an attempt to arrive at a philosophical notion of Jesus; they are also an attempt to express a philosophy of Christianity and to do so within philosophy of reli-

---

[1] Albert Schweitzer, *The Quest of the Historical Jesus*, trans. W. Montgomery (New York: Macmillan Publishers, 1961) from the German original *Von Reimarus zu Wrede: Eine Geschichte der Leben-Jesu-Forschung* (1906).

[2] Specifically his "Concerning the Intention of Jesus and His Teaching," a critical edition of which appears in *Reimarus: Fragments*, ed. Charles H. Talbert, trans. Ralph S. Fraser (Philadelphia: Fortress Press, 1970).

gion. The authors and works here studied are in a very real sense the first modern philosophies of religion and at the same time constitute its classical phase. But philosophy of religion must always be viewed in the light of the entire corpus or system of a thinker in order to grasp the role intended as well as the goal achieved.

Late eighteenth and early nineteenth century philosophy of religion stands as heir to the Enlightenment, with its determined liberation of thought from unquestioned belief. Yet those who, in Kant's phrase, *sapere aude* ("dared to know") were eventually courageous enough to reassess the early Enlightenment's facile dismissal of historical religion, and particularly of the Christian religion for its absurdities, crude rationalizations and rigid dogmatism. Not only had Christian history become a cause of embarrassment to modern intellectuals; in the dawning age of text criticism, earliest Christianity had become suspect for its troublesome scriptures. Ultimately, even Christianity's Jesus had become a stumbling block to intellectuals, at least guilty by association with his very own followers, while worse was intimated of them and him.

The momentum of Enlightenment philosophy of religion was to reject Christianity and its Christ and to replace them with a universal religion of reason that was so abstract as to protect it from compromise by history and human agents.

Not only did believers react but philosophers as well. Yet post-Enlightenment philosophy of religion is not philosophy of religion in the contemporary sense. The modern philosophy of religion that began with Descartes was penetrated and determined by a Christian culture that is no longer entirely ours. Hence, when late-eighteenth- and early-nineteenth-century philosophers pursue philosophy of religion, what repeatedly emerges is philosophical reflection in which the Christian religion—sometimes explicitly, other times implicitly—serves as the reference point, paradigm, and even the ideal, despite well-noted failings and little warrant for its privileged status. Not only did most major philosophical writers of the eighteenth and nineteenth centuries execute a philosophy of religion, but those who did so considered it an essential, crowning achievement of their philosophical programs.[3] All were aware of the theological applications of

---

[3]At the same time, philosophy of religion was just emerging in the early 19th century as an independent field within philosophy. And traditional university lectures reflect this. Kant, for example, lectured on rational theology, still a subdivision of metaphysics. And

their works and conceded nothing of import to the theologians. And while, for example, Kant diplomatically understated his theological claims and confined himself to arguing for the right of philosophy to enter the province claimed by theology, Hegel went much further, in this as in all else, and maintained that he was doing the authentic theology of the day—providing knowledge of God—since theologians had abandoned the task. If one wishes to judge the product strictly as philosophy of religion, one must note its important cultural limitation. But if one chooses to assess its philosophy of the Christian religion, which was at least part of the plan, one must judge each an extremely rich, suggestive, and provocative achievement for both philosophy and theology, then and now.

Four thinkers are examined in the chapters that follow, but also four types of philosophy of religion, each of which continues to be a source and to some extent a model for those who still attempt to think about the transcendent dimension of personal experience and human history in a meaningful, coherent way. The first two models, Rousseau and Kant, are the product of late rationalism; the second two, Hegel and Schelling, the product of speculative idealism. Needless to say, the four types considered in this study are by no means the only types of meaningful philosophy of religion. Each type has evident shortcomings and has been almost as noteworthy for the reactions it sparked as for the influence it exercised. Nor should this beginning, formative, and classic period of Continental philosophy of religion be the end. Moreover, there still are instructive lessons to be learned in passing through it sympathetically, circumspectly and, of course, critically.

The study of four philosophies of religion spanning the mid-eighteenth to mid-nineteenth centuries is also the examination of a significant event in the history of modern religious thought. Rousseau, Kant, Hegel, and Schelling were commited to no lesser goal than the philsosphical rehabilitation of Christianity and its Christ by finding the elusive philosophical formula for reconciling reason and revelation and then elaborating it in a philosophy of religion that would rearticulate the religion of Jesus in a pos-

---

his major work in philosophy of religion, *Religion within the Limits of Reason Alone,* was not a lecture series. However, Kant seems to anticipate the new field when, in the preface to the first edition, he suggests that the work might serve as a text in a course for theology candidates on the philosophical theory of religion. Hegel's Berlin lecture series (1821-1831) on the philosophy of religion certainly contributed to establishing philosophy of religion in its independence.

itive light, as against the destructive momentum and dark shadows cast by Enlightenment religious thought. This attempt to reconcile reason and revelation was, however, no modern apologetics, and traditional Christians were largely unpleased and unsettled by the results. For what becomes of Christianity and its Christ in the works of these philosophers occurs, of course, not for the sake of Christianity but for the sake of philosophy. The result is not always "orthodoxy"—that devilish shibboleth in religious thought. All four were aware that they were *not* toeing the reigning orthodox line. Sometimes they were confrontational about it, sometimes diplomatic. But each one, insofar as he believed that he had found a better way of articulating the truth of religion and of Christianity, sought to posit a new kind of orthodoxy. For that, the charge of "heretic" was and is raised.[4]

Rousseau, Kant, Hegel, and Schelling are not at all an unlikely company. No claim is made here, however, that the band of philosopher-theologians they represent is complete. At least two significant thinkers are omitted—Fichte and Schleiermacher.[5] Fichte, however, may be viewed as a transitional figure between Kant and Hegel, while Schleiermacher may be viewed as most essentially a theologian. But if the goal here had been a complete history of post-Enlightenment philosophy of religion, they surely would have found their place.

Late twentieth-century moderns must frequently strain their minds and imaginations to envision a century in which philosophy and theology were paramount in intellectual life. Even if religion had suffered nearly constant assault and apparently endless defeat throughout the Enlightenment, philosophy for its part was almost universally regarded as a valued contributor to the age's advance. Philosophy had freed men from ignorance, had systematized knowledge, and had begun a critique of society and religion. Negatively, it had helped stamp out the "infamy"—the fanaticism and superstition associated with established religion—in order to clear the way for the advance of reason and science. Positively (always the more diffi-

---

[4]Yet even if it were so, both heresy and orthodoxy have their place within a full history of Christian thought. And, following a suggestion of Ernst Bloch, one might even speculate that a history of so-called Christian heresies might provide real insight into and perhaps even an alternative view of what Christian religious thought has really been about.

[5]It is only to be expected that critics will make a case for others as well.

cult task), it had sought to articulate a new vision of the future based on a confidence in reason and science working in harmony.

Philosophers, however, were in honesty compelled to acknowledge that religion was not merely identical with the fanaticism and superstition that had grown up in and around it. There soon appeared philosophers who discerned wheat among the chaff and resolved to save it, not for the sake of the "wheat" itself but because of its sustaining, nourishing character. In this, Rousseau was the distinguished first, as he called a halt to the French Enlightenment's negative program in religion. In the end, he sought to save Jesus and Christianity from the deists and atheists, sometimes for reasons about which he himself seems unclear.

One might term Rousseau's response to Jesus and Christianity intuitive, even sentimental. For he saw in Jesus an admirable moral figure with whom he could empathize and even identify, and he recognized the contrast between this warm, human religious figure and the religion of increasingly cold reason that the *philosophes* were advancing. But his reembrace of Jesus and of Christianity pleased neither deists nor Christians, for it neither distanced itself sufficiently from Christianity to please the *philosophes* nor was it a clear enough return to the old foundations to satisfy the orthodox. Rousseau's direct criticisms of pretentious reason and of unreasonable religion sparked an unlikely alliance of *philosophes* and priests against him. Neither group perceived the ground-breaking significance of what Rousseau had written in the *Profession of Faith of the Savoyard Vicar*. The plea for reasonableness in religion and for tolerance of Christianity as *a* religion struck the churchmen as too little and the *philosophes* as too much. Christian circles rightly discerned no reinstitution of orthodoxy on rational grounds; *philosophes* correctly observed the trimming of reason's (and their own) pretensions and saw in Rousseau himself a prominent defector from their larger social program. The call, however, would be heard, taken up, and clarified in faraway Königsberg by Immanuel Kant who joined with Rousseau, while advancing beyond him, in a definition of religion as morality, the affirmation of Christianity as moral religion, and the salvation of its Christ as the teacher and personification of the highest morality, in spite of the lapses of Jesus' declared followers across the centuries. The Christ that they each affirmed, however, may more accurately be termed the *Chrestus,* the morally "useful," rather than the traditional *Christus,* the "anointed" of God.[6]

In Rousseau and Kant, religion, including Christianity, had been philosophically set on a new foundation—moral reason—that would, for a time at least, support only a streamlined edifice in place of the grand dogmatic cathedrals of the past. Gothic theologies could no longer count on support from philosophy and stood accused by reason of straining the foundations of any rational faith. And while Hegel soon discarded the modesty of a Rousseauean or Kantian program in philosophy of religion (and in philosophy more generally) to erect a baroque basilica without rival, it never stood entirely firm on its foundations and an eager wrecking crew appeared as soon as the master builder was interred within. Hegel's grandiose project, his precipitous proclamation of his success and his enemies' equally rash proclamation of his failure, as well as subsequent reconstruction attempts, have determined the course of much of serious philosophy and theology ever since. Overshadowed in the bombast and collapse of Hegelianism stands Schelling, straining to be different, pleading for a hearing and insisting on the living, free God of a free, fallen, and liberated creation.

In the movement from Rousseau and Kant to Hegel and Schelling, reason itself became redefined and rational religion with it. While for Rousseau and Kant reason at its greatest meant "moral reason," for Hegel and Schelling it meant "speculative reason." And from speculative reason even the "later Schelling" did not successfully free himself, despite his invocation of revelation. Nor does his category of freedom (which does distinguish him from Hegel in an essential way) veil the importance of speculative reason that binds him and Hegel together.

In Rousseau, moral reason leads to the sympathetic paring down of religion and of Christianity to natural religion. In Kant, it leads to the cau-

---

[6]The wordplay here has an ancient Roman origin that neither Rousseau nor Kant invokes or has in mind but that nevertheless is capable of expressing the important change that occurs in the Christological dimension of each's philosophy of Christianity. The Roman historian Suetonius's brief mention of a certain *Chrestus* in the *Vita Claudii* (25.4) reflects an apparent misunderstanding not only about the spelling but also possibly about the meaning of the title given Jesus. For *Christus* is simply the Latin of the Greek translation of Messiah, or anointed, while *Chrestos* means "the useful." Suetonius employs the title-name with apparently no meaning in mind. Rousseau and Kant, and many another, while holding nominally to Jesus the Christ, really mean Jesus the *Chrestus*—Jesus the (morally) Useful.

tious reconstruction of religion and Christianity within the limits of reason, where Christianity is assessed a totally natural religion and indeed its highest form. In Hegel, with the new vision of reason comes the dazzling prospect of religion and Christianity as the self-manifesting life of the absolute that philosophy alone is adequate to articulate and complete. Schelling develops his philosophy of religion around the principle of divine-human freedom. But in order to begin he has recourse to theological, rather than philosophical, presuppositions. Then, having accepted revelation by an act of faith, he returns to speculative reason in order to explicate its contents. The result sometimes strains to hold as reason-grounded but is still deserving of the hearing for which Schelling so passionately pleaded.

Thus, the chapters that follow set out to examine the philosophies of Christianity and the philosophical Christologies that resulted from the audacious attempts by four leading philosophers of the modern period to fulfill philosophy's program in a philosophy of religion and at the same time to save religion *from* philosophy and *for* philosophy. None is an unqualified success. Yet what they set out to accomplish is sometimes almost as rich in failure as in achievement. The influence, reaction, rejection and revival that each has generated, as well as the lessons of their failures, recommend them to critical attention still. But the extent to which each succeeded in making Christianity and its Christ worthy of serious intellectual reflection once again compels our respect and repays our instruction.

The arguments of eighteenth and nineteenth century philosophy of religion, moreover, continue to be echoed in our late twentieth century. Contemporary philosophy of religion has not really surpassed the eighteenth and nineteenth centuries on essential points, and one may dare suggest that the discussions of the eighteenth and nineteenth centuries' remain superior in certain respects, certainly in style, perhaps in form and ambition as well. Contemporary philosophy of religion, in its arguments for/ against/about God, religion and the human-divine encounter may (to paraphrase Whitehead) be only a series of footnotes to the classic philosophies of religion that issued from the post-Enlightenment. If this should prove so and if we deal today in texts that are largely "footnotes," then we surely have cause to engage in a sustained look at and examination of a group of original thinkers, as the present study proposes.

PART ONE

THE JESUS
OF MORAL REASON

ROUSSEAU
AND THE SAVOYARD JESUS

INTRODUCTION

The intellectual debates and literary tempests of every age eventually subside, and so the name Jean-Jacques Rousseau enjoys a calm in our times that the living man seldom knew. His influence extended in his lifetime as far eastward as Königsberg where legend has it that Immanuel Kant eagerly awaited his latest work. After his death his works continued to be read at least as far east as Tübingen where the young Hegel and Schelling were students at the time of the French Revolution. Nevertheless, Rousseau was soon afterwards ignored in Germany as he was either tarred with the excesses of the French Revolution or simply snubbed. And despite the important work of Ernst Cassirer (*Das Problem Jean-Jacques Rousseau*, 1932) and fellow neo-Kantians in pointing out his philosophical contributions, Rousseau is still much ignored in the philosophically and theologically influential German-speaking world. He was and is still read in France, but even there he had been generally associated with French Romanticism until Cassirer's interpretation began to have influence.

In opening Rousseau today, one is still struck by the sincerity and searching passion of his writings—often polemical, always personal, frequently lyrical, sometimes near pathetic. The question of his significance, however, remains to be asked anew, and specifically the significance of his religious thought. The answer to this question centers on Book IV of *Émile,* the epoch-making *Profession of Faith of the Savoyard Vicar* in which Rousseau argued that religion, and specifically the Jesus of Christianity, were too integral to be written off in the fashionable manner of the French Enlightenment. That the publication of *Émile* in 1762 led to the religious persecution of one who sought to liberate both religion and philosophy from myopia, of one indeed who attempted to locate a common ground to unite these sworn enemies, is all part of literary history in which Rousseau's *Confessions* also has its say. The *Profession of Faith of the Savoyard Vicar* endures as a complex and intriguing religious document from the age of the *philosophes*. Its reception was stormy, its reputation and influence immediately widespread. But it was more than a dramatic, literary piece in a dramatic, literary age. Its analysis of and reflections upon religion merit and repay our attention still. Moreover, perhaps no philosopher has articulated the suffering humanity of Jesus with a sensitivity and empathy equal to Rousseau's.

Rousseau is indeed a religious thinker, and by no means incidentally so. Rousseau is the first of a distinguished company of philosopher-theologians of the post-Enlightenment. He was also the least philosophical and the least theological of them, for he was a self-taught man. Both his education and his thought are more experimental and less systematic than might have been desirable, and the limitations of his schoolmaster surely show. Perhaps because of his lack of formal training he is all too quickly passed over, not so much by intellectual historians generally as by would-be successors to Kant and Hegel. In this, Rousseau might see yet another conspiracy against him. In examining Rousseau and his philosophy of religion,[1] we should like to take a cue from Kant, and from Kant as distinct from the Kantians. The sage of Königsberg knew better than his followers that Rousseau stands on his own. Moreover, he had the good fortune to know the writings of Rousseau before biography and autobiography made the task appreciably more complex. For Rousseau is surely a thinker whose thought needs to be saved from his life, even if he has seen to it that we can never fully disentangle the two. For our part we shall, in examining his religious thought, attempt to discern his merited and proper place, specifically with regard to philosophy of religion and its attempt to save Christianity and its Christ from superstition and from narrow rationalism and for philosophy.

---

[1] A distinction is made here between his philosophy of religion and his religious thought. A full consideration of the latter would necessarily include a discussion of the *Social Contract* that culminates in a discussion of "civil religion" (Book IV, chapter 8).

In inquiring into Rousseau's religious thought, all paths converge in the garden of the vicarage of Savoy. The *Profession of Faith of the Savoyard Vicar* is indisputably the central and most important of Rousseau's religious writings, and it is the only one of these that represents serious philosophy of religion. In the *Profession* one finds as clear and developed a position on religion—or any subject—as Rousseau was to make. But in it too one finds the problems that plague Rousseau intepretation: the imprecise language and fledgling concepts, the polemics, the paradoxes and *voltes-face*—and the grounds for the various debates they have given rise to, politically, theologically and hermeneutically. Here one finds Rousseau then not in a serene or pristine state but struggling and tattered, not in a carefully manicured systematic garden but in an intellectual state of nature. This is not, however, even remotely to suggest that the *Profession* was hastily written. In his classic edition of the work[2] Pierre-Maurice Masson describes how the document evolved throught the course of several re-writings. In combination with his *La Religion de Jean Jacques Rousseau,*[3] Masson presents a thorough account of the development of Rousseau's religious thinking that crystallized in the Vicar's discourse as well as of antecedent novels whose religious content influenced Rousseau (such as the novel *Cleveland* by the Abbé de Prevost that recounted the natural religion of a primitive people[4]), and contemporary religious statements that the *Profession* disputes (most notably Helvetius's *De l'Ésprit* of 1758[5]).

Rousseau interpretation has itself a long history, full of controversy. Unfortunately, many have tried to discover in or force upon Rousseau positions that were never quite his own. From his literary debut he has been prisoner and victim of fashions—from the deistic Parisian literary salons into which he made his first dramatic entrance after his prize-winning essay for the Academy of Dijon on the sciences and arts and from which he afterwards made repeated grand exits, to the French Romantics who claimed to be the offspring of Julie and Saint-Preux in Rousseau's novel *La Nouvelle Heloïse,* to the French Revolution that not without right claimed to

---

[2] *"La Profession de Foi du Vicaire Savoyard"* de Jean-Jacques Rousseau, critical edition, ed. Pierre-Maurice Masson (Fribourg/Paris, 1914). Hereafter cited as Masson, *Profession.*

[3] Three volumes (Paris: Librairie Hachette, 1916). Hereafter cited as Masson, *Religion.*

[4] Masson, introduction to *Profession,* xiii.

[5] Ibid., xxvi.

have inherited some of its political ideas from this most obedient servant of the king.

Ernst Cassirer, writing on the far side of the Rhine, must be credited with opening Rousseau to modern reassessment. As Peter Gay notes in his introduction to the English-language translation,[6] Cassirer, in imitation of Kant, set out to find the real rather than the alleged virtues of Rousseau and located them not in any formal system but in a dynamic center of thought with a rationalist concept of freedom. There is no making Rousseau a neatly cohering religious thinker, unless one simply ignores large parts of the very works one cites. The loose ends dangle in clear view. And if one would treat Rousseau critically and ultimately fairly, one must acknowledge them and ponder their possible significance while penetrating to the fundamental ideas and existential concerns out of which the *Profession* in particular evolved. Robert Derathé (*Le Rationalisme de Jean-Jacques Rousseau*[7]), who follows in the French branch of the Cassirer school, stresses the importance of morality in Rousseau's thought, while he seeks to save him definitively from the French Romantics and sentimentalist school. In doing this, however, he stresses the rational, as the title would suggest, but now at the expense of sentiment. He criticizes the sentimentalist interpretation he perceives in Masson's studies but fails to engage the difficult problem Rousseau was himself struggling with, namely, some accommodation between reason and sentiment. Such accomodation is a principal theme of the *Profession* and has important implications for the view of religion.

Rousseau is by no means without fault in the misinterpretations that have arisen. His works frequently begin with revolutionary precepts, for example, only to come to conservative conclusions. Such is the case in the first *Discours* that anathametizes the sciences and the arts only to locate salvation finally in the academy; equally in *La Nouvelle Heloïse* that preaches the emancipation of sentiment and the supreme rights of passion only to exalt in the end the traditional virtues of marital fidelity, family and social duty; and finally in the *Profession* itself in which the Vicar sets the stage for a scathing critique of religion and begins one, only to conclude

---

[6]Introduction to *The Question of Jean-Jacques Rousseau,* trans. and ed. Peter Gay (Bloomington: Indiana University Press, 1963; German original, 1932) 22; hereafter cited as Cassirer, *Question.*

[7](Paris: Presses Universitaires de France, 1948).

with a declaration of the need for religion and the indispensability of the Christian religion that moments before had seemed superfluous if not harmful.[8]

How account for these turnabouts? The simplest way has been the one most often taken: only read part of the work, or hold to that which one admires or would condemn, without accounting for the whole. This was certainly the general fate of *La Nouvelle Heloïse,* many of whose readers apparently never continued beyond the passionate letters of Part I to the ultimately moral and religious conclusion that was Part V. The impassioned critics of the *Profession* for their part must have read only the opening deistic positions and not the near-pious conclusion—except for those such as the author(s) of the *Mandement,* or Pastoral Letter, issued by the Archbishop of Paris, who proceeded maliciously to doubt its sincerity. The marginal comments of Voltaire in his copy of the *Profession* and also of the *Lettre à M. de Beaumont*[9] are instructive and often characteristically amusing in this regard. They indicate that fellow deist but personal enemy Voltaire could applaud Rousseau's antireligious polemics and endorse his deism but utterly fail to comprehend the possibility of an enduring sympathy for aspects of Christianity, to say nothing of an attack upon the party of *philosophes* to which Voltaire belonged. Voltaire read as a *philosophe* and a partisan, not as a philosopher. And he was not above citing his "edited" *Profession* in the campaign against *l'infâme.*[10] Rousseau's own marginalia, in drafts of the *Profession,* indicate that he was very deliberately trying to steer a course between the devout on one side and the intellectuals on the other, and thus to hold back from the dangers of superstition and fanaticism in the one group and atheism and immorality in the other. The Vicar's discourse makes it through and only Rousseau is damaged. Contemporaries did not appreciate, and did not even seem to perceive, what Rousseau was attempting, and sometimes one wonders whether Rousseau himself fully appreciated the radical challenge to both reason and religion that he was in the process of formulating.

Written during the controversial aftermath to the publication of *Émile* and the *Profession* contained within it, the *Mandement* and *Lettre à M. de*

[8]Masson, *Religion,* II:116.

[9]Cf. Ronald Grimsley, ed., *Rousseau: Religious Writings* (Oxford: Clarendon Press, 1970) which gives them in footnotes to Rousseau's texts. Hereafter cited as Grimsley, ed., *Religious Writings.*

[10]Masson, *Religion,* II:33.

Beaumont provide interesting commentary. Not only are they effective rhetorical pieces *ad hominem* but telling examples of how each blindly read and responded to the other—and at the same time of how correct each was in his essential objections. This time, Rousseau is more than victim.

PHILOSOPHY AND THE PHILOSOPHES

Given Rousseau's naive anticipation of a *Profession* well received in Protestant circles and officially tolerated in Catholic areas, one might well accept Rousseau's later assertion (in Promenade II of the *Rêveries du Promeneur Solitaire*) that the Vicar's principal intended polemic was against the *philosophes*. Moreover, the structure and content of the *Profession* would support this interpretation independently and thus confirm Rousseau's explicit claim. The *philosophes* and their style of philosophy were singled out for both the first and final attack of the *Profession*. In the opening pages, they were cited for their hypocrisy and personal interest in place of commitment to truth[11] and in the closing pages they were attacked for their own attack on religion and for the dangers posed by their atheistic stance.[12]

The *philosophes,* it should be recalled, had viewed themselves not just as thinkers but as a movement, with which Rousseau was perceived to be aligned. Any criticism uttered by a member outside the private salons was taken not as a difference of opinion but as an attack upon the party and its program, in effect as treason to the cause. Rousseau's stormy association with the circle of Diderot, Condillac, d'Allembert, and others is well known, and its intrigues have been chronicled on both sides. By degrees, the Enlightment leaders perceived and shunned Rousseau as a tortured, driven man and even as a threat to their intellectual equilibrium.[13] Diderot, five years before the publication of *Émile,* wrote in a letter to Grimm, ''I never want to see that man again; he could make me believe in devils and Hell.''[14] Rousseau fully intended his remarks in the *Profession* as an attack

---

[11]*Émile,* Everyman's Library (New York: Dutton, 1974; orig., 1911) 230; *Oeuvres Complètes de Jean-Jacques Rousseau,* ed. Bernard Gagnebin and Marcel Raymond (Paris: Bibliotèque de la Pléiade, 1959-) IV: 567-68. Hereafter cited in English as *Émile.* The French will be cited as OC, as will other volumes that have appeared in the Pléiade edition.

[12]*Émile,* 276-78; OC IV:632-35.

[13]Cassirer, *Question,* 91.

[14]Letter of October/November 1757, quoted by Cassirer, *Question,* 91.

upon both party and program, about which he had become increasingly skeptical and mistrustful.

Rousseau saw the need for articulating a reasonable alternative to the materialism of the *philosophes* and for undercutting the triumph of a sterile reason. He recognized that he was himself susceptible to the very negations of the *philosophes*. But Rousseau discovered in the experience of nature the power that took away the mist of intellectual doubts and that enabled him to believe. In the aftermath of his spiritual encounter with nature and his perceptions of a narrowly materialistic program in the *philosophes*, Rousseau felt the need to strike out at them publicly. His initial advocacy of deistic positions in the *Profession* only to reconstellate them in a new religion of reason that embraced so many externals of "the superstition" (as Enlighteners termed Christianity) confounded and provoked them. The *philosophes* did not sense challenge but they recognized attack, even if they subsequently went on to quote the Vicar for their own purposes. Rousseau's attack was an open one, unlike the subtle and radical challenge he threw down to religion in the category of conscience. For Rousseau, certain positions had to be refuted outright, such as those of Helvetius. The *philosophes* were not to be viewed as saviors of the modern world, as they flattered themselves to be, but as part of a larger unsolved problem—the social fall away from a state of nature—and as a sure indication of how the problem could not be solved. That many thought them the bearers of the solution and that they so proudly declared themselves to be such made it more imperative that they be exposed.

The attack began just after the opening words of the first discourse, with the existential confession of the inadequacy of Cartesian doubt when applied to existence[15] and with a denunciation of the *philosophes'* hubris:

> I found them all alike proud, assertive, dogmatic, professing, even in their so-called skepticism, to know everything, proving nothing, scoffing at each other.[16]

And of their egotism he wrote:

> Every one of them knows that his own system rests on no surer foundations than the rest, but he maintains it because it is his own. There is not one of them who, if he chanced to discover the difference between truth

---

[15]*Émile*, 229; OC IV:567.
[16]*Émile*, 230; OC IV:568.

and falsehood, would not prefer his own lie to the truth which another had discovered.[17]

Ideas alone lead astray, and in a remark paralleling his subsequent attack on Christianity for having created a jargon without concepts,[18] he accused the current philosophy of creating concepts without content:

> The chief source of human error is to be found in general and abstract ideas: the jargon of metaphysics has never led to the discovery of any single truth, and it has filled philosophy with absurdities of which we are ashamed as soon as we strip them of their long words.[19]

"Haughty philosophy leads to atheism," commented the Vicar in warning his young hearer against extremes, "just as blind devotion leads to fanaticism,"[20] and added, "Dare to confess God before the philosophers." For Rousseau, even more provoking than the dogmatism of the skeptics was the *philosophes'* undermining of morality. For Rousseau could not imagine a moral code without divine sanction and hence the atheism of the *philosophes* was morally abhorrent to him. (De Beaumont's attack on Rousseau ironically takes a parallel line of criticism.) In a striking footnote,[21] while agreeing with Bayle that fanaticism was more immediately dangerous than atheism, the Vicar/Rousseau went on to state his respect for the passion that was at the base of fanaticism and that, if properly directed, led to "the noblest virtues" while the irreligion of the argumentative philosophical spirit only enfeebled life and in the long run was more fatal.

The *philosophes* were taken as the concrete symbols of a narrow reason, which Rousseau believed was right to criticize the fanatical tendencies of the religious but that, as the price for removing fanaticism, impoverished the human spirit. True humanity begins where morality begins, and here Rousseau made clear his position that both reason and religion (Christianity) must submit to and be transformed by conscience.

LANGUAGE

Rousseau's language and terminology are admittedly problematic. The same Rousseau who wrote, "Systems of all sorts are over my head,"[22] was

---

[17]*Émile*, 231; OC IV:569.

[18]*La Lettre à M. de Beaumont*, OC IV:252.

[19]*Émile*, 236; OC IV:577.

[20]*Émile*, 277; OC IV: 633-34. The English translation is not literal; the French has "l'esprit fort," not "athéisme."

[21]*Émile*, 276; OC IV:632.

[22]Draft of a letter to Mirabeau, 25 March 1767, quoted in Cassirer, *Question.*

also aware of the difficulties posed by the words themselves, and so he wrote in a letter to Madame d'Epinay:

> Learn my vocabulary better, my good friend, if you would have us understand each other. Believe me, my terms rarely have the common meaning; it is always my heart that converses with you, and perhaps you will learn some day that it speaks not as others do.[23]

For Rousseau, the heart, which he assigns to the soul, speaks and can be said to have a voice that parallels that of nature. As spiritual heart, it is the organ of sincerity and naturalness and finally the organ and vehicle of conscience. And in this wise the heart of Rousseau seeks to converse with others.[24]

But the language of the heart goes much further. For the larger category "sentiment" is dependent upon this organ and conscience has thus not to do with *physical* feelings (although some emotional state such as exaltation may attend it in the body) but rather with *metaphysical* feeling in the sense that in conscience, considered as sentiment, one feels or prehends the metaphysical good. The radical distinction between mind and heart and their uneasy separation are reflected in the shifting emphases of the *Profession*. For the Vicar's religious system is ostensibly built around reason and yet obviously grounded in the heart. In addition, the Vicar is evidently as concerned with moving the heart of his young listener and larger audience as he is with impressing the mind through reasoned argument.

Cassirer stresses the importance of distinguishing, in Rousseau's language of sentiment, between mere sentiment on one side and judgments and ethical decisions on the other.[25] He goes on to note that sentiment by degrees rises from a special faculty of the self "to the original power of the self, from which all other powers grow and from which they must continually take nourishment lest they wither and die."[26] Rousseau is trying to break with the sensationalist psychology of his day and would seem to

---

[23]*Correspondence Générale*, II:266, quoted by Gay, introduction to Cassirer, *Question*, 14.

[24]Rousseau's "heart" is itself a problem. He is of couse not the first to speak in such imprecise terms. Augustine's *Confessions* has similar metaphors, for example, and perhaps the even more curious heart with ears and soul with marrow. Nor is Pascal to be overlooked.

[25]Cassirer, *Question*, 110.

[26]Cassirer, *Question*, 112.

be construing moral feeling as a higher than sensual feeling. Can there, however, be a hierarchical relation of feelings that have their centers in the radically different loci of soul and body? As he seeks to free his language from one set of limitations, he imposes another as he affirms a body-soul dualism and then extends it to sentiment. His language would suggest relationship, continuity and ascent between physical and moral feelings. Those sensitized to the "ghost in the machine" may wince at his language, especially as we read of "feelings of the soul" here. The most important religious concepts in Rousseau—conscience, heart and their relationship to reason—are caught up in this problem of Rousseau's language. But Rousseau has important notions to discuss, even if in troublesome terms, and this writer is prepared to agree with Derathé who finds in Rousseau only verbal contradiction and seeming disaccord in formulations but a consistency, if surely an evolution, of thought.[27]

THE PROFESSION OF FAITH OF THE SAVOYARD VICAR

The *Profession* is a small theological novel inserted into the larger *Émile*. It is not Rousseau's only attempt to compose a religious statement: there is, for example, the "Morceau allégorique sur la Révélation" of 1756-1757 that was left incomplete. Nor is it the sole religious testament: the dying Julie makes a profession of faith in *La Nouvelle Heloïse* which Rousseau, in the *Confessions,* says is "exactly the same as that of the Savoyard Vicar."[28] Within *Émile,* the *Profession* is to present the culminating religious education that is part of the larger educational program advocated by the work. It is not a statement of dogmas, but a sharing of personal beliefs in a near-theatrical setting designed to evoke solemnity and move the soul.[29] The figure of the Vicar (modeled after the abbés Gatier and Gaime whom Rousseau had known) is a transparent veil for Rousseau himself who here did not desire to make a religious confession as such. By placing his name on the book, he wished, however, to avoid what he considered the cowardly anonymity of Voltaire and others in publishing material touching upon religion. Formally, Rousseau claims he is the youth

---

[27]*Le Rationalisme de Jean-Jacques Rousseau* (Paris: Presses Universitaires de France, 1948) 4. Hereafter cited as Derathé, *Rationalisme.*

[28]*O.C.* I:407. (English: J. M. Cohen, trans. *The Confessions of Jean-Jacques Rousseau* [Middlesex: Penguin Books, 1954] 379.)

[29]Masson, *Profession,* xx.

to whom the *Profession* is addressed (and there is an autobiographical basis for this character), but no one is thus distracted from the true author of the Vicar's views.[30] The Vicar's religious statement is very much a profession, not only before his impressionable young listener but also before the two enemy camps of *philosophes* and religious dogmatists.[31] Each part of the *Profession* addresses a camp, but it is the second part, which attempts to combine deism with heartfelt Christianity, that is ultimately more significant.

The educational project of *Émile* is not unconnected with Rousseau's most famous work, the *Social Contract*. And this is perhaps underlined by the fact that both works were published in the same year, 1762. The projects are not directly related, but Book IV of the *Social Contract* does provide a link to Book IV of *Émile*. For Book IV, chapter eight of the *Social Contract* contains Rousseau's famous discussion of civil religion. There Rousseau outlines the kind of religion that will best serve the interests of society. And while Rousseau considers a Christian republic to be impossible, he stops short of rejecting Christianity itself. What he in effect outlines is the neutralization of Christian dogma and its otherworldliness in a deism whose state-defined articles of faith will foster sociability. The religion of the *Profession of Faith of the Savoyard Vicar* is not this state deism but is a Christianized deism instead. As such, it may be taken to represent that form of Christianity that may be imparted to the young and that is compatible with the state. There is no doctrinal conflict between the two. The difference consists in the central place accorded Jesus of Nazareth as the teacher of moral religion and as example. In stressing Jesus as a pristine figure of sincerity and self-transparency, Rousseau is at the same time pointing to the necessity of individual self-recovery in order for a reformed society to escape corruption. In this sense, the Christianized deism of the *Profession* may be said to extend and apply the idea of religion outlined in the *Social Contract*. To say this, however, is not to disguise the *Social Contract's* criticism of Christianity's essential otherworldliness and the

---

[30]Ibid., xxxiii-xxxiv. The Vicar and the narrator of *Émile* are not beyond contradicting each other, as many have noted. The former is a priest, the latter a philosopher of nature. Where their views do not coincide lie new difficulties for interpreters but an underlining of the separate composition and integral nature of the *Profession* section of *Émile* (= Book IV).

[31]Ibid., ix.

view of its founder as a teacher of a spiritual kingdom incompatible with
the notion of a civil society.

STYLE

The *Profession* is very much a work of rhetoric, but it seeks to persuade us even more to its method and sincerity than to its content. Nonetheless, teachings are presented with deliberateness and sometimes with
subtlety.

In his celebrated philippic, the *Lettre à M. de Beaumont,* Rousseau re-
viewed the *Profession* in this way:

> The Profession of the Savoyard Vicar is composed of two parts: the first,
> which is the larger, the more important, more filled with new and striking
> truths, is intended to combat modern materialism, to establish the exis-
> tence of God and natural religion with all the power of which the author is
> capable.

(He goes on to attack his clerical critics for ignoring this part and for thereby
indicating that they are not really concerned with the cause of God.)

> The second [part], much shorter, less even, less deeply [gone into], pro-
> poses some doubts and difficulties about revelations in general, according
> our own [revelation], however, its certain truth in the purity and holiness
> of its doctrine, and in the very divine sublimity of him who is its author.
> The object of this second part is to render each in his religion more hesitant
> to accuse others of bad faith in theirs, and to point out that the proofs of
> each are not so very demonstrative in the eyes of all that one should treat
> as blameworthy those who do not see there the same clarity.[32]

One does not expect to find in Rousseau's open letter to the Archbishop of
Paris an objective review of the work that had prompted the pastoral letter
and condemnation. But despite its rhetorical interest, Rousseau's letter does
convey a sense of what he wished to emphasize in the *Profession*. To
Archbishop de Beaumont, he stressed Part I; to a Voltaire he would stress
Part II. For ourselves, we must seek where the first principles and final
emphasis more truly lie.

The literary spontaneity of the Vicar's profession quite simply belies
the evolution of faith and composition that it represents.[33] The work is an
attempt by Rousseau to respond to the felt need to give propositional, if

---

[32]Grimsley, ed., *Religious Writings,* 300-301.

[33]All quotations from the English translations of the *Profession* are taken from the
Everyman's Library edition, as cited above, note 11.

not systematic, form to his religious belief as a man of reason and sentiment. Once the reader penetrates to the wellsprings of his faith, he may perhaps see what the rational structure obscures or even disguises; that the sources of the central beliefs are in sentiment (with all the ambiguity and special senses of that term), while reason—in the sense of intellectual reason—is used to pare down traditional Christian beliefs to bare essentials. Even the apparent grounding of Part I in reason does not ultimately distract one from the lack of logical order in the exposition.[34] Masson observes that the genuine novelty and originality of the *Profession* would be more striking if Rousseau had *not* imposed a logical order of sorts on the exposition but had instead been faithful to the order of feeling—of heart and experience—that is, to the order in which he discovered his central verities for himself. If we look for the order of feeling, we should not first hear the Vicar's examination of the value of sense and the activity of judgment in the first discourse. For the principal doctrine, verity, and experience that this new gospel would declare is that "In the beginning is conscience." All moral maxims are derived from this discovery, and their true source always remains nature and not the deductions of philosophers. This is not to say that Rousseau utterly breaks with the philosophy or rationalism of his times. Despite his criticism of the *philosophes,* he still shared many of their views and he largely agreed with the religious critiques of his day. The work evidences this, and these points of agreements are the reason that the *Profession* was incorrectly denounced as a typical deist tract. It is in his heart far more than in his mind that Rousseau parts from their company, and this heart will not be without effect in modifying and regrounding his deism, as will be especially noted in the discussion of his method below.

Why then the rationalism of Part I (which has never impeded interpretations of Rousseau as an irrationalist)? Is it a mere concession to, or rhetorical deception for, the rationalists and deists who would subsequently be attacked? Rousseau was, in this, more likely following convention than engaged in a ruse. It is also very conceivable that Rousseau simply did not perceive how daring it would be in the eighteenth century to proclaim a faith that began not with a well-argued epistemology and understanding of the universe that required a god to order it but rather with an intuitive feel-

---

[34]Masson, *Religion,* II:82.

ing of the good and of its source as given in and with conscience. For, had he fully appeciated how novel his deism was, one can only suppose that he would have considered a more direct, and thus even bolder, course. In saying this, one must stress that Rousseau's rationalism is not mere decoration, disguise or rhetorical device but an authentic part of his faith, with an essential collaborative and complementary function to that of conscience. As one comes to see the nature of reason and conscience in his thought, one also comes to recognize that while his is not typical eighteenth-century rationalism, his is also not a nineteenth-century indulgence of sentiment.

The opening pages of the *Profession* indicate that the faith to be professed is a product of a whole and very human person. Before we hear of his beliefs, we learn of the Vicar's lived-out faith: his personal morality and humanity, his detachment from doctrinal formulations yet faithfulness to traditional outward religious expression. And we are told his essential motivation for formulating a creed: his need for peace and repose; his inability to sustain a life of Cartesian doubt.[35] Part I opens with a declaration of the true function of religion, followed by a Rousseauean theory of sincerity. The following subsection reveals the Vicar's epistemology in matters of religion, which aims to justify only what he feels the need to know, and his theodicy, which justifies God and leaves man the author of all evil. (This position was much more fully developed in the *Letter to Voltaire on Providence* that figures prominently in eighteenth-century attempts to justify the deity in the shattering aftermath of the Lisbon earthquake.) Only toward the end of Part I does the reader come to what will ultimately prove the most essential in this faith: conscience, the infallible guide and instinct of the soul. The ending of Part I is an attack upon prayer that, although linked to Rousseau's theodicy of all-is-right-on-the-whole, would seem to belong more properly to Part II, except that Part II deals with uncertainties in religion, whereas prayer is rejected with the full certainty of Part I.

In Part II the *Profession* begins the seemingly erratic turns that have generated so much discussion about the true nature of the Vicar's faith. A

---

[35]Cf. also Søren Kierkegaard, *Johannes Climacus, or De Omnibus Dubitandum Est*, trans. T. H. Croxall (London: Adam and Charles Black, 1958). In this work of 1842-1843 and unpublished during his lifetime, Kierkegaard, in the character of the pseudonym Johannes Climacus, gives us a rather charming satire on the attempt to live out a life of Cartesian doubt.

rationalist critique of positive (revealed) religion is followed by an affirmation of the heart—and thus not reason alone—as the highest court in judging religion. The Vicar then goes on to establish the criterion of practice for evaluating religious groups (much as in the manner of Lessing's *Nathan the Wise*) and, after seemingly having undercut Christianity for the inhumanity of the doctrine of the damnation of nonadherents, he goes on to wax both eloquent and sentimental about the gospel and Jesus. In the following section he declares himself a skeptic in theory, a believer in practice, and goes on to give another rationale for his self-described Christianity profession, namely, saving the trunk at the expense of certain branches, and then issues the ecumenical admonition to stay with the cult of one's fathers. In his summation, the Vicar declares that he has given reasons for faith and doubt. But these are, we find upon reflection, traditional reasons for doubt and novel reasons for faith, at least in the modern period. The important mediating principle in this is the heart's affirmation of faith stances that would be unjustifiable on the basis of intellectual reason alone.

METHOD

Any eighteenth-century reader of the *Profession* who had been prematurely persuaded by its opening pages that it was to be a typical deist tract must have been surprised when it did not culminate in the standard rejection of claims about revelation, the gospel and the person of Christ but suddenly—and without any explicit preparation for such a departure—affirmed them because the *heart* of the speaker responded to their content and significance. This development in the work troubled many of its first readers and has puzzled not a few interpreters since then. Yet, as Masson astutely observes, Rousseau tells us plainly in the text what his method is. If one hears it, one ought not to expect that the Vicar's discourse will automatically follow the destructive path of a deist consideration of historical religion, or at least that it will follow such a path the whole way. And if one listens to the Vicar with care, one can puzzle out the inclusion of a pious regard for Jesus where one would expect conventional deism. The enduring limitation or frustration for any Rousseau interpreter will be that, even allowing Rousseau's premises and observing his process of arriving at conclusions, one will never succeed in making the movements with him. For the Vicar's heart is his alone, even while it includes universal conscience. One may *think* his thoughts, and even think them through where he may not have done so, but one cannot readily duplicate the interaction of mind and heart that is claimed. Yet if one does not have Rousseau's heart and private intuitions, one's heart may imitate Rousseau's method in at least one respect—in being patient with surface disturbances for the sake of reaching calm depths.

Rousseau strains to bring his mind and heart together on the subject of religion. Nonetheless, the reader observes them to some extent on separate courses. For the deist thinker, God would be merely the cosmic horologue—a philosophical hypothesis; but Rousseau, the veritable son of a clockmaker, proclaims with fervor and piety belief in the Father of all men—in sum, a deism of the mind and a "theism" of the heart. With mind and heart, Rousseau is attempting to reconcile two hitherto incompatible faiths: simple, intellectual natural religion in the first instance, traditional Christianity in the second. In trying to bring together the tenets of eighteenth-century rational religion with the mythological world of New Testament faith statements, his commitment to the former entails bringing the latter more into conformity with it. And the *Profession* fully reflects the interaction and subjugation. But the "heart" that allows Christianity to be maintained in the face of intellectual reason finally subsumes both. Here the "heart" is understood as conscience and what emerges is a religion of conscience, still natural but no longer hostile to historical religion.

The Vicar's method is simple and straightforward. It is clearly not Cartesian and might better be understood in contrast to the Descartes who would accept as evident only what could be presented and understood by the mind so clearly as to be beyond doubt.[36] Rousseau begins his review of religion with an eye and an ear—and finally with the feeling of the heart—for all matters that have a *personal* interest for him. And he is finally willing to accept as "evident" all doctrines, and all in necessary connection to such doctrines, to which in the "sincerity of his heart" he cannot refuse consent.[37] What is not of personal concern and urgency can be left in an intellectual limbo state: Rousseau will not torment himself trying to explain what he considers to be of little practical consequence (that is, of consequence for morality). Of course, what is plainly absurd must be rejected. These are the guiding principles. The "sincerity of his heart" does not make Rousseau a sentimentalist, for it refers to conscience. Rous-

---

[36]Cf. Masson's discussion in *Religion*, II:86ff.
[37]Ibid., 87.

seau's method in effect posits moral intuition and moral content as the highest source and content of religion and as the supreme criterion for judging historical religion. Intellectual reason takes second place, but an important place all the same. Morality and praxis thus formally guide the review of religion. For the rest, in the true gospel spirit, Rousseau is content to let wheat and chaff grow together rather then risk destroying society's moral staple in an excess of rationalist-deist zeal.

ROUSSEAU AND THE VICAR'S CHRISTIANITY

Christianity suffuses Rousseau's thought. Christian themes, motifs, and references abound. Rousseau reaffirmed his allegiance to Christianity when his orthodoxy was questioned,[38] deeply wished to be regarded as a Christian, and with apparent sincerity believed himself to be such and in the true spirit of Geneva Protestantism. If he deviated from Protestant belief, he could defend his position in noting that individual interpretation was the hallmark of Protestantism. He was a devoted Bible reader, at the end of his life displaying increasing sentimental enthusiasm for it,[39] and in his bedridden old age used to read the *Imitation of Christ*.

Masson's *La Religion de Jean-Jacques Rousseau* has been criticized for trying to take Rousseau to the Church of Rome for a second time. Whether or not Masson presses Rousseau this far, he plainly tries to keep Rousseau numbered among Christians. He construes his theism and morality as unconsciously Christian rather than philosophical[40] and asserts that the *Profession,* which to some seemed only to gather together all the negative thought of the eighteenth century about religion, is thoroughly penetrated with the Christian spirit.[41] (Masson, however, never defines this spirit nor does he ever indicate any norms or beliefs for one's qualifying as a Christian.) In the Vicar's remaining a Catholic despite his warm view of Protestantism, Masson claims to find in Rousseau a lingering feeling for the cult he briefly adhered to and, despite the rational absurdities in Catholicism that the Vicar points out—such as transubstantiation, the respect

---

[38] And adds in *La Lettre à M. de Beaumont* that he is not dependent on miracles in order to be a Christian. OC IV:990.

[39] Masson, *Religion,* II:240.

[40] Ibid., 113.

[41] Ibid., 110-11.

of one who sees more than idolatry therein.[42] But Masson's analysis is more thorough than his own conclusion would suggest, and so he also observes that Rousseau's was a "Christianity without dogmas" rather than a "theological Christianity,"[43] and finally admits that "Christianity was for him a kind of sentimental supplemental to the religion of conscience."[44] And while still terming Rousseau's position Christianity, he goes on to a grand summation:

> The religion of Rousseau is a Christianity that is not only without doctrinal discipline—I would not say without mysteries, because it jealously holds on to the mystery of Providence, the mystery of the soul, and of the immortal soul—it is also a Christianity without history which suppresses time and space about Jean-Jacques and leaves him in a tête-à-tête with a kindly Jesus. It is also a Christianity without redemption and without repentance, from which the feeling of sin has disappeared, and of which Jean-Jacques is at one and the same time the priest and even the new Christ. However, in this religion that guards so lively a confidence in one God "common father of men," that has let slip away the sense of human weakness but retains that of unhappiness, that cries over a lost paradise, that considers earthly life as a passage toward the true fatherland, and that awaits so firmly just reparation in the time to come, one cannot say that Christianity is dead. This is perhaps no longer the faith of Christianity; but these are, at least, its hopes.[45]

Such thinking would seem determined to make Rousseau Christian. Christians themselves do not agree on minimal belief. Rousseau affirms and recognizes the moral content of Jesus' central teachings, and the goodness and pathos of Jesus himself. But he denies elaborations of the meaning and identity of Jesus in the history of Christian theology. Most emphatically, he denies original sin and all that follows from this: historical salvation begun by a savior and a god become incarnate in order to redeem. Rousseau does not speak with the theological language of sin, but he certainly has a parallel category, even if it is a "social fall." (On this point, Masson, as quoted above, is simply wrong when he says that "the feeling of sin has disappeared" without repentance. This would be to ignore the effort the socially fallen individual must make to reattain self-transparency.) Rousseau is moved with tenderness and sympathy for Jesus, but this is Jesus the

---

[42]Ibid., 112.
[43]Ibid., 155.
[44]Ibid., 270.
[45]Ibid., 294.

man, not the anointed of God. And, while Rousseau breaks new ground in eighteenth-century philosophy of religion even to make a place for the founder of Christianity, in the end Jesus is acknowledged only as the admired, gentle-but-firm teacher of moral lessons accessible to the sincere heart of everyman. For Rousseau, this is positive and ought to be enough. For the deist party, it was too much, while for the orthodox it was of course still far too little.

Derathé views him as a deist à la Voltaire, despite attempts to be seen a sincere Christian:

> Despite his respect for the Gospel and the fervor of his religious feeling, Rousseau professes a religion that does not go beyond the limits of natural religion.[46]

Kierkegaard, among the modern orthodox critics of Rousseau, observed in his *Journals* that Rousseau is the example of what it means not to be well-read in Christianity, while the more contemporary Karl Barth locates Rousseau's essential break with Christianity in the denial of original sin.[47] In Rousseau, he remarks, "the Church doctrine of original sin has seldom . . . been denied with such disconcerting candour and in so directly personal a way."[48] This is to view Rousseau as a modern Pelagian. Rousseau would counter, as he did in his "Open Letter to Archbishop de Beaumont," that, once one is baptized, original sin is wiped away. His method would suggest that, for the rest, it is not a practical point worthy of disputation. For, whether having passed through the valley of sin and then the cleansing waters of baptism or simply having crossed the open plains of nature, one is where one is and must—on one's own—go further. The orthodox do not accept this as a moot point and stress instead the permanent aftereffects of original sin upon the will and thus the continued need of God's grace for salvation. (Rousseau was quite simply Socratic on this old

---

[46]Derathé, *Rationalisme*, 61.

[47]Kierkegaard writes, "Incidentally, this is an example of what it means not to be taught and brought up in Christianity. . . . [H]e is so totally ignorant of Christianity" (*Journals and Papers*, vol. 3 [Bloomington: Indiana University Press, 1975] 773 [no. 3837]; *Papirer* X^4 Z 223 [1851]). The context is a reference to Rousseau's failure to understand the collision between doing the good and suffering for it, in the Christian sense that Kierkegaard understands.

[48]Karl Barth, *Protestant Theology in the Ninteenth Century: Its Background and History*, trans. J. Bowden and B. Cozens (Valley Forge: Judson Press, 1973) 224 (translation of *Die Protestantische Theologie im 19. Jahrhundert* [1946]).

theological point and believed, with Socrates, that the cause of evil was ignorance that could be overcome with knowledge, and he stressed instead the social and exterior sources of evil.[49])

Rousseau, as Masson notes, does share Christianity's hopes, but without a Christ who is to fulfill them, and he subscribes to a notion of providence, although of a deistic kind. He was "theistic" in his view of the deity he adored and occasionally sensed in nature in direct intuitions. If there is a core of orthodoxy Rousseau shares with Christians, it consists of a theism akin to Christianity's and a dualism shared by both. But these are facets of almost all Western religious thinking, whether pagan or Christian or humanist. Rousseau knew that he shared central tenets with Christians but did not recognize the fact that they are not uniquely or especially Christian. Other deists thought of themselves as reformers, calling Christianity back to a frank acknowledgment of its essentials that they simply termed "natural religion." Rousseau could not do without the qualification "Christian" and his insistence upon it accounts in part for his attachment to Christianity and Jesus.

Rousseau's view of and bond with Christianity contains much that is culturally conditioned. Even his Vicar's review of Christianity proceeds from the philosophical culture of the day. For the *Profession* sets out in the expected manner of a treatise concerned with philosophy of religion, especially of a rationalist, deist cast. Part I sets out to discover a religion worthy of allegiance and arrives, not at all surprisingly, at natural religion. Even if Part II sets itself the task of considering problems in religion, there is no reason—except cultural—for centering upon Judaism, Islam and Christianity, less reason still to break forth into the celebrated paean to the Gospel and its Jesus. One understands how this development comes about by keeping in mind the personal method of selection of themes. The Vicar/ Rousseau discusses Christianity, Islam and Judaism because they are the historical religions of the West. Islam and Judaism are not serious competitors of European Christianity in Rousseau's time, of course, and they seem included more in an Enlightenment spirit that wished to portray Christianity as one religion among others. The Vicar discusses Christianity in some detail because his *heart* responds to it—by turns a heart that is moral and sentimental. While the mind of the philosopher arrives in Part

---

[49]Pierre Burgelin sees Manicheanism, rather than Pelagianism, as the temptation in Rousseau, Cf. *Existence,* 415.

I at natural religion grounded in conscience, his heart responds warmly and positively in Part II to what his own cold reason would have him reject. The heart wins. Were Rousseau and his Vicar part of a different moral-religious culture, one would have to suppose that Rousseau would hymn another scripture and another moral teacher. For Christianity in essence merits no special position within the Vicar's very limited phenomenology of revealed religions, and sentimental eloquence about Jesus cannot obscure the fact. For Rousseau the *philosophe,* in summation, the religion of universal moral reason is the true faith. The heart of Jean-Jacques Rousseau, citizen of Protestant Geneva and Christian Europe, responds to New Testament morality and drama, as his culture still expected, but not to "New Testament faith" from which it was freeing itself.

In the *Social Contract,* Rousseau made plain his view of Christianity as a spiritual religion that is not an adequate basis for political society. Moreover, the suggestion is plain that Christianity as spiritual religion is a threat to a well-ordered human society.

> But this religion, having no specific connexion with the body politic, leaves the law with only the force the law itself possesses, adding nothing to it; and hence one of the chief bonds necessary for holding any particular society together is lacking. Nor is this all: for far from attaching the hearts of the citizens of the state, this religion detaches them from it as from all other things of this world; and I know of nothing more contrary to the social spirit.[50]

The Vicar never denies this view of Christianity. Instead, he fastens upon other elements in it and dismisses the otherworldliness that may be historical but that, in human history, is simply impractical. In the *Social Contract's* indictment of Christianity as an obstacle to political society, its founder does not escape blame. But, for the *Profession,* Jesus can and should be saved for this world.

CHURCH

When one considers Rousseau's expressed views of the church, it becomes difficult to understand how any interpreter might argue for Rousseau's drifting back to the Catholic church. Rousseau unequivocally rejected church authority—certainly a central teaching of Roman Catholicism—and made no secret of his low opinion of clergymen. Were one to

---

[50]Trans. Maurice Cranston (Baltimore: Penguin Books, 1968) 182; OC III:465.

ignore the "Open Letter to de Beaumont," Rousseau's position would still be strongly antichurch. But his "Open Letter" makes the evidence overwhelming. Of course, the *Lettre à M. de Beaumont* is a polemical piece and this factor must be counted. In it, Rousseau sought to win friends in the Church of Geneva by his jibes at the Church of Rome. But even Geneva had become enough of a self-interested institution not to be thus flattered. Rousseau had made it clear that he had no sympathy for traditional Christian doctrines and that the institution with its claims to authority was both a perversion of the gospel and a violation of individual freedom and responsibility. And while freedom and responsibility were central to the Reformers, reaction to Rousseau in Protestant areas indicated the extent to which free individual interpretation of the Scriptures was truly to be allowed. The churches of both Rome and Geneva heard the attack not only upon doctrine but also upon church, and reacted predictably.

Rousseau nonetheless clung to the church, and his *Confessions* relate the importance he attached to being received back into the faith of Geneva after his Catholic period and then, during the *Émile* controversy, to being admitted to communion in a local church. In the second of the *Lettres de la Montagne,* he indicates what he truly sought in the church, namely, a fellowship of souls—*une atmosphère évangélique*—where he could fraternize in the "freedom of the children of God" with other souls enamored of Jesus.[51] Church and fellowship were in the end a personal need, not a reflection of acceptance or esteem for doctrine, theology and the institution built around them.

How far the reformed churches had deviated from the spirit of *sola scriptura* and individual interpretation Rousseau pointed out in castigating those who had acquired all the rejected habits of the past: the need for ecclesiastical bodies and with it the need to dominate.[52] He does not suggest that the churches disband and states that if the *Profession* of the Vicar were widely adopted one would see changes not in external cult but rather in the hearts of churchpeople.[53] This implies de-emphasizing, rather than abolishing, the institution and reemphasizing the notion of an assembly. Rousseau never indicates (as Kant subsequently did) that the church could positively serve to reinforce the moral faith that is the essence of his reli-

---

[51]Masson, *Religion,* II:162.
[52]Ibid., 163.
[53]Ibid., 166.

gion, although such a position would follow easily from the Vicar's remarks. But faith is always a very private matter for the archindividualist Rousseau, and thus he overlooks practical cooperation among individual admirers of Jesus in bringing about the Kingdom of God. One goes to church for fellowship, but fellowship is not conceived as related to religion in any essential way. The Vicar never comments on a possible civil role of religion, a topic that Rousseau took up in the final pages of the *Social Contract* the same year. The Vicar's notion of Christianity harmonizes well with the practical civil religion of a political society, as sketched by Rousseau. But the Rousseau of the *Social Contract* notes real problems posed for an earthly commonwealth by the spiritual teachings of Jesus. A religious assembly that orients one away from this world is there severely criticized.

When one compares the positions and conduct of Rousseau to Kant as regards the church, one cannot but ironically observe that while Kant had the positive notion of church it is Rousseau who goes to service and sacrament. Kant, for his part, ostentatiously left the academic procession in Königsberg as it reached the church doors. Whereas Kant affirmed the practical value of a particular faith in leading to moral faith only to step out of the processional line, Rousseau conceded no practical function for the Christian church and then insisted on entering even when those inside sought to bar him.

REVELATION

Rousseau's position on revelation, while paradoxical, was sufficient to provoke both Rome and Geneva. More than any other stance in the *Profession,* it sounded the theological call to arms against the heathen writer who had put his name on his work. In this Rousseau went beyond his attack upon the central authority of church so dear to Catholicism to a de facto assault on the foundations of Protestant Christianity. And his ultimate expression of respect and limited acceptance of revelation did not successfully conciliate.

In characteristic eighteenth-century fashion, the *Profession* had initially established reason as the criterion for judging religion but then amended this position in the proclamation of conscience as the highest authority. The casual reader who pauses at this point in the document might think himself observing another deist exercise at reconstructing natural religion or at making Christianity reasonable. Even the declaration of the role of conscience would not in itself necessarily direct one away from such a reading. The Vicar had issued the standard criticisms of revelation: the problems for the modern scientific mind brought about by miracle claims, the contradictions found in purported testimony and the logical vicious circle that is established when miracles, prophecies and testimony are invoked to support each other. On the positive side, the Vicar affirmed reason and its discernment of a will and higher intelligence that order the universe,[54] man's freedom to act and his animation by an immaterial soul,[55] and a kindly providence. Most of the arguments were really quite familiar, even if distinctive due to the Vicar's context and tone. The attack upon orthodox religion was appreciated, as Voltaire's marginalia indicate. Book revelation is, in short, of more than questionable value when it is bound to so many difficulties of proofs, logic, and laws of nature. The cry becomes "How many men between God and me!"[56]—expressing in a phrase both the problems caused by human witnesses and scribes and also their ultimately superfluous nature. For God does not need Moses and a hundred other intermediaries in order to speak to Jean-Jacques Rousseau,[57] since he can and does address him directly through reason and conscience. And in the interaction of reason and conscience one discovers for oneself all that is required, rather than having it revealed by a complicating exterior agent. A rational God, after all, would be practical and not impose needless, distracting hermeneutical chores upon those eager to discover and do his will.

God speaks directly, and all would be simple if people would listen to "the immortal voice from heaven" and to their own "divine instinct"[58] rather than to human voices. But insincere men abound who, not even sure of their own authority, attempt to speak in the name of God:

> As soon as the nations took to making God speak, every one made him speak in his own fashion, and made him say what he himself wanted. Had they listened only to what God says in the heart of man, there would have been but one religion upon earth.[59]

What is meant is not natural religion as generally understood—the simple religion of universal reason—but the transcending, ennobling, elevating,

---

[54]*Émile*, 236-37; OC IV:574-75.
[55]*Émile*, 241; OC IV:583.
[56]*Émile*, 261; OC IV:610.
[57]*La Lettre à M. de Beaumont: O.C.* IV:987 (Grimsley, ed. *Religious Writings*, 291).
[58]*Émile*, 254; OC IV:600.
[59]*Émile*, 259; OC IV:608.

innate religion of conscience, which is precisely the voice from heaven and the divine instinct mentioned. Without so many other voices and the effort required to distinguish among them, he noted with irony, he would be freer to serve his God.[60]

Eighteenth-century religious thought was working up the courage to proclaim reason as the true revelation, and Rousseau shared this view, in modified form.[61] Reason remained decisive, but it was conscience—as moral reason—that was emerging as the supreme revelation and Rousseau was bolder than his contemporaries in expressing his conviction.

Jean Starobinski, in *Jean-Jacques Rousseau, La Transcendence et L'Obstacle*, would say that the only revelation that in the end matters is that which occurs immediately in conscience—direct, irrefutable, universal, always heard even if not always heeded.[62] Starobinski speaks of a "double lived revelation" that also serves as the reconciliation of the particular with the universal: it consists, first, of being and knowing the self and, second, of seeing and possessing the truth. The two aspects taken together constitute the fullness of revelation. Starobinski further distinguishes between the stages *dévoilement* and *révélation* in existence. For Rousseau, *dévoilement* (unveiling) is the attempt to come back to one's original pristine self-transparency, while *révélation* would be the subsequent activity of manifesting the recovered natural state.[63] This is at least wholly Pelagian, if not unchristian in outlook. It does not deny human failure and need for recovery but emphasizes that the wherewithal for restoration is already present and that the original, natural state of self-transparency can indeed be recovered by human effort alone, a state in which the voice of conscience will be heard with pristine clarity.[64]

In both senses of revelation (that is, as universally accessible conscience and personal witness), the individual plays an active role. To be

---

[60]*Émile*, 261; OC IV:610-11.

[61]Hegel would make the claim resoundingly in the 19th century, but with an amended notion of reason. Among 18th-century writers, Lessing must certainly be cited. In his *Education of the Human Race* (1780) he was unmistakably moving in the same direction but refused in advance the hubris constituted by this implicit conclusion in his own thought.

[62](Paris: Gallimard, 1971) 97-98.

[63]Ibid., 101. The term *dévoilement* is Starobinski's and not Rousseau's. Starobinski's distinction seems valid, nonetheless, even in unexplicit in Rousseau.

[64]The orthodox would want to counter that the human condition after *divine* forgiveness is *greater* than the original state. This is the "felix culpa" motif, according to which the fall of the first Adam merited a "second Adam" who brings the race infinitely more.

• 28 • THE JESUS OF MORAL REASON

told what is contained in canonical books is an unworthy passivity. For one must open and read for oneself the "book of nature" inscribed in the soul. In this, Rousseau goes far beyond his claim of reaffirming the Protestant principle of personal interpretation of the Scriptures. For the essential scripture and essential source of revelation we now find together. And once we understand that conscience is part of a higher reason, we shall see that reason has really become revelation as early as Rousseau.

Even while Rousseau went beyond contemporaries who stopped short of the affirmation of reason as revealer and revealed, as both subject and content of revelation, he felt the need for reconciling his standpoint with the Christian revelation. Everything the Vicar tells us and every implication of his thinking is to dismiss the Christian gospel as superfluous, if not harmful to healthy reason. Yet, like Nathan the Wise in Lessing's later drama of the same name (1779), the Vicar begins a discourse on the three revelations and "book religions," (namely, Judaism, Christianity and Islam), and, much in the manner of Nathan, after showing Christianity's case to be weakest, goes on to establish a criterion of judgment reminiscent of the tale of the three rings: "To judge a religion rightly, you must not only study it in the books of its partisans, you must learn it in their lives."[65] But the Vicar goes further, to an attemped accommodation with the gospel. Having established reason, as God's gift, as the proper judge of dogmatic claims (God would insult man to give him a fine tool and then refuse to let him use it[66]), and having effectively used reason to undermine Christian faith claims, the Vicar offers his incongruous conclusion about revelation: that he neither accepts nor rejects it, while he remains convinced of its truth. He reflects further that it would be incompatible with God's justice to be obliged to accept an historical revelation in order to be saved[67] and adds, in caution, that he wishes his view to be understood as subjective. In his defense, the Vicar might invoke here his "method" which would remind us that he will not torment his mind about matters of no practical consequence. But he would distract no one thereby, and one might be tempted even to question his sincerity in this refusal to be consequent in his thinking. For when the Vicar argues in favor of banishing Christian mission-

---

[65]*Émile*, 266; OC IV:619.
[66]*Émile*, 264; OC IV:614.
[67]*Émile*, 271; *OC IV:625*.

aries, he does not shy away from his conclusion or its "objective" worth when he says,

> Not only does this seem reasonable to me, but I maintain what it is that every wise man ought to say in similar circumstances.[68]

When all would seem to lead to the rejection of the Christian Book, why does he halt the march of reason and then, in an about-face that mollified no one but that is apparently sincere, go on to praise the gospel and its Jesus? The answer lies, one again, in his heart. For although the New Testament is "full of incredible things repugnant to reason, things which no natural man can understand or accept,"[69] he declares in the next breath that "the gospel indeed contains characters so great, so striking, so entirely inimitable, that their invention would be more astonishing than their hero."[70] The characters of the gospel and its teacher appeal with force. The mind must reject absurd claims about the characters (such as divine incarnation and resurrection from the dead) and remain at least dubious about much else, but the heart (= sentimental heart) responds to other contents and finds them moving expressions consonant with the intuitions of conscience (= moral heart). Hence if the Book is accepted in any sense as a revelation, it is as the words of a natural man who has uncovered (*dévoilement*) the highest truths and exhibits (*révélation*) them in his life. In this, we may view Rousseau as a forerunner not only of Kant but also of Hegel. This is surely not orthodoxy's meaning of revelation and Rousseau knew that full well. But it is powerful and appealing in its appreciation of the struggling humanity of Jesus.

JESUS THE CHRESTOS

In essence, the interpretation of Jesus presented by the Vicar amounts to rejection of the *evangelium de Christo*.[71] Neither the gospel nor its Jesus is accepted as anything approaching divine providence's vertical descent into human affairs. Moreover, they are plainly discounted as anything more than human.

Nor is this obscured by the rhetorical flourish of the ode to Jesus or by the famous comparison of Jesus and Socrates, both of which comprise an-

---

[68]*Émile*, 270; OC IV:623.
[69]*Émile*, 272; OC IV:627.
[70]Ibid.
[71]Cf. Burgelin, *Existence*, 434.

other surprise turn in the apparent direction of the *Profession*. But the turn is brief, if sharp, and undertaken so that the *heart* of Jean-Jacques Rousseau can offer recognition to another who has been sincere and responsive to his own and so that natural religion makes some place for the historical Jesus, but equally so that the *philosophes* might be annoyed and undermined.

In contrast, the few words about Jesus in the *Social Contract* suggest a strikingly different figure. There he is described not as a moral teacher but as the founder of spiritual religion. In saying this, Rousseau is not embracing a more traditional view of Christ but, from the standpoint of one concerned about the organization of the proper society, issuing an indictment of Christianity.

> Jesus came to establish a spiritual kingdom on earth; this kingdom, by separating the theological system from the political, meant that the state ceased to be a unity, and it caused those intestine divisions which have never ceased to disturb Christian peoples.[72]

The Vicar does not recognize Jesus as a teacher of otherworldliness. The spiritual values that he represents for the Vicar are sincerity, self-transparency, and moral struggle in a corrupt and corrupting world. The Vicar has in fact ignored or simply neutralized the troubling view of Jesus in the *Social Contract*. And, in so doing, he has perhaps dissolved the problem Jesus would there pose to a pluralistic earthly society. For the *Profession* stands for spiritual values that have a place in a political society and that pose no threat to it. Moreover, the figure of Jesus himself provides an additional richness: a model of moral living and a witness to the possibility of successful moral struggle even in the most hostile social context. The *Profession* simply ignores what the *Social Contract* viewed as essential to Jesus' actual teaching. In so doing, the *Profession* rescues Jesus from the spirituality of otherworldliness and plants him firmly in the spirituality appropriate to this world. Jesus can be saved for a world that can profit from his example. And it is the Jesus of this world—a moral and practical rather than historical Jesus—that the *Profession* finally hymns.

Before the ode to Jesus, the Vicar's discourse had clearly dismissed any claims by or about any man to be the "channel of the sacred will," of the "divine majesty," rejected as adequate credentials of alleged super-

---

[72]*The Social Contract*, trans. Maurice Cranston (Baltimore: Penguin Books, 1968) 178; OC III:462.

human status "certain private signs, performed in the presence of a few obscure persons, signs which everybody else can only know by hearsay"[73] and miracle stories that describe the Christ in his ministry, as well as any other miracle but the unchangeable order of nature. (Other miracles, as exceptions to the law of nature, are simply unworthy of God.) Before the sentimental turn then, much about Jesus had already been denied—most essentially his being the Christ or "anointed of God," "Messiah." Implicit is exclusion of any claim that the gospel is in any sense witness to Jesus as the Christ or anointed.

However, once the *evangelium de Christo* is rejected, its moral content and exemplary teacher are affirmed and praised—not by intellectual reason, which was reduced to respectful silence in this instance while compelled to outright attack upon much of the surrounding narrative. Intellectual reason tolerates the Jesus portrayed in such a compromising medium and in such compromising company. This may seem little, unless one is familiar with the philosophical backdrop against which this deed of religious tolerance for the historical Jesus was carried out. Against the intolerance of the *philosophes* and their dismissal of everything and everyone in the gospels, Rousseau's is a daring and provocative act, a radical turn in Enlightenment philosophy of religion that heralded and began the philosophical rescue of Jesus, that is, the salvation of Jesus by philosophy, for philosophy, and from the *philosophes*.

Manuscript drafts of the *Profession* indicate that Rousseau had originally written a strong polemic about the Christ, that he then deleted it and added the comparison of Jesus and Socrates in order to underline just how far he was from conventional deism and the party of the *philosophes* and, thus, how much at heart a Christian.[74] The final, published version stresses the unique achievement of Jesus in the historical context: not the fulfillment of Jewish expectations of Messiah but the realization in his person of the type of the good man as imagined by Plato. The Jesus who was an island of (Greek) wisdom amidst (Jewish) fanaticism, of simple (Greek) virtue amidst a degraded (Jewish) nation,[75] is one who has risen above his

---

[73]*Émile*, 262; OC IV:612.
[74]Cf. Peter D. Jimack, *La Genèse de la rédaction de l'Emile de Jean-Jacques Rousseau*, in Theodore Besterman, ed., *Studies on Voltaire and the 18th Century*, vol. 13 (Geneva: Institut et Musée Voltaire, 1960), but also Masson, *Profession*, which has the most complete treatment of the *Profession* text.
[75]*Émile*, 272-73; OC IV:626.

background to heroic stature and risen higher than the Socrates who was merely the product of his more enlightened moral context. Jesus' accomplishment is greater than Socrates' because Jesus started out at a lower point, because in a morally baser society.[76] The content of Jesus' accomplishment is not different from Socrates' but only the process of achievement and the cultural starting point. And the final argument for the "superiority" of Jesus—stresses a Rousseau who will increasingly claim proof of his own moral goodness in the wrongs done him—is the contrast between the calm death of Socrates amidst friends and the lonely agony of Jesus' crucifixion: "Yes, if the life and death of Socrates are those of a philosopher, the life and death of Christ are those of a God."[77]

Rousseau's Vicar, who has retained the term "Christ" while discarding its meaning, should have expressed himself in Latin rather than in French. Had he done so, we might read *mors divi* and not *mors dei*. For the divine being intended is not of the kind who inhabits the upper regions or descends exceptionally therefrom, but rather a superior mortal who by his deeds is elevated, divinized. Such a distinction in the Vicar's discourse would have blurred the rhetorical effect intended, to be sure. Rousseau profits instead from the ambiguity of the term "god," although religious critics were not won over. The meaning of Jesus, then, is not that in Jesus of Nazareth God became man but that man becomes godlike in the Jesus who lived and died as the suffering servant of the religion of conscience.

He who accepted the *evangelium Christi* saw in its teacher one worthy of imitation. And an "Imitation of Christ" is not unreasonable to Rousseau or his Vicar. But, as Starobinski observes on this point, "The imitation of Jesus Christ, in Rousseau, is the imitation of the 'divine' act by which a solitary human conscience becomes the source of truth or transparency to a truth come from outside."[78] And the greater one's moral witness, the more painful one's rejection by one's people—so reflects a

---

[76]The anti-Jewish implications of such remarks will not escape the 20th-century reader. Rousseau is by no means the only writer who, in wishing to put down Christianity, insisted on placing Judaism and Jews even lower. At the same time, his lofty estimation of the Greeks reflects a cultural trend that finally culminated in the "tyranny of Greece over Germany."

[77]Ibid. The French reads "sage," for Rousseau has no intention of making Socrates a *philosophe*. Hegel too finds great significance in the abjectness of Christ's death, in the *Lectures on the Philosophy of Religion;* cf. chapter 3 of this work.

[78]Jean Starobinski, *Jean-Jacques Rousseau: La Transparence et L'Obstacle* (Paris: Gallimard, 1971; orig., Paris: Librairie Plon, 1957) 89-90.

Rousseau thinking not only of Socrates and Jesus but also of Jean-Jacques Rousseau. While the prophetic power is surprising (and also ironic in one who dismissed prophecy), the sentiment of a slightly megalomaniac Rousseau is not. The reader of the *Confessions* and *Correspondence Générale* knows this side of the author all too well. More important than the place of Rousseau, who might thus situate himself between Socrates and Jesus, is still the ultimate place of Jesus in Rousseau's religious system. This consists of Jesus as teacher, example and witness. As Starobinski notes,

> The Christ of Rousseau is not a mediator; he is only a great *example*. If he is greater than Socrates, it is not by his divinity but by his courageous humanity. Nowhere does the death of Christ appear in its theological dimension, as the act of reparation that would be at the center of human history. The death of Jesus is only the admirable archetype of the just man calumniated by his people. Socrates did not die in loneliness [*solitairement*], while the greatness of Christ comes to him from his loneliness [*solitude*.] He offers the most edifying example of the destiny of the exception which Jean-Jacques suffers and himself desires.[79]

Starobinski's retention of the term "Christ" entails some of the same ambiguity as Rousseau's use of it.

The end result is that the anointed of God, the Christ of Christianity, is not "rejected and despised" (as he had been in previous French Enlightenment thought) but merely dismissed. Exit the Christ of faith, only to have enter the Jesus of the (moral) heart who finally emerges as the morally Useful (*Chrestos*) of the Vicar's faith.

ROUSSEAU AND THE VICAR DEBATED

1.HEATHEN OR HERETIC?:
DE BEAUMONT'S PASTORAL LETTER AND ROUSSEAU'S REPLY

Out of the furor aroused by *Émile* came the *Mandement* (Pastoral Letter) issued in August 1762 by Christophe de Beaumont, Archbishop of Paris, and then in March 1763 Rousseau's equally famous reply, the *Lettre à M. de Beaumont* (Open Letter). De Beaumont himself would seem to have had little to do with the composition of the Pastoral Letter, as common practice for such documents and de Beaumont's own subsequent indications of regret for *ad hominem* remarks would suggest. The stinging

---

[79]Ibid., 88-89.

personal attacks on the honor and good faith of Rousseau led the citizen of Protestant Geneva to draft in late 1762 an acid reply to Paris's Catholic archbishop. Its principal nonliterary, nonpsychological interest lies in the emphases given to contents of the *Profession*. It adds nothing substantially new to the faith of the Vicar but rather underlines the Vicar's negations and affirmations, while defending his own personal honor. Both the *Mandement* and the *Lettre à M. de Beaumont* still prove lively reading, and one may observe a bit maliciously that the objections of both are well founded. Each betrays a nonobjective and utterly unsympathetic reading of the other writer, but this is not surprising, given the genre in which each was writing. For each addressed and was interested in persuading a far larger audience. (The *Mandement* was not addressed directly to Rousseau, while Rousseau's open letter both formally and ironically addressed his formidable adversary with all his titles: "Archbishop of Paris, Duke of St. Cloud, Peer of France, Commander of the Order of the Holy Spirit, Proviseur of the Sorbonne, etc.,"[80] acknowledging them exactly as the *Mandement* lists them, except for the claimed source, namely, "divine mercy and the grace of the Apostolic See.")

The *Mandement* proceeds through twenty-six numbered paragraphs to attack the dangerous teachings of *Émile,* the character of its author and the diabolic quality of those sections of the *Profession* that seek an accord with traditional Christianity. The author of the *Mandement* accuses Rousseau of speaking of the excellence of the gospel only to destroy its dogmas and of depicting the beauty of virtue only to extinguish it in the heart of the reader.[81] The *Mandement* author is committed to the church doctrine of original sin and would disagree with the entire spirit of the Enlightenment which Kant, in a well-known phrase, defined as "man's release from self-incurred tutelage."[82] He posits as alternatives *either* the tutelage of the gospel and revelation as interpreted by the church *or* moral chaos, and argues against what he believes to be the rationalist orientation of Rousseau's work. Invoking St. Paul against the modern pagan philosopher he discerns beneath the Vicar's robes, he writes that reason alone loses itself

---

[80]*O.C.* IV:925 (Grimsley, ed. *Religious Writings,* 236).

[81]Quoted in Grimsley, ed., *Religious Writings,* 217.

[82]"What is Enlightenment?" in *On History,* trans. and ed. Lewis White Beck (Indianapolis: Bobbs-Merrill Co., 1963) 3; *Kants Gesammelte Schriften* (Berlin, 1910-1972) VIII:35.

and that the proper and best use of reason consists in submission to revelation.[83] The *Mandement* reads Rousseau badly on this and fails to recognize his own criticisms of reason alone. Moreover, it never engages the
Vicar's teaching on the submission of reason to conscience which is the
special teaching of the *Profession* and the true locus of the challenge that
the *Mandement* senses in the Vicar's modern rationalist faith.

In paragraph XXVIII, the Archbishop's Pastoral Letter delivers its dramatic summation:

> [W]e condemn the aforesaid book as containing an abominable teaching
> that would reverse natural law and destroy the foundations of the Christian
> religion, [as] leading to disrupting the peace of the state, [and] to setting
> subjects in revolt against the authority of their sovereign; as containing a
> great number of propositions respectively false, scandalous, full of hate
> for the church and her ministers, contrary to the respect due to Holy Scrip-
> ture and the traditions of the church, erroneous, impious, blasphemous and
> heretical.[84]

We see in this not untypical reaction from Christian quarters that Rousseau's deism is the provocation, along with its critique of Christianity, and
that the radical moral religion envisioned by the Vicar, grounded in conscience and yet positing itself as consonant with the essence of the gospel,
is apparently not perceived. Had the *Mandement* understood clearly, or
wished to do so, it might have retorted that Rousseau's religious morality
was itself the product of the gospel and that his philosophical hubris made
him refuse to recognize the true source of his own insights. A plurality of
revelations has long been a difficult thought for Christians and the *Mandement* seems deaf on more than one level to the declaration of an ever new,
universal yet individual revelation claimed by Rousseau.

Rousseau, for his part, responded as a true son of the Enlightenment,
not understanding the fears and vested interests of more traditional Christians. His Open Letter rightfully replies to the personal nature of the
Mandement's charges, but his self-indulgence elicited from Voltaire (in his
marginal comments to the published letter) the quip: ''You begin by
speaking of yourself, and you speak only of yourself. You're not
shrewd.''[85] Where he does rise above wounded ego, Rousseau delivers his

---

[83]Grimsley, ed., *Religious Writings*, 221.
[84]Ibid., 229.
[85]Quoted in Grimsley, ed. *Religious Writings*, 230 n. 2; OC IV:927, at line 24.

own *ad hominem* attack on de Beaumont, not for bad character but for slander. He would portray himself as a good Genevan Protestant brazenly attacked by a foreign Catholic (and, in this, conveniently pass over his longtime residence in France and the Protestant condemnations that issued from Holland and Geneva itself), as one devoted to Scripture and dutifully employing reason and the right of individual interpretation. In his continued attack on the doctrine of original sin and in his defense of educational methods in *Émile,* he cleverly remarks that the work and its educational theories were destined for those baptized and hence washed free of original sin,[86] and leaves it to the strange logic of theology to account for the origin of present vices in the original sin from which Christians have supposedly been washed clean. His attacks on miracles are sharpened. He accuses those who interpolated miracle stories of obscuring the teaching of the gospel and adds that he himself has no need of miracles in order to be Christian. And, in his renewed attack on human testimony as sufficient grounds for accepting book revelation, he wittily calls attention to a recent volume of impressive signed testimony concerning vampires![87]

Having underlined his break with so much held dear by Christians, he leaves his own Christianity and salvation to a Higher Judge. He presumes at the same time that his good name is numbered among the elect and on a list from which it cannot be erased by human authority.[88] To be included on such a list, he reasserts, he need not be orthodox or dishonestly toe the orthodox line. For the essential in religion, he stresses, consists of practice and whoever is good, merciful, charitable, and humane believes enough to be saved.[89] This is the affirmation of the heart of his religion. (Voltaire here observes, "This is to be *just,* not Christian."[90])

He affirms reason and then attempts to affirm revelation, noting the difference between rational religion and revealed religion as consisting of that between understanding *and* believing on the one side and *not* understanding but nonetheless accepting and believing on the other.[91]

The *Mandement* and *Lettre à M. de Beaumont* taken together represent the conflict between an insecure orthodoxy and a deism still invoking the

---

[86]OC IV:938 (*Religious Writings,* 243).
[87]OC IV:987 (*Religious Writings,* 292).
[88]OC IV:961-62 (*Religious Writings,* 265).
[89]OC IV:962 (*Religious Writings,* 266).
[90]Quoted in *Religious Writings,* 266 n. 1; OC IV:962, at line 21.
[91]OC IV:990-91.

name Christian—or reinvoking it. It is a public argument, a battle for the minds and hearts of the times. The *Mandement* sees the *Profession* as a dangerous work for traditional and institutional Christianity from the hand of a deist who brazenly affixes his name to it and becomes not only an identifiable target but also a reachable one. Rousseau, for his part, repeats and sharpens his criticisms of church and revelation and underlines the essential in religion, namely, moral practice, about which his mind and heart concur, while insisting on the ties, if not the tangle, of his religion with the Christianity from which his heart will not let him free. In a sense, Voltaire's observation is correct: "This is to be *just,* not Christian." But Rousseau was insisting that Christianity find a way to become this other and also that whoever wished to be just could and should remain Christian and an imitator of Jesus, the suffering servant of conscience.

2. RATIONALIST OR ROMANTICIST?: THE ROLE OF CONSCIENCE

Rousseau's attack upon the *philosophes* has frequently been cited as evidence in favor of a nonrationalist interpretation of his thought. But opposing any such view stands the deist-rationalist content of the *Profession,* to say nothing of its condemnation by de Beaumont and others precisely as rationalism. Nineteenth-century interpreters read Rousseau as a romantic, and this projection of the nineteenth century upon an authentic figure of the eighteenth has for too long impeded objective assessment.

Romantic

Views of Rousseau as a protoromantic are both exaggerations and distortions, while not wholly without foundation. And such a frequently cited remark as that of Hume—that Rousseau had only felt during the whole course of his life and that in him sensibility had risen to unexampled pitch[92]—distorts both Rousseau and Hume when it is invoked to portray Rousseau as the father of French Romanticism instead of expressing Hume's exasperation with a very difficult house guest.

No one can deny that Rousseau used the language of feeling and that he often expressed himself imprecisely. But if one looks carefully at the contexts of his words, seeks out his presuppositions, and follows his thoughts through to their conclusions, one cannot but recognize that,

---

[92]Quoted by Frederick Copleston in *A History of Philosophy,* vol. 6, pt. I (New York: Image Books, 1964) 78.

whatever the limitations that remain, Rousseau had an utterly different self- and worldview from that of the romantics, and nowhere is this truer than in his religious thought.

To invoke the life of Rousseau here, as romanticist interpreters frequently do, is to confuse biography with thought. There is certainly much in his life and in the *Confessions* to suggest romantic inclinations, but the language of feeling alone is not enough to include Rousseau in that other era. Against his own protest, Jean-Jacques Rousseau *was* a man of his times, even when he opposed its trends and leading figures. And his optimistic, committed belief in the efficacy of reason is the hallmark of his eighteenth-century stance. If he criticized others' use of reason and noted its limits, he did not thereby become an irrationalist, and the thrust of his criticism is not to abandon reason but to enlarge and thus enhance it.

But those who insist on the romanticism of Rousseau should be answered, and what better ground than the fields about that country home near Vevey from which the love story of Julie and Saint-Preux moved the tender hearts of the eighteenth century and where, some claim, they sired a brood of romantics? But these "children" of Julie and Saint-Preux are, in the end, worse than illegitimate; they are pretenders to the honor. If one reads only the first parts of *La Nouvelle Heloïse,* as undoubtedly many of the eighteenth century did, one perceives the dominance of romantic tendencies. That *La Nouvelle Heloïse* began as a romantic daydream of Rousseau, which he then partially lived out with Sophe d'Houdetot and Saint-Lambert, is fully conceded. But as in life so in his creation, he finally escaped the romantic consummation toward which it was proceeding and ended it on a moral, religious note. If the work had followed through its apparent logic, its reasonable romantic conclusion might have seen either some kind of earthly happiness for Julie and Saint-Preux in their sublimated passion or else their tragic death—as Rousseau had originally contemplated ending their afternoon boating excursion. To have said this is to concede that Rousseau was in the process of writing a romantic novel. But the fact remains that it was *not* such a novel that he ultimately published. Both his romantic self-indulgence and the characters that issue from it are reformed in the religious, moral conclusion that he attached to the work. In the light of the conclusion, the first parts of the novel, dominated by *amour-propre,* portray a passion that is revealed in retrospect as destructive.[93] The ending that Rousseau finally used casts the novel into dialec-

---

[93]Starobinski, *Jean-Jacques Rousseau,* 140.

tical form and changes it from a not untypical tale of futile passion into the edifying history of the progress of souls, in which duty triumphs over passion.[94]

For Julie did not expire out of love for Saint-Preux, nor indulge in any form of love suicide, nor did she drown tragically in a boating accident. Instead, she contracted a fatal illness after leaping to the rescue of her child who had fallen into the water. In this, she symbolically cleansed herself as she simultaneously accomplished a heroic task as mother. Thus the tragic ending, if it is such, has its basis in morality and duty, not in passion. And Julie's final words, after her own profession of faith as reported by Saint-Preux, speak of a culmination of their love in the hereafter where *virtue* will unite them. Considered in its published form then (and even if one perceives the ending as somewhat incongruous), the novel must be viewed as portraying the dialectic of passion and virtue. Its romance and sentimentality must be viewed in the light of the ending and thus the full context of the work subsumes them into a higher order.

Furthermore, in her heroic leap, Julie must not be construed as acting on the basis of sheer feeling. The character development in the novel will not support such interpretation and Rousseau plainly rejected feeling as the basis for moral action. Julie is a mother doing her duty to her child, and she is intended in this to be an example of Rousseau's ethics. Ernst Cassirer, who began the twentieth-century rescue of Rousseau from the romantics, adds that

> Rousseau's ethics is not an ethics of feeling but the most categorical form of a pure ethics of obligation (*Gesetzes-Ethik*) that was established before Kant.[95]

Moral intuitions located in the heart are not to be confused with traditional descriptions of the heart as the seat of passion. Heart triumphs over passion, both in *La Nouvelle Heloïse* and in Rousseau's thought generally. It also triumphs over intellectual reason. Rousseau opposed both the cult of feeling and the cult of intellectual reason with the divine intuitions of conscience. And given the nature of conscience and its relation to reason, this leaves us a Rousseau who is neither a nineteenth-century romantic nor a typical eighteenth-century rationalist. Conscience and the foundations of

---

[94]Ibid.
[95]Cassirer, *Question*, 96.

ethics, even if described in the language of the heart, are not the product of physical feeling. If we grasp this, we avoid a misinterpretation of Rousseau and move closer to appreciating his accomplishment within eighteenth-century thought in which, as Cassirer notes, Rousseau not only opposed a one-sided rationalist culture but "in opposition to the predominant opinion of the century—eliminated feeling from the foundation of ethics."[96]

Rationalist

Rousseau regarded the *Profession* as a rationalist creed even while it attacked the rationalists and rationalism of his day. Once Rousseau has been rescued from the romantics' and irrationalists' undue claims upon him, the task becomes that of specifying the nature of his rationalism. Here Rousseau has not left us a simple task, although surely an important one. For Rousseau was not merely prescribing moderation in the face of the times but attempting to establish reason on a firmer, wider base. This may finally mean an enlarged reason, but in this we shall have to proceed cautiously and confine ourselves to what the texts support.

The most emphatic case for Rousseau's rationalism is found in Robert Derathé's work.[97] In it, Derathé seeks to complete the work of Cassirer by rescuing Rousseau from lingering sentimentalist interpretations in France. Derathé is aware of the sentimentalist aspects in Rousseau—the voice of nature, the role of experience and feeling as true teachers—and argues for its reconcilability with the "divine flame of reason," "the true guide."[98] According to Derathé, error arises when interpreters construe the relationship of feeling to reason as one of primacy rather than as simple anteriority.[99] Primacy, he declares, finally goes neither to feeling nor reason but to the moral life which maintains an equilibrium between the two.

The development of reason has several stages, in Rousseau's view: the prerational (passive registration of sensation),[100] *raison sensitive* (formation of simple ideas by comparison of various sensations),[101] and *raison*

---

[96]Ibid., 89.
[97]Derathé, *Rationalisme*.
[98]Ibid., 4.
[99]On this point, Derathé considers Masson, Maritain, Brunschwicg, and Lassère among the guilty. Cf. *Rationalisme*, 4-5 n. 3.
[100]Ibid., 25.
[101]Ibid., 26.

intellectuelle (marked by introduction of complex ideas).[102] For those who equate the rational with the totally abstract, even the second stage might be considered still prerational, for it essentially involves response to physical sensation. But Rousseau made no such equation. When he elsewhere spoke of reason, it was abstract intellectual reason to which he referred, both when he criticized excesses and praised its proper role. Intellectual reason does not exhaust the sense or possibilities of reason for Rousseau. And as one perceives that intellectual reason is itself only a stage and that it requires fulfillment in order to be whole, one must ask about the relationship of the new development or stage that completes the foregoing stages to reason. Only the third stage is abstract, and so neither the development nor higher stage need necessarily be abstract. *Raison sensitive* is allied with physical feeling and suggests that another form of *raison* might also be allied with another type of feeling, namely, moral feeling.

Reason is completed in conscience, which Rousseau did not explicitly mention as a form of reason while at the same time he clearly distinguished it from intellectual reason. Yet Rousseau's use of three stages of reason, completed by conscience, suggests that conscience is not only the culmination of reason but a fourth stage, a *raison morale*. The term suggests the reasonableness of reason's submission to a higher authority that can now be understood as part of reason itself.

Reason leads to conscience. He made the point polemically in the reply to de Beaumont when, in contrast to the *Mandement*'s assertion that reason properly leads to the gospel, Rousseau maintained that reason never abandons itself to an exterior authority but rather submits to conscience and together with conscience goes on to judge religion and the gospel. Unless conscience is understood as not only intricately but also *essentially* tied to reason, to a reason that includes intellectual reason (and of course anterior stages) with conscience, submission on the part of (intellectual) reason would represent self-abandonment, even if to another authority interior to the self. Rousseau did not use the term ''moral reason'' but ''conscience'' functions as such, and understanding conscience as moral reason is in the end not only warranted by the text but required.

In religion, intellectual reason would indicate only what doctrines would be like, namely, plain, clear, and strikingly simple.[103] If left at this, Rous-

---

[102]Ibid., 28.
[103]*Émile*, 264; OC IV:614.

seau's religion would quickly reduce to natural religion of the familiar Enlightenment kind. But a higher faculty enters and responds to the content of positive (revealed) religion, without in any way compromising the essential reasonableness of the universal affirmed. This is the new turn that Rousseau gave to deism in the *Profession* and is what led—despite difficulties with Scripture—to the ultimate affirmation of the gospel. Rousseau viewed Christianity first in the light of intellectual reason and then in the light of higher, moral reason, and the result was that he affirmed Christianity in a new way at the very point where one would have expected dismissal. The moral intuitions of the heart having responded to the moral teaching and teacher of the Gospel, Rousseau's heart went out to embrace the gospel and affirm Christian revelation in a way that was disconcerting to most of the rationalists and religious of his century. For in the gospel he found a morality taught and embodied in a rare, pristine fashion, one worthy of affirmation no matter the absurd human interpolations. And, while conscience intuitively responds to higher truths, intellectual reason might be scandalized were it not reassured by this higher reason.

Intellectual reason alone cannot affirm the gospel as the Vicar did. Yet, when the Vicar spoke, neither was intellectual reason constrained nor abandoned nor outraged when subsumed beneath conscience and its affirmations, but took up its proper role and listened to a higher voice. Rousseau went even further when he said that reason only comes into its own when allied with conscience. If reason is limited to intellectual reason as its highest form, then in theory the use of intellectual reason ought to be sufficient. But, in practice, intellectual reason unguided by a ''higher power'' leads one astray. This might sound as if Rousseau were about to agree with de Beaumont and call for grace. But the higher power that is needed is conscience, and Rousseau was thus in effect saying that for reason to be sufficient it required conscience as moral reason.

Rousseau is a rationalist, but with Rousseau rationalism is transformed as it is elevated above intellectual reason. The same purity of heart that is the condition for the emergence of conscience is also the *sine qua non* for the proper exercise of reason, and there is no *saine raison* in a base heart.[104] Conscience is the necessary guide without which reason leads to error and excess. But the interrelationship of intellectual reason and conscience is

---

[104]Derathé, *Rationalisme,* 7.

more intricate still. For intellectual reason is also the power by which the primitive instinct for the good develops into full conscience.[105]

Rousseau emphatically distinguished between "reason" and "conscience" in that by the former he meant *intellectual* reason. Yet the two require and complement each other in any *saine raison*. Reason, as intellectual reason, develops conscience, and conscience then guides intellectual reason. God gives us conscience in order to live the good; reason in order to know it; and, the Vicar added, freedom in order to choose it. Conscience without intellectual reason would be blind love of the good, while intellectual reason alone, without the perfecting sentiment of conscience, would be knowledge of the good detached from action and in imminent danger of hubris and error.

"My rule of giving myself over to sentiment more than to reason is confirmed by reason itself," declared the Vicar. This can be restated: "My rule of giving myself over to sentiment more than to *intellectual reason* is confirmed by *reason-that-has-become-whole (saine raison)*." The heart— and thus conscience too—has its reasons; and intellectual reason, having taken its place in a *saine raison,* knows them.

If conscience can be termed "moral reason," then the rationalism of Rousseau would at last seem beyond dispute. He is then the advocate of a new rationalism—one that encompasses both "mind" and "heart." His body-mind dualism in the end blocked his developing a concept of reason to encompass the whole person, the category of *raison sensitive* notwithstanding. But such a broadened rationalism, beyond intellectual reason and even beyond a recognition of the limits of intellectual reason to a *saine raison* that includes conscience as *raison morale,* is a significant advance. The affirmation of sentiment in Rousseau then is finally an affirmation of reason, but not the narrow reason of the *philosophes.* Rousseau wished to do more than oppose their social program and narrow rationalism. He wished to formulate a whole reason that would lead to a better society of moral individuals. The language of sentiment and the language of reason are both employed, but not until one realizes that Rousseau was in the process of articulating a wider notion of reason does one see how they work together.

---

[105]Ibid., 112.

ASSESSING ROUSSEAU'S RELIGIOUS THOUGHT

ESSENTIAL TEACHINGS OF THE VICAR'S FAITH

Conscience

The first and central doctrine of Rousseau's reformed, rechristianized deism is *conscience*. It is the original and most important source of religious knowledge for Rousseau and has a double primacy. For it is both a source of self-knowledge and a direct link to the deity, giving us some knowledge of deity as well. It reveals everything essential about humanity, the deity, and their interaction. And from it there follows that for Rousseau theology is fundamentally ethics.

Neither tradition nor book revelation can rival the fundamental and universally accessible revelation inscribed in the human heart. Tradition and book revelation may serve to echo the divine voice and only to that extent have utility and worth.

In the hymn to conscience in the fifth of his *Lettres Morales* Rousseau extols conscience:

> Conscience, conscience, divine instinct, heavenly immortal voice, sure guide of a being ignorant and finite yet intelligent and free, infallible judge of good and evil, *sublime emanation of the eternal substance* which renders man like unto god, it is you alone which constitutes the excellence of his nature.[106]

The remainder of this hymn of praise is identical in the *Lettres* and in the *Profession:*

> In thee consists the excellence of man's nature and the morality of his actions; apart from thee, I find nothing in myself to raise me above the beasts—nothing but the sad privilege of wandering from one error to another, by the help of an unbridled understanding and a reason which knows no principles.[107]

---

[106]OC IV:1111. Our emphasis. This version is distinguished from the *Profession* by the emphasized phrase. Why the *Profession* (1762) omits this suggestive phrase contained in the *Lettres Morales* (1757-1758) is unclear.

[107]*Émile*, 254; OC IV:601. This is still somewhat short of the deifying role of consciousness in Hegel. (Cf. chapter 3 of this work.) Noteworthy in the elevating role of "conscience" is that French has only one term for both "conscience" and "consciousness." German has *Gewissen* and *Bewußtsein* respectively.

Conscience is the principle of transcendence in Rousseau's religious thought, raising men above the beasts and to a full humanity that is god-like. Conscience is thus not only a divine principle but a *divinizing* principle as well. The language of the heavens indicates not only the source of this principle but the final destiny of him who fulfills that high calling.

Knowledge of conscience is the knowledge of one's divine origins, of one's enduring links to the divine and of one's divine destiny. It is the power that confers dignity on every individual and renders submission to the authority of another unnecessary and unworthy. It makes one religiously self-sufficient, without need of priest or prophet or other human intermediary, and without need of the all-high revelation of conscience duplicated—or more likely distorted—in a book.

It is at the same time the sure guide and fulfillment of reason, transforming and enhancing previously attained stages of reason by conferring a wholeness upon them. Conscience becomes thereby the mediating principle between religion and reason, taking up both in an uneasy synthesis that includes historical religion. Conscience finally and self-consciously smudges the pure abstract simplicity of natural religion's relation to reason when it affirms elements of historical Christianity.

Through the simple yet decisive principle of conscience, the religious thought of Rousseau rises above the deism of Voltaire and would see itself as also rising above the Christianity of the church, all the while claiming continuity. The *Profession* proclaims reason and revelation, philosophy and Christianity, reconciled, despite the protests of contemporaries who will not see and who desire no reconciliation. That each term—reason and revelation—has been altered in achieving the new harmony is quite plain in retrospect.

While conscience is the fundamental religious experience in Rousseau's thought, there is still place for something like mystical experience, a subject about which Rousseau was quite cautious. One finds mention of it not in the *Profession* of the Vicar but in the profession of the dying Julie of *La Nouvelle Heloïse*.

The professions of Julie and of the Vicar are compatible, as Rousseau himself insists. But Julie's mystical inclinations and the particular nature of her mysticism are noteworthy, especially in the final section of the novel that seeks to transform the work into an ethical piece. Saint-Preux expresses the essential view of Rousseau, which is that of the skeptic in matters of mysticism[108] because it potentially leads to to the neglect of ethical duty. Rousseau thus goes less than the whole route with the heroine. In his other works one might be tempted to see in him a "nature mystic." But this would be a misinterpretation of the way he understood his immersions in nature. For nature, in his view, is only the occasion, not the source, of religious feeling, and Rousseau is not a pantheist. Nature becomes the stimulus for raising the heart to God. Even the "matinée à l'anglaise" in *La Nouvelle Heloïse,* when Julie, Saint-Preux and Wolmar briefly experience a level of immediate communication, is not mysticism. But the "death mysticism" of the Julie who happily, patiently waits for the lifting of the veil that separates her from final union with God is unmistakable, even if union itself is to take place only in the beyond. The highest level of mystical union attainable by those on this side of the grave consists in the revelation of conscience—immersion in nature and the *matinée* experience notwithstanding. The God of this world is the *deus absconditus* and one cannot hope for union with him while alive. At the same time, the death mysticism motif underlines Rousseau's dualism. For mystical unity is the joining of spirits, not bodies, and not even embodied spirits. Thus, given the fact of the soul's imprisonment in a body, one cannot expect the real union of the soul with the divine until soul is freed from body, which is precisely how Julie understands her approaching death and why she welcomes it.

The mysticism of Julie finally serves to underline the importance of conscience, which is the highest access to the divine in this world, even as it points up the role of body-soul dualism that accounts for the limitation imposed by fleshly existence.

Reason-Sentiment

The second major teaching follows from the first, namely, the compatibility and even complementarity of sentiment and reason. For conscience as both moral sentiment and moral reason is not understood as a bridge built between the two but as the deeper ground that has united the two essentially and from the beginning. Neither the role of reason nor that of sentiment is thereby in any way diminished, and each continues in its eighteenth-century functions in religion and society.

---

[108]Masson, *Religion,* II:75. This is also the view of Kant: cf. chapter 2 of this work.

Natural Goodness of Man

The essentially pagan affirmation of the natural goodness of man takes its place as a central doctrine and premise of Rousseau's religious thought. In contrast, the position of orthodox Christianity is not that man is originally evil but that his natural state of innocence was destroyed by original sin. This Rousseau emphatically and repeatedly rejected. Human fallibility is accepted, but not the unrecoverability of the natural state. Were it otherwise, conscience would not function unimpeded, nor would its voice be always clearly audible to the attentive listener. It was thus for Rousseau a necessary doctrine in order to ensure the sovereignty of conscience in the human sphere. (The implications of an "original sin" or "radical evil in human nature" became clear in Kant's religious thought which thus broke with Enlightenment thought in a more fundamental way.)

In addition, while this doctrine might at first seem to make God responsible by default for patent evil in the world, it is really intended to solve the problems of theodicy in Rousseau's religious system by making evil a problem of ethics rather than of metaphysics. Man is responsible for all evil insofar as he deviates from his natural goodness. And he can fully and freely return to his natural state. Thus the triumph of good and the destruction of evil do not depend on God who might be blamed for not acting sooner if it were he alone who could act, but on man who must simply come back to himself and who is fully able to do so.

The Exemplary Humanity of Jesus

Appended to the essential teachings of the Vicar's faith is a hard-fought place for Jesus as moral teacher, example and hero. The Jesus who rose above a corrupting and morally backward society, who attained naturalness in an unnatural social order, who exemplified sincerity and self-transparency in a world of lies and self-deceit, and who paid the price that corrupt society exacts from those who thus dare to be a child of God—this Jesus cannot be ignored and must not be dismissed. He commands our respect and our audience to his divine words and human deeds and prompts our imitation of him.

CONCLUSION

How may we finally evaluate the thought construction that houses Rousseau's philosophical view of religion? The various elements that he seeks to bind together in the Vicar's profession have been observed and catalogued. Most prominent among them are intellectual reason, conscience, and Jesus as both instance and teacher. How might one metaphorically imagine the result? As architecture, one might see it as an intellectual Mannerist church, where the pediment and frieze would be lovingly carved representations of the Sermon on the Mount, situated above Doric columns of reason that also adorn the edifice. Drawing closer to it, our imaginary observer would increasingly wonder about the construction and even begin to suspect merely a Renaissance facade attached to a simple meeting hall, for which the half-columns of reason would serve as embellishment but not as support for the edifice. At the same time, he would perceive in the Jesus of the frieze that he might be more divine than Socrates but that he is neither an Olympian nor the Son of God. Scrutiny of the edifice would eventually reveal that the rationalsm and piety are not mere facade elements—neither ornamentation nor purposeless additions—but that, however curiously combined, they constitute the true exterior of the edifice. Why such a peculiar construction? the architectural purist might ask of an unperturbed mannerist Rousseau. One might even see in it adequate materials for two entirely different temples. Why did the architect insist on their being joined, despite the prevailing canons of the day?

One might go on to imagine the nature of any service to be held within. The center of the construction would indicate what to expect. The simple meeting hall enclosed by pillars of reason and representations of piety make it clear that neither Roman ritual nor Calvinist preacher has place within, but instead only the simple, quiet religion of the heart.

The edifice has three units: rationalism, Christianity and the cult of the heart. The last, core of both imaginative edifice and of Rousseau's religious thought, is his special contribution. And his broad—if sometimes vague—notion of the heart makes it unique. While the rationalism and Christianity might seem merely a problematic exterior, they are indeed integrated elements of the structure, not an appended and hence not a potentially removable facade. What holds the elements together is conscience, revealed in the heart, including and transforming first reason and then Christianity into a novel form of natural religion.

Thus viewed, Rousseau's is a strange and unique complex, housing an unusual faith. But if it is not the "faith of our fathers," it is not on that account bad faith. What is most striking is that Rousseau felt the indispensable need both of rationalism and of Christianity in the religion of conscience and that conscience does not remain a bare principle but reaches out and incorporates these near-sworn enemies of the eighteenth century into itself. Noteworthy too is the manner in which reason and religion/ Christianity relate to conscience. For each submits to conscience independently. In the Vicar's *Profession,* religion submits to reason also, in order to weed out absurdities, but finally submits separately to conscience. The *Profession,* which appeared to so many a critique of religion and whose strongest polemic was reserved for the *philosophes,* really attempted to humble, chasten, and reform both religion and philosophy in a new order.

Conscience is manifestly the heart of Rousseau's vision of religion. For Rousseau, conscience is religious experience of an elevated and privileged kind. And he who has had it is unprepared to negate anything in which its echo is found, hence not only in reason but also in the gospel of Christians. From a more objective and thorough philosopher of religion, one might well expect other instances to have been discerned and discussed. But these are the echoes that Rousseau heard, and he tried only to show that their apparently contrasting voices contain the same reality.

The *Profession,* which is the most complete statement of Rousseau's religious view, is a serene and unsettling document: serene in the tone and good faith of the speaker, unsettling then and now for the reflective listener who asks about interrelationships and the ultimate direction of the doctrines set forth. It was unique in its eighteenth-century context for the imposed and uneasy peace that it attempted to enforce upon reason and Christianity, unique too for the powerful subjectivity of its author. Its overly ambitious program obscured its true nature and seems to have left the author himself less than clear about the radical reordering he was proposing. Rousseau set out to make a statement that centered on practical religion rather than on dogmas. At the same time, he wished to be faithful to the natural religion of reason both as he understood it in a timeless dimension and as his contemporaries had articulated it. He wished, in addition, to avoid rejecting historical Christianity insofar as it echoed timeless verities. To do this, he ignored the supernatural claims of the New Testament and the history of the cult and of the institutions such claims gave rise to.

As Rousseau himself noted in the *Lettre à M. de Beaumont,* the *Profession* was a plea for tolerance. It was also an argument for containing superstition and fanaticism and in support of the sincere religiousness of those who do not hold to strict orthodox belief. But the *Lettre* could mislead one into overlooking a toleration of increasing importance for Rousseau, namely, religious toleration on the part of rationalists who disparaged Christianity. The more important plea, before the widest audience, is thus for a toleration of Christianity itself.

At the same time, the *Profession* set out a clear hierarchical order among Christianity, reason, and conscience in which the last, as moral reason, has first place. The *Profession* thus had several novel points to make in its time: conscience as the fundamental religious knowledge and principle; intellectual reason as subordinated to conscience and tolerant of Christianity; and a place for Christianity as religion where one might have expected it to be viewed as superfluous or harmful. Rousseau would not deny Christianity, at least insofar as Jesus and his Gospel teachings are concerned. He affirmed the elements he viewed as Christianity's core and as held in common with the universal religion of reason/conscience. The historical religion—whose historicity was simply ignored—was not on that account ever construed as indispensable or necessary, nor was it ever explicitly cited as a help in making known the content of the ideal religion, as it would later be viewed by Kant. The true radicalism of Rousseau in his intellectual context was his refusal to reject Christianity at the same time as he identified a sufficient and universal source of revelation in conscience.

The *Profession* is thus the first modern philosophical plea for the limited acceptance of Christianity, and its obvious sincerity in making its plea distinguished it in an eighteenth century given to posturing. It would find many parallels down to the present, but it would have no imitators, not least in its emphasis on the actual suffering humanity of Jesus.

The *Profession* and the religion it articulated are finally limited to the subjectivity of Rousseau. One hears a contented declaration of timeless faith and completely misses any formal attempt to leap across the famous ugly ditch[109] separating the rational and the historical. And thus how Rousseau can move from the pure religion of reason (intellectual and moral) to a complex and compromised historical faith and then back again, all the while affirming and identifying both on the same basis, is a secret that lies in the *heart* of Jean-Jacques Rousseau. Conscience may be the category to bring intellectual reason and intellectual religion together, but *historical religion* is a problem unsolved.

---

[109]Lessing's, of course.

What remains of Christianity after intellectual reason pares down superstition and mythology and after moral reason/conscience affirms ethical teaching and teacher is a Christianity shorn of history, but not of its historical Jesus—essentially a subdivision of natural religion lovingly tolerated in spite of questionable aspects of New Testament faith. Christianity is understood certainly not as the *new* religion or covenant replacing the old, nor even as a particularly valuable expression of the old. Quite modestly, it is judged as *a* religion, but emphatically and radically within a deist context it is judged positively. Having done so while invoking reason, Rousseau demonstrated that his was not the rationalism of the *philosophes.* It was the faint beginning of a wider rationalism. But, on the other side, his was obviously not the Christianity of the orthodox of his day. Rousseau would probably easily have agreed with the first assertion and refused the latter. However, the text of the *Profession* substantiates both. There is no way to bridge the gap or disguise the leap from a moral religion grounded in the supreme revelation of conscience to a Christian religion tied to historical persons and historical events. Rousseau never recognized the gap or leap that his intellectual attempt constitutes. The eighteenth and nineteenth centuries would witness many similar attempts. Historical Christianity and its book remain a permanent stumbling block, even for philosophical followers of Jesus. One may close one's eyes and open one's heart, as the Vicar does, but sincerity alone does not dissolve the *scandalon,* and we who have listened to the Vicar have also surely heard him stumble against it.

In the end, Rousseau breaks with eighteenth-century orthodoxy. In saying this, this writer finds himself substantially agreeing with the arguments of those who condemned *Émile,* while certainly rejecting the mean spirit in which they were written. Heresies are of course always relative and frequently valuable, and Rousseau is merely a heretic to the ruling Christian theology of the day. Judged by the larger and unofficial canons of "Western religious thought," he is eminently orthodox. For the principle tenets of the latter include deism/theism, dualism, and a general moral orientation. The constellation takes decidedly different forms and hierarchical arrangements among Christians, non-Christians and anti-Christians in the West. In his dualism, Rousseau is at one with Plato, St. Paul, and René Descartes in subscribing to a theory of the creation and radical nonidentity of spirit and matter. This idea his opponents shared as well. Difficulties arose because the author of *Émile* found himself on the losing side—politically but not intellectually—in a periodically repeating theoretical battle on how spirit is saved. He never doubted that it could be or is saved, even if he did deny its fall and hence need of salvation.

Pelagianism is the essence of his "heresy." From it, as much as from reason's scrutiny, follows the superfluity of certain traditional and fundamental Christian doctrines (such as incarnation and atonement), and in denying them Rousseau left the church for the salon. That he personally preferred the company of simple church folk to Parisian intellectuals is only one of the many pradoxes between his life and his thought.

His religious thought is distinguished by a new constellation of the essentials of Western religious thinking: morality rises to preeminence in the category of conscience, while deism takes second place. Dualism plays its usual role. In the final analysis, Rousseau was not only faithful to dualism but thoroughly trapped in it while trying, with only partial success, to contain its effects on human self-understanding. In this, he was a mainline Western religious thinker. Dualism is in fact nothing less than fatal in his thinking. For his dualism made it ultimately impossible to reconcile reason with the realm of feeling, try as the category of conscience might. Rousseau fully saw the limits of intellectual reason in practical life (and thus also in religion). He strained to get beyond the intellectual reason of his time, without ever constructing a critique of reason (but certainly not without influence upon the philosopher who later did).[110] Rousseau pressed toward a new, enlarged rationalism that he never clearly articulated. He pushed erratically and sometimes violently out from the narrow confines of the Enlightenment self. And perhaps his category of conscience even briefly reversed the ever-narrowing effects of this Western dualism and might be said to expand the notion of the self in his vaguely defined notion of sentiment in relationship to reason and conscience. Yet his thought never arrived where its dynamism seemed directed, and he never broke free to a new articulation of reason and the self. In this, Kant and Hegel would go

---

[110]Immanuel Kant, of course, in the *Critique of Pure Reason*. This is not to suggest, however, that Rousseau influenced Kant in this work. For such is plainly not the case. It is in a general sense true, nonetheless, that Rousseau influenced Kant in a general way rather than in any particular work, but the influence revolved around the emphasis to be given ethics in philosophical thinking. Cassirer and others have credited Kant with "thinking through" the thoughts of Rousseau where he himself did not (just as others have credited Freud with thinking through his feelings). Rousseau's influence should be noted but not unduly emphasized.

much further, and each in his way be acclaimed and denounced for it. Yet for all its limitations, the new Christianized deism that Rousseau sought to articulate has its place of distinction in eighteenth-century religious thought. On some points, it does not advance as far as Kant, but it is still more than a trial run at Kantianism, as neo-Kantians have come to concede. Rousseau's philosophy of religion is ultimately "less" Christian than Kant's, but also less in danger of what others perceive as an atheistic drift in Kant. Rousseau's "heart" is able to check his "mind" more effectively than Kant's, and he clings—sentimentally—to the Jesus that in Kant dissolves into a symbol. The Christianity and Christ that Rousseau would hold on to are part of a Christianized deism that was to be the exterior form of the religion of conscience.

In responding to the theses and vagaries of the *Profession*, the respective camps of *philosophes* and religious applauded the perceived polemic against the other, denounced the attack upon their own camp and missed all that was new in the work. While they perceived the proclamation of faith to the *philosophes* and rationalism to the religious, they failed to discern the reformation and sublation of both in conscience. The proclamation of rational religion with standard deistic content was of course not novel, even if still provocative. And faith, then as now, had its partisans self-appointed to censor or censure those who deviated in the smallest detail.

The historical significance of Rousseau's *Profession* consists largely in the fact that in it Rousseau confronted and successfully opposed Enlightenment religious thought with the saving category of conscience, with the unobscurable moral grandeur of the human Jesus, and with the conviction and personal force of Jean-Jacques Rousseau. He was among the first moderns to insist on viewing Christianity positively while refusing to leave the rationalist camp, and he was a forerunner of the Idealist tradition that returned to a positive view of Christianity. He is in a sense a transitional figure between the rationalist natural religion of the Enlightenment and the moralized Christianity to follow. But he was not merely the precursor of Kant. For better or worse, his position, his beliefs and his reasons for them were his alone.

The *Profession of Faith of the Savoyard Vicar* is not a great philosophical document, although it is correctly deemed a classic. There are, apart from the role of conscience, no commanding insights, nor is there any development of principal ideas. It is, as its title proclaims, the profession of the religious convictions and affirmations of one man, arrived at through diverse sources (self-education, Bible reading, reason and reflection), sanctioned by his heart, and held uneasily together in lonely personal insistence. Its enduring attractions, in addition to its literary merits, are its intellectual sincerity in grappling with religion and its powerful insistence on the person of Jesus to Enlightenment Europeans prepared to embrace a more universal form of religion.

It is thus a great statement of an incomplete intellectual engagement of religion. Philosophically its success is circumscribed, yet it is a succinct and rich expression of a position more widely shared than Rousseau himself realized. And in its attempt to preserve religion by reason and from reason, the question is whether his effort may not unwittingly be in advance of some of the philosophically superior attempts that succeeded it, in its simple understanding of the religion it professes, but even more in its refusal to think religion through to dissolution.

• 2 •

KANT AND THE JESUS
OF REASON ALONE

INTRODUCTION

The transition from Rousseau to Kant in religion is far less pronounced than in other areas in which their philosophical thought might be analyzed and compared. While their styles and programs are otherwise strikingly different, they share significant positions in religious matters. Their fundamentally positive evaluation of religion, of Christianity in particular and despite all its faults, distinguished them in the Enlightenment, while their topical interest in such theological problems as theodicy and the reasonableness of faith identify them as men of their times. One can fully understand neither Kant nor Rousseau apart from their eighteenth-century context, its intellectual presuppositions about the power of human reason and its critical attitude toward religion, and particularly toward one historical religious faith in which reason had exposed and dismissed irrational elements and special claims grounded in a revelation inaccessible to reason.

Knowledge of God, justifying God before reason and the individual before God, and then understanding the individual in relationship to institutions claiming a special status before the deity are but a few of the characteristic subjects of Enlightenment and Kantian religious thought. Throughout, the central problem for Kant is reconciliation of wayward man with the unchanging moral law. Kant's understanding of the matter parallels that of Christian theology and occasionally seems to approach traditional Christian church teaching, as for example, concerning original sin.

Yet the definitions are in the end Kant's own, and not the church's, as is evidenced in his concept of the radical evil in human nature and equally in the concept of the purposefulness of the world.[1]

While sharing the spirit of Rousseau's reflections on religion, Kant ultimately parts company with him. His doing so is also the point of his break with Enlightenment thought. As one might expect of Kant, it is a gentlemanly break, undisguised by polite manners but also free of acrimony. It occurs in the articulation of the concept of radical evil where, in the almost Zoroastrian combat between good and evil philosophically restaged in *Religion within the Limits of Reason Alone,* its implications shape the dramatic structure of the work and, in the process, Kant's philosophy of Christianity.

If Rousseau makes it difficult to disentangle thought from biography, Kant might make it deceptively simple. And yet it would distort our grasp of Kant, of the formative influences upon him and of certain emphases in his thinking, to ignore his origins and education. For German Pietism is a decisive influence and stands in a dialectical relationship with Enlightenment religious currents in his thought. Kant's parents, we know, belonged to a pietistic religious circle and entrusted their son's education to the "modern" school headed by F. A. Schultz. There he spent eight formative years (1732-1740) in Königsberg's Collegium Fredericanum that was strongly allied to the tradition of Philipp Jakob Spener, August Hermann Francke, and the pietism of Halle from the time of its establishment in 1698.[2] But the Enlightenment spirit was also present in Königsberg, especially at the University where Martin Knutzen first served Kant as the model of an accord between enlightened *Wissenschaft* and pietist religious faith.[3] Kant thus received stimulus and critical insights from both quarters.

---

[1]An immediate and notable difference between original sin and fall into radical evil is that Kant nowhere seems to entertain the possibility of a higher purpose served by fall into sin. In the 19th century, Kierkegaard, in his own effort to penetrate the mystery of human evil through his pseudonym Vigilius Haufniensis, suggests a higher relationship to God potentiated by the Christ-event that resulted from human fall. Kierkegaard's work otherwise parallels Kant's consideration of evil on several points. On Kierkegaard, cf. also Vincent A. McCarthy, *The Phenomenology of Moods in Kierkegaard* (The Hague: Martinus Nijhoff, 1978) 39-40.

[2]Uwe Schultz, *Immanuel Kant in Selbstzeugnissen und Bilddokumenten* (Reinbek bei Hamburg: Rowohlt, 1965) 9-10.

[3]Hermann Noack, Einleitung: "Die Religionsphilosophie im Gesamtwerk Kants" in I. Kant, *Die Religion innerhalb der Grenzen der blossen Vernunft,* ed. Karl Vorländer, 7th ed. (Hamburg: Felix Meiner Verlag, 1961) xiii.

The one also served to free him from the hold of the other. For the *Aufklä-rung* distanced him from Pietism and made him suspicious of emotionalism in religion to the point of reticence to discuss religious experience at all, whereas Pietism countered the naive optimism of the Enlightenment with the sobering recognition that something in human nature undercuts the unending progress promised by the age of reason and that human effort would not be enough to overcome this hindrance. Kant thus moved toward a religious position characterized by a chastened rationalism in the service of moral progress. But his dark assessment of the human condition also expressed itself in skepticism about purity of motives and the very possibility of moral progress, such as in the *Foundations of the Metaphysics of Morals* in which he anticipated the doctrine of radical evil found in *Religion within the Limits of Reason Alone.*[4]

A rationalist in religion, Kant preferred to term his position "moral theism" rather than "deism."[5] However, with the Enlightenment, he rejected the anthropomorphisms of traditional theism and other conceptual excesses unworthy of humankind finally come to rational maturity. Thus he dismissed all prayer or currying favor with the divine and took a position that sometimes went beyond mere skepticism about claims of direct divine intervention in human affairs.[6]

Some see lingering traces of religious awe as underlying Kant's reflection on immortality and infinity and detect its roots in his pietist heritage.[7] Others see in the Critical Philosophy itself a "religious outlook."[8] A religious outlook is doubtless present. But when one acknowledges Kant's explicit moral emphasis in a formulation such as "the starry heav-

---

[4]*Kants gesammelte Schriften,* Akademie Ausgabe, 28 volumes (Berlin, 1910-1972) IV: 407, 432; noted by Jean-Louis Bruch, *La Philosophie Religieuse de Kant* (Paris: Aubier, 1968) 47-52. (Hereafter citations of *Kants gesammelte Schriften* will be abbreviated KgS and with the appropriate volume and page numbers: e.g., this citation would be KgS IV: 407, 432.)

[5]Cf. *Lectures on Philosophical Theology,* trans. Allen W. Wood and Gertrude M. Clark (Ithaca: Cornell University Press, 1978) 30; *Vorlesungen über die philosophische Religionslehre,* KgS XXVIII: 2, 2, 1002, passim. Cf. also Allen W. Wood, *Kant's Moral Religion* (Ithaca: Cornell University Press, 1970) 164.

[6]C. C. J. Webb, *Kant's Philosophy of Religion* (Oxford: Clarendon Press, 1926) 20-21.

[7]Noack, Einleitung: "Die Religionsphilosophie," xx. One might interpret Kant's reaction to the idea of immortality—for it is an *idea* and not experience that prompts his poetic utterance—as closer to Romanticism than religion.

[8]Wood, *Kant's Moral Religion,* 2.

ens above me and the moral law within me,'' one hesitates before going too far and astray.[9] Suffice it to say that it is a far simpler task to discern Kant's position from his negative utterances about religious subjects than to do so from the occasional misty expression of a religious sense. Even as he was neither deist nor atheist, Kant was finally neither a pietist nor a mystic.

Kant's religious position developed along lines inherited from the *Aufklärung*, with its demand for reasonableness in beliefs and eventually a more far-reaching identity of reason and religion. It also proceeded from Pietism and the traditional Christian views contained in it. From both *Auflärung* and Pietism he inherited a fundamental concern with morality, and this emerges as the emanating center point of his religious thought. Yet in the doctrine of radical evil that so startled rationalist contemporaries, Kant illustrated the intellectual distance between the salons of the *philosophes* and the sober world of Königsberg, while in the discussion of overcoming radical evil, he evidenced his distance from Pietism and the reigning orthodoxy as well. In the end, we witness a Kant who accepted the Pietistic insight into human depravity without abandoning Enlightenment hope for moral progress, who was thus beyond the naiveté of natural religion but also beyond the sense of helplessness in sin that characterizes Pietism. The rational, moral religion that he set forth in *Religion within the Limits of Reason Alone* came to terms with Christianity and with his pietist heritage but not without self-consciously reinterpreting their teachings according to a hermeneutic of practical reason that explicitated the moral truths recognized as the essential content of doctrine. Kant's hermeneutic has been much criticized in theological circles and, for his Scripture interpretation, as Hans Frei notes, ''Kant had the privilege of seeing almost everyone, no matter from what hermeneutical school, united against him.''[10] But he remained adamant in the application of his hermeneutical principle nonetheless.

One of the possible advantages of his hermeneutical principle, from his own point of view, is that it disposes with the need of acquaintance with biblical hermeneutics. Indeed, Kant's knowledge of the theological literature of his time, and of theological literature in general, appears to have

---

[9]The famous phrase is from the *Critique of Practical Reason*, trans. Lewis White Beck (Indianapolis: Library of Liberal Arts/Bobbs Merrill, 1956) 166; KgS V:161.

[10]*The Eclipse of Biblical Narrative* (New Haven: Yale University Press, 1974) 263.

been scant. The absence of theological references in *Religion within the Limits of Reason Alone* is in striking contrast to references to the religious practices of Iroquois and Mongols and to Oriental religions. Yet one of the important theologians of the twentieth century would indirectly defend Kant's ignoring theologians of the eighteenth. Karl Barth, in his history of *Protestant Theology in the Nineteenth Century,* states that the theological initiative in the eighteenth century was in the hands of the "enemies," namely, the philosophers.[11] Kant knew these enemy-theologians well of course and shared their camp, and in this sense one might say that Kant is well-read after all in the significant and influential religious thought of his time, as well as being an important contributor to it and all its camps.

While Kant's religious thought is a valuable mirror of the religious debates of his time and while *Religion within the Limits of Reason Alone* has had great influence in theological quarters, his religious thought is not universally well regarded. On the theological battlements stand the critics of his heterodoxy, while on the philosophical side are to be found not a few critics of his persistent interest in religious subjects and in the Christian religion particularly. Some have speculated that if Kant had never written or published *Religion within the Limits of Reason Alone* his place in philosophy and his influence in continuing philosophic discourse would be precisely what they have become on the basis of the Critical Philosophy alone (of which his religious writings are not formally a part). In this view, *Religion within the Limits of Reason Alone* adds nothing to Kant's philosophy, and some have even suggested that it is its weak point. This charge should be entertained but not accepted. One must nonetheless concede that Kant's religious thought is not complete. He had no intention of writing a formal theology in the modern sense and as distinct from philosophical theology. Like Rousseau—and unlike Fichte, Hegel, and Schelling—he did not begin as a theologian or student of theology. Nor, like Rousseau, did Kant leave a complete religious system or philosophy of religion. *Religion within the Limits of Reason Alone* represents only a partial engagement of religious subjects, even if it contains the essence of Kant's reflections on religion. Yet at the same time *Religion within the Limits of Reason Alone* is the first modern philosophy of religion, an enduringly important example of the confrontation between reason and religion and a

---

[11]Quoted by Bruch, *La Philosophie Religieuse de Kant,* 256; *Protestant Theology in the Nineteenth Century* (Valley Forge: Judson Press, 1973) 136-38.

thought-experiment of a very high order. And while his philosophy of religion is not a part of the Critical Philosophy as such, it is significant that his only major work completed after the three Critiques and the first work of philosophical doctrine is on the subject of religion. (It is not, however, an application of the Critical Philosophy to religion. This is more nearly accomplished in Fichte's 1792 *Attempt at a Critique of All Revelation*.)

Religion within the Limits of Reason Alone does not formally engage the God-problem and, in fact, presupposes the reader's familiarity with earlier publications dealing with it.[12] The Critical Philosophy's shaking of the foundations of metaphysical knowledge had extended to God as well, and the *Critique of Pure Reason* had refuted metaphysically grounded demonstrations of the existence of God and had destroyed all pretense to knowledge of God, while carefully noting that the nonexistence of God could also not be proven.[13] The God of the *Critique of Practical Reason* was the postulate of morality and not its determining ground; God was simply recognized for the sake of morality. For reason cannot conceive the attainment of the highest good, the object of duty, unless there is a highest intelligence.[14] God's existence is thus required, not as a ground for obligation but rather in order to *understand* how the highest good may be achieved.[15] Reason must conceive of God in order to comprehend how the moral law may be fulfilled and how virtue and happiness (the *summum bonum* or highest good) may be achieved; but it need not conceive of God in order to grasp the content of the moral law or in order to act upon it. This can be done on the basis of reason alone.[16] The God-idea is posited to serve the human passion for understanding. But the "symbolical anthropomorphism" of a God-idea gives us only knowledge of our own mind, of its needs and mode of functioning, and no knowledge whatsoever of the reality of God. The rift thus brought into view is expressed in Kant's oft-cited phrase that he has destroyed *knowledge of God* in order to make room

---

[12]Here we leave out of account the *Opus Posthumum* that has been variously interpreted: by some as a move toward a personal God (e.g., Adickes), and by others as the dissolution of the God-concept into a mere symbol of the categorical imperative. Cf. Wood, *Kant's Moral Religion*, 10-11; also Frederick Copleston's fine but frequently neglected "Kant Volume": *A History of Philosophy* (New York: Image Books, 1964) VI:II:171-83.

[13]Cf. James Collins, *God in Modern Philosophy* (Chicago: Regnery, 1959) 192.

[14]*Critique of Practical Reason*, 128-36; KgS V:124-32.

[15]*Critique of Practical Reason*, 130; KgS V:125.

[16]For a fuller discussion of the God of Kantian thought, cf. Collins, *God in Modern Philosophy*, chapter 6.

for *faith*.[17] In the *Lectures on Ethics,* he added that "Religion has no need of a speculative study of God."[18] For Kant then, knowledge of the reality of God is neither possible nor necessary. But the God-idea is useful, and through the postulates of practical reason we may learn what God is for us as moral beings.[19]

God-related subjects are found in other writings as well. The final paragraphs of the *Critique of Judgement* (1790) extended the God-postulate of the Second Critique to guarantee the moral purposefulness of the world. Kant thus moved from teleology to theology, but the latter remained contained within the former and foreshadows the containment of a "purposeful Christianity" in a larger system of religious/moral purposes in *Religion within the Limits of Reason Alone.*

Kant took up the important eighteenth-century topic of theodicy in his 1791 essay "On the Failure of All Philosophical Theodicies."[20] Theodicy has been a stock subject in philosophy of religion. It was, in addition, a recently ignited issue in Kant's time subsequent to the 1755 Lisbon earthquake that shook Enlightenment confidence in the "best of all possible worlds" and called its purported ruler into question as well.[21] And if the philosophical trial conducted in this essay did not disprove moral wisdom, it did conclude that

> The result of this trial before the tribunal of philosophy is that no theodicy so far proposed has kept its promise; none has managed to justify the moral wisdom at work in the government of the world against the doubts which arise out of the experience of the world.[22]

---

[17]Preface to the 2nd ed. of the *Critique of Pure Reason,* trans. F. Max Müller (New York: Anchor Doubleday, 1966) xxxix; German: B xxx.

[18]Trans. L. Infield (New York: Harper and Row, 1963).

[19]Cf. Wood, *Kant's Moral Religion,* 151.

[20]This essay, like Book One of *Religion within the Limits of Reason Alone,* appeared in the *Berlinische Monatschrift.* It appears in English translation in Michael Despland, *Kant on History and Religion* (Montreal: McGill-Queen's University Press, 1973).

[21]Cf. Voltaire's *Poem on the Lisbon Earthquake* and Rousseau's *Letter to Voltaire on Providence* for two opposing eighteenth-century interpretations. Kant, in his 1755 *Theory of the Heavens,* had found something positive in the earthquake in that it led to the discovery of mineral springs in East Prussia! This is, of course, exactly the line of thinking so wonderfully scorned in Voltaire's *Candide.* Cf. Despland, *Kant on History and Religion,* 18. Kant himself could write satire and write well, as he demonstrated in his 1766 "Dreams of a Spirit-Seer" that seemed to attack vision, visionaries, and claims of direct revelations but that was equally aimed at metaphysical claims to knowledge of the deity.

[22]Despland, *Kant on History and Religion,* 290; KgS VIII:262.

And the essay ultimately concluded that, since only supersensible knowledge could be a base for proof of the moral wisdom of the creator, theodicy is not a task of science but a matter of faith.[23]

In the early 1780s, Kant delivered a series of lectures (published by Pölitz in 1817) entitled "Vorlesungen über die philosophische Religionslehre," or "Lectures on the Philosophical Theory of Religion."[24] The title is doubly interesting: first, in that it is an inexact description of the subject matter of the lectures, which are really more concerned with rational theology; second and more importantly, in that the title ("Philosophical Theory of Religion") was also the title originally intended for *Religion within the Limits of Reason Alone*.[25]

The Lectures neatly summarize Kant's religious thought up to the publication of the *Critique of Pure Reason*. They proceed through a discussion of the various types of rational theology and provide a statement of Kant's philosophy of religion that fills out that of the later work. At the same time, the Lectures also provide a chart for locating the discussion of *Religion within the Limits of Reason Alone* within Kant's religious thought as a whole and serve as a bridge to the later work, even if that was not their intended purpose.

The Lectures divide rational theology (or what would today be termed "philosophical theology" or "natural theology") into two parts: speculative and moral. The speculative is further divided. The *transcendental* includes ontotheology and cosmotheology. Both of these are concerned with a concept of God as first cause and represent, for Kant, the position of deism. The *natural* includes physicotheology, or speculation on the relationship between God and nature. From this a theistic conception of God emerges, either as author of the world (*Welturheber*) who acts as architect and provides form or creator (*Weltschöpfer*) who brings forth the material that constitutes the world.

---

[23]Ibid., 293; KgS VIII:267.

[24]The English translation, by Wood and Clark, cited above, is called "Lectures on Philosophical Theology."

[25]The lectures are included in KgS in vol. XXVIII, 2nd half, part 2, 993-1126. Other versions of the same lecture series also are included in the same volume, viz., the *Natürliche Theologie Volckmann* and the *Danziger Rationaltheologie*. While the Pölitz version is the best known, there is, as Gerhard Lehmann notes in the Einleitung to the volume, no reason to make the Pölitz version the norm, as Kurt Beyer did in his 1937 Halle edition of the lectures. As the most-cited version, it is the natural first choice for a translator, but Wood and Clark have no more grounds than this for selecting it alone.

Kant then proceeds to a discussion of *moral* rational theology and its conception of God as world ruler (*Weltbeherrscher*), a position that the Lectures characterize as moral theism and that is closest to Kant's own. In the discussion of moral rational theology, Kant states that morality leads to religion. This is repeated in the first preface to *Religion within the Limits of Reason Alone* and provides a link with his later work.

The Lectures define theology as "the system of our knowledge of the highest Being,"[26] and in this sense the lectures are a rational *theo*-logy, a rational reflection upon *God*. The end point of the "Lectures on the Philosophical Theory of Religion" becomes the starting point of *Religion within the Limits of Reason Alone*'s moral theism. And, in retrospect, the Lectures allow us to note the qualitative change introduced into Kant's reflections on religion that results from the inclusion of radical evil. For those who would interpret Kant's position in *Religion within the Limits of Reason Alone* as ultimately deism, it must become clear from a reading of the Lectures that Kant himself regarded his God-concept as theistic. (Kant would of course equally object to his position's being called atheism. Interpreters can, however, cite passages of the *Opus Posthumum* with an atheistic drift.[27]) *Religion within the Limits of Reason Alone* has a markedly different approach. It is concerned with understanding moral progress aided by religion that is both natural and historical. The work remains thoroughly anthropocentric and practical in its inquiry.

Kant made a further refinement among types of theology in the sometimes ironic pages (part one) of his 1798 *Strife Between the Faculties* when he distinguished between biblical and philosophical or rational theology. There Kant not only defended the right of philosophy to enter the theological and biblical arena, as he already had done, but suggested philosophy's superiority, and, for those who discerned a more subtle message, its unique legitimacy.

Kant's religious writings up to 1793 form a unit. This is not only because they belong either to the pre-Critical Philosophy or to the Critical Philosophy itself (with the exception of the 1791 "Failure of All Philosophical Theodicies" that is closer in spirit to his 1793 work), while *Religion within the Limits of Reason Alone* belongs to the second part of Kant's

---

[26]KgS XXVIII, 2, 2:995.
[27]E.g., cf. KgS XXI:25; also XXI:27; a later remark (XXIII:108) goes in the other direction.

program, namely, the construction of philosophical teaching based on the Critical Philosophy. It is also because *Religion within the Limits of Reason Alone* is, as its preface indicates, a work independent of the Critical Philosophy. It is not a "fourth critique," nor is its teaching on radical evil in any way deducible from the Critical Philosophy (even if Kant had already expressed a sense of human fallenness). This is to suggest that the doctrine of radical evil was not only a departure from Enlightenment religious thought but a significant turn in Kant's own thinking. It eventually re-shapes his religious thought by bringing philosophical reflection into confrontation with a *historical* faith that is ultimately viewed as a practical necessity in the actualization of true religion, rather than the deviation or encumbering superfluity it appears to be in other Enlightenment authors.

Because of the role of radical evil, the concept of religion in *Religion within the Limits of Reason Alone* is a significant modification, while finally no break, with the religion that one would otherwise deduce on the basis of the *Critique of Practical Reason* and in light of the First Critique. It alters the theory of justification and entails a shift from the individual to the social plane. Moral advance is no longer understood as an individual matter, nor can it be. For, because of an individual, historical fall that is universally repeated and that has permanent consequences, the individual must take part in a collective moral effort and finally requires a "supersensible supplement." Such involvement also takes each individual beyond the realm of private acts of will to the concrete plane of history where collective moral effort will either succeed or fail.

LITERARY ASPECTS OF
RELIGION WITHIN THE LIMITS OF REASON ALONE

Religion within the Limits of Reason Alone was not originally planned either in its present form or with its present title. Kant initially had intended to publish four separate but connected essays on the subject of religion in the *Berlinsche Monatsschrift* in which he had previously published numerous small essays. The first essay of the project, "On radical evil" (Book One of the present work) was published as intended. It was first submitted to the Berlin censor by the editor Biester in February 1792 at the author's request, although the Monatsschrift was then published in Jena and the censor's approval was thus not required. The censor cleared the essay, since it was judged to be of only scholarly interest, and it appeared in April 1792.[28] When the second essay, submitted in June 1792, was refused publication permission on the grounds that it went against the teachings of the Bible, Kant, who supported the authority of the state but opposed the conservative censorship policies of Wöllner, found an alternative publication route in submitting the three unpublished essays to one of the University faculties empowered to pass on religious subjects. Thus, with the *imprimatur* of the philosophical faculty at Jena, he finally had all four essays published in their present unified form in Königsberg.[29] This was not, however, to be the end of Kant's difficulties. In October 1794, he received a letter expressing the king's displeasure, mentioning *Religion within the Limits of Reason Alone* by name and threatening the aged Kant with "highest disfavor" if he did not put his "talents and authority" to other use. In Kant's reply, the philosopher promised the king to refrain from all public statements on religion, and this he did until the king's death in 1797, at which time the edict of Wöllner was also cancelled.

Karl Vorländer recounts that the originally planned title was "Philosophische Religionslehre," and that the work carried this while in press.[30] In his preface to the first edition, Kant recommended to candidates in biblical theology "A special course of lectures on the purely *philosophical* theory of religion . . . , with such a book as this, perhaps as the text."[31] Jean-Louis Bruch finds this title a more accurate designation of Kant's thoughts, while he finds the present title more indicative of the work's

---

[28]Cf. Theodore M. Greene, "The Historical Context and Religious Significance of Kant's *Religion*," in *Religion within the Limits of Reason Alone*, trans. Theodore M. Greene and Hoyt H. Hudson (New York: Harper and Row, 1960) xxxiii-xxxiv, hereafter cited as *Religion;* also cf. Karl Vorländer, "Zur Entstehungsgeschichte der Schrift über die 'Religion innerhalb der Grenzen der bloßen Vernunft'," section B of Noack, Einleitung: "Die Religionsphilosophie," xlvi-xlvii.

[29]Kant had also apparently considered Göttingen, Halle, and Königsberg itself. Cf. Karl Vorländer, *Immanuel Kant: Der Mann und das Werk*, 2nd enlarged ed. with an essay "Kants Opus Posthumum" by Wolfgang Ritzel, ed. Rudolf Malter (Hamburg: Felix Meiner Verlag, 1977) xlix.

[30]Noack, Einleitung: "Die Religionsphilosophie," lii. This is of course the title of Kant's Lectures on rational theology. "Philosophische Religionslehre" is the accurate description of the work's content.

[31]All references to the English translation of Kant's *Religion within the Limits of Reason Alone* are to the Greene-Hudson translation cited above. References to the German text will be to the "Akademie Ausgabe" of *Kants Gesammelte Schriften* (see note 4 above). Preface to the first edition, 10; KgS VI:10.

method than of its object.[32] The original title, with the term *Lehre* (theory/teaching/doctrine) also clearly sets the work apart from the Critiques. *Religion within the Limits of Reason Alone* is manifestly not the fourth critique that some expected. If there is such a work,[33] it is Fichte's 1972 *Attempt at a Critique of All Revelation,* a work with its own literary history.[34] *Religion within the Limits of Reason Alone* appeared one year later and shows how much farther Kant had gone beyond a theory of religion based on the Critical Philosophy. Kant also went well beyond Fichte's very modest conclusion that revelation *may* be possible, as Kant's own work asserted a decisive, historical revelation.

In *Religion within the Limits of Reason Alone* Kant stressed reason's role in assessing religion but at the same time proclaimed the legitimate place for religion within the reflections of reason.[35] To this extent, it agreed with Rousseau's *Profession of Faith of the Savoyard Vicar.* It did not suggest the true starting point for a fruitful, positive consideration of religion within the limits of reason alone. For this had already been done in the *Critique of Practical Reason* in the postulate of God as the guarantor of the fulfillment of the telos of the moral law, namely happiness.

FIRST REACTIONS

The Berlin censor Hillmer, who had approved book one as suitable for a learned, discerning readership, had given some indication of the troubles to come when he refused the second essay the *imprimatur.* The king's official displeasure apparently shook Kant deeply, if one may judge from his reply. There Kant stated that his intention in *Religion within the Limits of Reason Alone* had been to criticize not Christianity but the religion of reason whose practical sufficiency but speculative inadequacy was demon-

---

[32]*La Philosophie Religieuse de Kant,* 13, 35.

[33]On the model of the Brahms First Symphony that has been called "Beethoven's Tenth."

[34]In brief: the young Fichte wrote *An Attempt at a Critique of All Revelation* as a kind of letter of introduction to the older and famous Königsberg philosopher. Kant was impressed with it and suggested its publication, without having fully read it then or thereafter. Kant's own publisher issued the work and left Fichte's name off the title page. Because of the publisher and "critique" in the title and because a work on religion was awaited from Kant, the readers of the first edition attributed it to Kant as the expected "Fourth Critique." Fichte's career was also thus quickly made. The story is recounted in several places. Cf. introduction to G. Fichte, *An Attempt at a Critique of All Revelation,* trans. Garret Green (Cambridge: Cambridge University Press, 1978).

[35]Cf. Karl Barth, *Protestant Theology in the Nineteenth Century: Its Background and History,* trans. J. Bowden and B. Cozens, (Valley Forge: Judson Press, 1973) 280.

strated in the work.[36] The controversy and exchanges are somewhat reminiscent of the Rousseau-de Beaumont exchange over the faith of the Savoyard Vicar. As with Rousseau, a critique of Enlightenment religion may have been the pronounced intention, but the theological critics did not err in discerning a radical critique of the Christian religion.

Criticism of Enlightenment views on religion did not pass unnoticed by the *Aufklärer*. Most were surprised by them. Some were angered and let it be known. The best-known condemnation was expressed in a letter from Goethe to Herder in which Kant was charged with having

> ignominiously dirtied [his philosophical mantle] again with the shameful spot of radical evil, so that Christians too can feel they ought to kiss the hem of it.[37]

And Herder accused Kant of going further with radical evil than Christian scripture itself.[38] They had not objected to the *Critique of Practical Reason*, although it had suggested a religious position distinct from deism—moral theism. But the program of *Religion within the Limits of Reason Alone* and its unpoisoned view of Christianity may have suggested intellectual treason. The opening words of the First Preface—*"Die Moral"*—may have sounded appropriately "enlightened," but they must have soon been put on guard as it walked in the steps of the Second Critique to an encounter with religion ("Morality thus leads ineluctably to religion"[39]). It soon became clear that Kant's consideration of religion would go beyond the Second Critique's God-postulate to reason's reacceptance of one of Christianity's most "un-Enlightened" teachings, namely, the radical evil in human nature, even if its inclusion was surely on reason's terms. On the other side, traditionally minded religious readers would have been on guard against the proponent of practical moral reason who claimed no need of religion even as he demonstrated morality's inner dynamic in its direction. Modern readers will have different concerns and different questions. Does one, for example, find in Kant's *Religion within the Limits of Reason Alone* Christian concepts in Kantian terminology? Or does one there

---

[36]Cf. T. M. Greene, "The Historical Context," xxxv; also the Vorrede to *Der Streit der Fakultäten* in which Kant includes the king's letter and his own reply.

[37]Letter of 7 June 1793. *Goethes Briefe*, Band IV (Berlin, 1923). Translated in Despland, *Kant on History and Religion*, 169.

[38]Cited by Bruch, *La Philosophie Religieuse de Kant* 75, from *Herders Sämtliche Werke*, ed. B. Suphan (Berlin, 1880) XX: 138, 220, 222.

[39]*Religion*, 42; KgS VI:6.

discover a secular philosophy cloaked in Christian language? And, if one could arrive at a consensus definition of either ''Christianity'' or ''philosophy,'' could one term the moral theism and the precepts of Jesus as described in *Religion within the Limits of Reason Alone* the one or the other? Is Kant's treatment of Christianity in any way deducible from the Kantian philosophy or is it a surprise turn resulting from his fall into the concept of radical evil?

STYLE

Religion within the Limits of Reason Alone might be described as ''dry,'' but interpreters such as Webb see this as positive, as placing the moral emphasis in shaper relief.[40] Karl Barth remarks that

> Nobody . . . brought into the open the theological viewpoint, thought and intent of the eighteenth century with so much determination, in such concrete and logical terms with so unemotional a clarity (in contrast to Rousseau), and with such an unfreemasonly candor (in contrast to Lessing) as he did.[41]

Religion within the Limits of Reason Alone too has its unexplained sudden shifts (most notably from theoretical religion to historical faith) and obscure utterances, and it even has its own language of the heart.[42]

The work cites no theology, although it frequently refers to the Bible. In fact, it cites no literature on religion, not even Kant's favorite philosophers of religion, including Rousseau, whose *Profession* in *Émile* he knew well, but also Leibniz, Locke, Shaftesbury, and Hume. In striking contrast to absent theological citations stand anthropological references to the religious attitudes, behavior, and beliefs of faraway peoples.

The four books into which the work is divided follow a logical and dramatic order from radical evil to resolution. Each book also has a ''parergon,'' or appendix concerning matters not directly discussed in each respective book.[43] But the sequence of the books does not fully indicate all

---

[40]Webb, *Kant's Philosophy of Religion,* 115.

[41]*Protestant Theology in the Nineteenth Century,* 267.

[42]One might remark that the German-speaking world usually pardons this kind of license in German as profundity (*Tiefsinn*), while dismissing it as obscurity in French (or any other language, except Greek). Kant too had a language of the heart, even if it does not lead to the quaint physiology one finds implicit in Rousseau.

[43]Despland, *Kant on History and Religion* (p. 203) quotes from Plato's *Statesman* (302B) where a parergon is defined as ''something aside from the subject we had proposed for ourselves.''

the subject matters to be discussed. For there is an unexpressed unity constituted by the one subject matter that is constantly referred to but never systematically addressed: the Christian religion. Christianity stands in the background of the entire work, frequently enters the discussion indirectly and occasionally more directly. But in neither fashion is its entry adequately accounted for. Formally, it is just one example of a historical faith. However, Kant has no hesitation in asserting the superiority of Christianity to Judaism and Islam (in contrast to both Lessing and Rousseau who set moral performance as the measurement, and deferred judgment). Traditional Christian categories seem to guide the work and its dramatic development. Hence we find reflections paralleling the doctrines of original sin, atonement and Christology, ecclesiology, and grace. Yet the work is never near to becoming a systematic theology. When the content of the categories is examined, one realizes that this is, as is to be expected, a *philosophical* theology. Kant omits discussion of religious experience, and this is no minor matter. *Religion within the Limits of Reason Alone* is therefore incomplete, and Kant's religious thought with it. It thus stands as an unfinished philosophical theory of religion, the incomplete reflections of a great thinker on religion but the first systematic modern attempt to understand religion and particularly historical religion in a positive, sympathetic—while always critical—fashion, and an essay that would serve as a paradigm in philosophy of religion.

The role of symbols and Kant's symbolic understanding of Christian materials (the "experiment" he announces in the Second Preface to the work) are a highly significant aspect. In this, Kant was able to make a genuine advance beyond the deists who had rejected too many facets of Christianity out of hand. Through symbolic interpretation of doctrines, Kant went beyond simple apologetics and made a case for Christianity as practically advantageous.[44] In so doing he anticipated Bultmann and demythologization in our own century, as well as Tillich's existential interpretation of Christianity. Moreover, in so proceeding, Kant believed that he was uncovering the deeper truths of Christian doctrine and thus saving them from the murky theology that had enveloped them.

But it is radical evil that is the most prominent, most startling (to secularist contemporaries), and most decisive philosophical idea in the work.

---

[44]Ibid., 151.

Its role is underscored by its being Book One (and it could hardly be otherwise, given the dramatic, rather than systematic, nature of the work's philosophy of religion). It influences the entire work. It goes beyond the mythical account of evil in the *Conjectural Beginnings of Human History*. There naive reason, in its pristine weakness, was depicted as disturbing a primordial animality, with evil resulting. It sometimes seems to render the work a closet morality play, a philosophical version of the conflict between good and evil. Interpreters disagree on how the concept comes to crystallization and expression in Kant's thought. Barth, for example, sees it as a natural part of Kantian thought,[45] where others see its roots in his personal disposition rather than in his system itself.[46] Most would agree, however, that it disturbs the otherwise clear and rounded Kantian system and alters the understanding of religion that would otherwise issue.[47]

Radical evil modifies the second of Kant's "four questions" (What can I know?, What ought I to do?, What may I hope?, Who is man?). It alters the third as well, according to Kant himself in a letter of 4 May 1793 in which he wrote that the task of *Religion within the Limits of Reason Alone* was to account for the third question.[48] The work has multiple tasks, but accounting for hope is prominent among them. Yet what I may hope is determined by the fact of radical evil. Hermann Noack views hope as the central concept of Kant's philosophy of religion, in which God is the founder, preserver, and completer of the moral community.[49] In this view, what one may hope is God's will that evil be overcome, rather than human triumph in struggle against evil—a hope that depends upon God rather than any individual or any union of individuals. But because it depends upon no individual, including the historical Jesus of Nazareth, it finally diverges from theological hope. For Christian hope is generally understood as a lively confidence in the victory over evil and is tied to the historical Jesus. In the

---

[45]*Protestant Theology in the Nineteenth Century,* 297.

[46]Cf., Bruch, *La Philosophie Religieuse de Kant,* 28.

[47]But Allen Wood claims that Kant's thought requires this concept to fill in lacunae in his discussion of the moral perfectibility of man vs. the dialectical threat to this in works up to the time of *Religion within the Limits of Reason Alone,* Cf. Wood, *Kant's Moral Religion,* 208.

[48]In his oft-cited letter to Karl Friedrich Stäudlin: *Philosophical Correspondence 1759-99,* trans. A. Zweig (Chicago: University of Chicago Press, 1967) 205; KgS XI:414.

[49]Cf. Noack, Einleitung: "Die Religionsphilosophie," lxix. I disagree with the emphasis on hope and see radical evil as the central determining theme that affects all further notions, including of course the important notion of hope.

absence of Jesus in Kantian hope, the Christological centerpiece of Christian theology thus disappears, as Noack also observes.[50]

Kant's notion of hope includes morality (*Sittlichkeit*) and happiness (*Glückseligkeit*), but the latter term does not mean earthly happiness or pleasure as a reward for fulfilling duty. Indeed any such happiness or pleasure would run the danger of corrupting the base of morality, as the *Critique of Practical Reason* observes.[51] One must hope and indeed one can hope, and such hope is practical. For it honeys the rim of the cup of duty and cuts short the danger of despairing of ever being well-pleasing to God, precisely the despair that could result from the consciousness of radical evil.

The impact of radical evil extends to the development of the notion of (religious) community. Moral community figures prominently in Book Three of *Religion within the Limits of Reason Alone* and one notes that it effectively supplants the Christian church in serving as the model of a people well-pleasing to God. The ideal of the ethical commonwealth is an "invisible church" that is the archetype for the visible historical church.[52] And the Christian church plays a purposeful, indispensable role in the creation of this higher community.

The social emphasis and requirement of formation into a community modeled on the archetype of the ethical commonwealth in order to resist evil is a development in *Religion within the Limits of Reason Alone* of what many see as the implicitly social character of the moral law itself.[53] That is, the individual recognizes that the moral law is binding not only on himself but also on others, that his own fulfillment of the moral law is a social matter, and that the highest good is a common good most effectively struggled for in community.

The concepts of hope and ethical commonwealth are finally joined and inextricably bound to the concept of radical evil, not only because they cannot be thought out apart from radical evil but because radical evil seems to block the hope of being well-pleasing to God and to restrict the ethical commonwealth to a "beyond." The role of moral community in *Religion within the Limits of Reason Alone* and the attendant social dimension is a new and important development in Kant's thought of how the moral law

---

[50]Ibid.
[51]*Religion*, 92; KgS V:89.
[52]Cf. Noack, Einleitung: "Die Religionsphilosophie," lxix.
[53]Cf. Wood, *Kant's Moral Religion*, 191.

may be acted upon, if never fully actualized. Radical evil does not alter "What ought I to do?," for I still have the duty to will the good, but it effectively curtails my ability to do what I ought, on the basis of an original choice against the good, and this limitation finally extends to the community of morally struggling individuals as well. It also unites them in a common hope. But both the hope and the need to hope in the face of an imperfectible moral order are rooted in the fundamental notion of radical evil.[54] *Religion within the Limits of Reason Alone* thus becomes the analysis of morality within the bounds of radical evil.

RELIGION WITHIN THE LIMITS OF REASON ALONE AS THE CONTEXT OF A PHILOSOPHICAL CHRISTOLOGY

It would be a misrepresentation of both Kant and his *Religion within the Limits of Reason Alone* to suggest that his central interest was to provide a philosophical rationale for Christianity and its Christ. *Religion within the Limits of Reason Alone* has the far more ambitious goal of scrutinizing all religion from the standpoint of moral reason and penetrating to its central and deepest truths.

Kant was, of course, aware of his philosophical presuppositions about reason and morality. He made some attempt to rise above cultural narrowness by inquiring about religion beyond the three monotheisms of the West, but he did not break the hold of European Christianity upon him and his thought. For this reason, perhaps, Christianity and its Christ figure more prominently than they otherwise would or ought. Yet Kant had, at the same time, an obvious special interest in Christianity. He evidenced this in the attention he devoted to illuminating the truths of practical reason contained in its particular doctrinal and scriptural formulations, and in appreciating the symbolic role of its Christ. Indeed, the unnamed Jesus receives considerable attention in the work. Thus only a willful reader can ignore the Christian cultural backdrop to the philosophical drama of *Religion within*

---

[54]I follow Bruch (*La Philosophie Religieuse de Kant,* 247) in this line of interpretation as regards the centrality of radical evil. I also agree with Bruch that other interpretations have validity. Where does one finally place the emphasis? Radical evil is the determining fact, hope is the practical matter, and the ethical community is the goal. Dramatic order favors the climactic category. (And this is where Albert Schweitzer places the emphasis: *Die Religionsphilosophie Kants von der Kritik der reinen Vernunft bis zur Religion innerhalb der Grenzen der blossen Vernunft* [Tübingen, 1899].) Hope is central. Radical evil is primary —perhaps, in the last analysis, primum inter pares.

the Limits of Reason Alone on the one hand and its positive emphasis to Christian doctrines, symbols and forms on the other. If these are limitations of the work as philosophy of religion, they nonetheless add their own richness to it.

RELIGION AND MORALITY

The very first word of Kant's work on religion is "morality" (*Die Moral*). The preface to the first edition thus announces the work's orientation. It asserts the independence of morality from any idea of God needed to understand one's duty and from any incentive needed to do it. It makes clear that the concept of religion to be developed, if not deducible from the preceding Critiques, will be harmonious with them. Morality, in sum, is free of religion and will guide the inquiry into religion. But morality, according to Kant, "leads ineluctably to religion."[55] Kant's meaning is that the idea of morality leads to the ideas of religion: thinking out the problem of being fully moral—of recovering oneself from fall into self-love and from the corruption of the base of all maxims—leads to ideas that religion has already expressed. (It will also ultimately lead beyond them to a purer idea of religion.) Kant confesses that, in the end, he cannot think the fulfillment of moral duty without thinking God. Many can grasp the moral law without God or religion, but he cannot realistically conceive of man's overcoming radical human weakness without God. Beyond that, he suggests that historical religion (or more precisely, historical faith) is a practical requirement for those seeking to fulfill the moral law, even if he would at the same time suggest the dissolution of historical faith into the single ideal form of moral religion.

Recalling the Second Critique, Kant links the concept of morality with religion and happiness but emphasizes a proper hierarchical relationship. The gospel of practical reason is quite clear: "In the beginning" is the idea of morality, and from it arise the ideas of the highest good and of happiness. These ideas in turn give rise to the idea of God (1) as the theoretical guarantor of the idea of the highest good and (2) as the practical guarantor of the happiness that does not come about in experience or observation.

Religion within the Limits of Reason Alone thus opens by positing a noumenal religion that will be compared to the historical reality, not for the sake of testing or reforming the concept but rather for the sake of find-

---

[55]*Religion,* 5; KgS VI:6 Cf. also the extended footnote in Kant's text.

ing the authentic element in historical religion in order to allow full maturation.

THE CONCEPT OF RADICAL EVIL

Book one is moral reason's expression of the philosophical truth contained in the Christian doctrine of original sin. At the same time, it establishes a pattern that is repeated in each of the three succeeding books where one or more Christian doctrines are singled out for philosophical restatement. This does not occur formally but takes place in fact. Kant moves on from original sin to atonement, forgiveness, ecclesiology and beyond, in what is at one and the same time a logical progression of Christian teachings and of moral philosophical truths. For the drama and the problem of morality—of good overcoming evil—follow from original sin/radical evil.

This is not to suggest that the doctrine of original sin and the concept of radical evil are identical. They most certainly are not, and Kant makes their differences plain.

Kant's introduction of the concept is a radical departure from Enlightenment religious thought, as already noted.[56] He stresses the good that is the natural state and that is known a priori and contrasts it to evil that is not a mere deduction or postulate but an observable reality. In the face of Enlightenment optimism about mankind and its progress, Kant points to the evil in the human condition that undercuts it all.

Is man good or evil by nature then? The question must be reposed to be answered correctly.

> When we say, then, Man is by nature good, or Man is by nature evil, this means only that there is in him an ultimate ground (inscrutable to us) of the adoption of good maxims or of evil maxims.[57]

He is originally and fundamentally good and destined to be fully restored to the good, but he has become evil—individually and universally (which of course does not mean "collectively").[58]

---

[56]While Kant and Rousseau share many positions as regards religion and morality, and while Rousseau himself broke with the Enlightenment, on this issue Kant and Rousseau take opposite sides. Indeed, on this particular point, Rousseau is the culminator of Enlightenment thinking, in his steadfast denial of original sin.

[57]*Religion*, 17; KgS VI:21.

[58]Again a difference from Rousseau who acknowledged a "social fall." For Kant, every one is individually responsible for his own actual fall.

The relationship between good and evil in man is clarified by the distinction between the "predisposition to good" (*Anlage zum Guten*) and the "propensity to evil" (*Hang zum Bösen*). Good is a predisposition and the original orientation; evil is a propensity that has developed. This distinction rules out any misinterpretation of good and evil as somehow equal in status. Kant was no Enlightenment pagan in outlook, but neither was he a modern Manichean.

For Kant, the choice of evil is an intelligible act that is intelligibly known and subsequently confirmed by experience. A choice of evil is the necessary inference to explain two conflicting but fundamental points: on the one side, the observation of evil, and, on the other, intuition of the moral law within. If there is a moral law which I ought to follow, then I must be able to do so, and for this I must be free. (Freedom here is not an intuition but a postulate.) If I am free, I must also be responsible for the evil that I see and that I do, and thus I must be guilty. (Moral guilt is, for its part, not an intuition but a deduction.) But I find myself unable to fulfill the moral law. Struggling against inclinations to evil, I am nevertheless unable to undo an original offense that I must have commited. I find my freedom limited, and only I can be responsible for this, or else my freedom has no meaning. I know myself as a being with the moral law engraved in my heart and yet as one who does evil or at least has done evil. In a rational universe, how else can I understand my condition, insofar as I can understand it at all? Rousseau's notion of the corrupting effect of society will not explain the corrupted heart untouched by society. For all men have chosen evil, and no exception can be found, even if we could find someone in a presocial state.

Of note is the fact that Kant's discussion of the relationship of good to evil and of how repeated evil acts come about on the basis of one original choice in no way sheds light on the original choice itself.[59] It becomes, in fact, increasingly incomprehensible the more one reflects upon it, just as surely as it becomes a necessary inference from examining the human condition. Kant, like Genesis, cannot tell us *why* evil was chosen, only *that* it was chosen. We are thus brought back not only to the fact of evil but to a philosophical version of the Christian teaching of the mystery of evil.

---

[59]While still not totally satisfying, Kant is still clearer than Kierkegaard in the *Concept of Anxiety,* where his pseudonym *Haufniensis* claims to make a psychological investigation only to proceed with a priori "observations."

Kant's concern in examining the radical evil in human nature is not the satisfaction of intellectual curiosity about original evil but rather the practical matter of understanding how one may fulfill the moral law. His examination of radical evil is thus an intellectual exercise carried out for the sake of achieving a practical realism in one's hopes and in one's conduct with regard to the moral law. The first act of evil is not empirically known but is reliably known nonetheless. Subsequent acts can be known empirically and not just intelligibly. But the first act is no less real for that. Indeed, the problem is that it is all too real and constitutes the root dilemma. For even if a second act could be successfully avoided (and this is the closest that fallen humans can become to moral perfection on their own), the offense of the first act remains and constitutes a humanly insurmountable stumbling block. Practical reason will thus have need of religious ideas in order to get around it.

Kant has confessed the sobering reality of radical evil in human nature. But he has subscribed to neither the Genesis expression nor the derived Christian teaching. In fact, he calls the notion of an ''inherited sin'' (*Erbsünde*) the most inept solution that has been proposed. He agrees with the progression sketched in Genesis: an original innocence and goodness out of which evil arose on the basis of a free choice. And he would not disagree with the notion that Adam sinned. Indeed, the first human must have sinned, in the same way that I have. Adam has the dubious distinction of being the first. But his sin and mine are the same.[60] The term ''original sin'' might be less troublesome, except that it means the sin inherited from Adam. Kant's notion of radical evil is everyman's original sin, the product of his own misused freedom that has placed self-love above the moral law.

Kant thus accepts the form of the Christian teaching on an original fall. But he rejects the content because it is imprecise and dismisses the theological term because it reflects the imprecision. He corrects the teaching by universalizing it, not just in its consequences, as the theological doctrine did, but in its origins, as reason demands.

THE POSSIBILITY OF GRACE

Kant restated his position that morality leads to religion when he wrote:

Reason, conscious of her inability to satisfy her moral need, extends her-

---

[60]Cf. Kierkegaard's development of this line of thinking in the *Concept of Anxiety*. Kierkegaard too dismissed the idea of an ''inherited sin.''

self to high-flown ideas capable of supplying this lack, without, however appropriating these ideas as an extension of her domain.[61]

Radical evil has pointed up the inability, and the idea of grace is the natural result. But, as if to underline the danger of the idea, it is kept at arm's length, as it were, by being confined to one of the parerga that follows each of the four books of *Religion within the Limits of Reason Alone*. Grace is not an idea of reason, to be sure, and the theological notion of grace is not entirely desirable. It must be pared down by practical reason, even as it never achieves any status beyond a hoped-for possibility.

Since human experience offers no clue about how mankind can restore itself to its original goodness and thereby fulfill its predisposition to the good, the suggestion of possible supernatural arises. But moral reason cannot entertain any notion of supernatural aid that leaves man in an unworthy passivity. If there is any grace, man must first act to make himself worthy of it and then actively lay hold of it. In addition, any such grace must be accessible to all and be available at an identifiable point in one's striving. Practical reason thus requires a grace idea that is at least semi-Pelagian.

The problem that elicits speculation about grace is this: How can a man who has made himself evil by nature make himself good? To pass from an evil nature to good is as incomprehensible as the original fall from innocence into evil. Yet because the original incomprehensible lapse was possible (because actualized), so may reascent into the good be possible.[62] It should at least not be impugned.

The grace that may be possible is that of finding favor in God's sight, of being found well-pleasing although one has not made oneself totally well-pleasing (because one is unable to fulfill the moral law completely, either retroactively or at every moment). For the grace of being judged well-pleasing, moral reason demands that man must have come as close as possible to restoring the purity of the law as the supreme ground of all maxims, within the permanent limits imposed by radical evil. This entails the heroic effort necessary to bring about a revolution in one's cast of mind and then the ongoing struggle to reform sensuous nature.

The meaning of grace—if there is grace—is that God counts the inner revolution, or turning back toward the good, as sufficient to one's being

---

[61]*Religion*, 47-48; KgS VI:53.
[62]*Religion*, 40; KgS VI:45.

counted well-pleasing and then, on the basis of merit gained in the wrenching of the will, aids in the continued battle against sensuous nature. Any assistance is thus earned, even if it remains a grace. Grace never means gratuitous forgiveness or undoing of radical evil. Radical evil, precisely because radical, is permanent in its effects and grace may thus be conceived as a small supersensible supplement and practical hope in the conflict between good and evil.

THE UNNAMED CHRIST
AS PERSONIFICATION OF THE GOOD PRINCIPLE
AND OF MORAL STRUGGLE

Conflict between good and evil is the universal human condition. It is a battle waged along lines sketched by the ethical monotheism that Kant never mentions but to which he and Western monotheisms seem much indebted: the religion of Zoroaster. Were Kant to have embraced the Zoroastrian representation, we would expect his emphasis to be the great cosmic battle between good and evil as really the sum total of all individual struggles. For Kant emphasizes that the individual and thus each person's struggle is decisive.

But Kant does not follow out a Zoroastrian scenario of the battle. Instead, he fastens upon what he takes to be the Christian representation of the same battle, symbolically expressed in the life and death of the Christ who is never mentioned by name. Indeed, Kant expresses the conflict between good and evil in what amounts to practical reason's reinterpretation of the Fourth Gospel. From his own standpoint, Kant is simply uncovering deeper philosophical truths expressed in Scripture. Kant thus exploits Christian symbols in the work of practical reason as he explores at considerable length the powerful symbolism of Christianity's hero in the struggle against evil.

The conflict between good and evil takes place in a world viewed as good, even though the locus of battle is matter. In emphasizing good as the initial state, Kant goes beyond his assertions in Book One to declare that the idea of mankind in its complete moral perfection is God's Word, present in him throughout eternity.[63] Enlightened by practical reason, we can now retranslate the prologue of the Gospel of John to read, "In the beginning was the idea of mankind in its complete moral perfection."

---

[63]*Religion*, 54; KgS VI:60.

Kant goes on to note the necessity of speaking metaphorically of this elevated idea as *coming down* from on high, of its presence among men as rather a "state of *humiliation* of the Son of God." An instance of this idea, he affirms, would have to be conceived as not only discharging all human duties and spreading goodness by precept and example but also as taking upon him every affliction, even the most ignominious death.[64] Thus the idea becomes represented in an individual.

Kant asserts the ability of everyman to conform to the idea, because he *ought* to do so; and, before ultimately conceding the reality of a historical instance, dismisses any *need* for a special empirical instance of the idea:

> We need, therefore, no empirical example to make the idea of a person morally well-pleasing to God our archetype; this idea as an archetype is already present in our reason.[65]

We each have our own Logos. To require historical instantiation of God's Logos is unbelief for Kant, and it is worse still to demand such a figure working miracles. For the moral law requires that each instantiate the idea. Thus if an instance of moral perfection should appear, it can and should be regarded as of natural origin. Supernatural origin cannot absolutely be denied, but it is of no practical value and would in fact be a drawback, since supernatural elevation would undermine any hopes of imitation. In a term that Kant does not use, a superhuman Son of God would be ἄχρηστος, "useless."[66]

The idea is present in everyman, but so is radical evil, and the reality of the latter seems to block the realization of the former. One cannot become perfectly well-pleasing to God, precisely because of the inalterable fact of radical evil, but one become *essentially* well-pleasing. The original deed can never be wiped out. But it can be atoned for. And the birthpangs of the new man are considered as counting for required atonement and con-

---

[64]*Religion*, 55; KgS VI:61.

[65]*Religion*, 56; KgS VI:62.

[66]The return of the Son of Man to heaven is also interpreted symbolically. Cf. *Religion*, 119-20; KgS VI:128-29. A footnote points out that reason cannot find a better example for imitation than the life narrated in Scripture but declares the stories of resurrection and ascension a sequel to the true, moral story—a sequel naturally unacceptable to reason unless interpreted symbolically as ideas of reason. For a fuller discussion of the moral usefulness of Jesus, cf. Vincent A. McCarthy, "Christus as Chrestus in Rousseau and Kant," *Kant-Studien* 73 (1982) Heft 2:191-207.

stitute the only morally acceptable solution.[67] This takes place in the sufferings undergone in the revolutionary change of heart in which the order of the moral incentives is reversed and restored.

Christian expressions suffuse Kant's philosophical description of atonement as he writes, for example, of the "death of the old man" and the "crucifying of the flesh." Kant does not satisfactorily explain why there should be lingering effects, however. The original fall took place in the perversion of the order of the moral incentives, and this is reversed by the change of heart that is accounted moral goodness. That there are aftereffects requiring vigilance and struggle in sensuous nature is, however, evidenced in experience, even if the reason for their endurance is unclear.[68]

Kant thus makes evil first too physical and then too spiritual. Since the battle with sensuous nature goes on even after the revolutionary change of heart, evil maintains a physical presence even after the essential spiritual conquest of evil by the will. But when it comes to wiping out the debt of evil, Kant makes its effects too spiritual. For, according to Kant, it is only necessary for me who has done evil to undergo the suffering of conversion, or moral rebirth. The evil that I may have done in the physical world, and which may still affect others, goes unmentioned. Does it really satisfy justice that only *I* undergo change?

The solution of the problem of enduring debt witnesses a reintroduction of Christian language in a strange-sounding passage that philosophically expresses a "Lamb of God" motif:

> And this moral disposition which in all its purity (like unto the purity of the Son of God) the man has made his own—or, (if we personify this idea) this Son of God, Himself—bears as *vicarious substitute* the guilt of sin for him, and indeed for all who believe (practically) in Him; as *savior* He renders satisfaction to supreme justice by His sufferings and death; and as *advocate* He makes it possible for men to hope to appear before their judge as justified.[69]

In this passage, Kant begins with the moral disposition, allows personification of it as a synonym, and then slips into the New Testament story of atonement. Such language does not clarify Kant's philosophical teaching

---

[67]*Religion*, 68; KgS VI:66-74.

[68]A possible reason could be that one does *not*, after all, succeed in reversing the incentives back to their original order and that hence the struggle goes on. But Kant does not consider this.

[69]*Religion*, 69; KgS VI:74.

at all; it rather confuses it. But it witnesses the power of Christian categories and expression for Kant and his will to assure a place for the Christ in the religion of practical reason.

One might have expected moral reason to be hostile to the idea of atonement, for it is one of Christianity's principal stumbling blocks for rationalists. Yet Kant does not exclude the notion, and even finds it serviceable, so long as practical reason interprets and controls it. Kant recognizes it as a central doctrine of Christian ecclesiastical faith and, in Book Three, refers to atonement again in terms that make its perceived potential dangers clear. Atonement, as it has been frequently understood by theologians, can lead to passive faith, for which humans have a propensity in any case. The only doctrine of atonement that practical reason can accept is one in which God provides a final grace after one has merited it through improvement in one's way of life. If atonement is taken to mean another's merit being applied to wipe away my offense and substituting for my own efforts, it is an offense to reason that must be rejected as unworthy of moral religion. Yet Kant concedes that one can never make oneself totally well-pleasing to God. He is open to the idea of atonement, even vicarious atonement, as a supplement to an individual's moral struggle but never as a substitute for it. But Kant is firmly against the requirement of faith in such atonement. The sole duty is always a good course of life. Reason alone is sufficient to teach that, if one does all in one's power, the love of good will make good any deficiency in one's deed.[70] A teaching about the grace of atonement (as complement to individual effort) is only necessary in order to make the process of moral perfection intellectually graspable. Belief in atonement may be practical, and may even be regarded as necessary to *understand* salvation, but to be saved one needs to *do* good works and does not need to think or believe atonement. Kant firmly distinguishes between what one can practically do and how one must think about the process in order to understand it. The two elements constitute a recognized apparent antinomy: an idea of atonement which might be a scandal to reason and the seeming requirement of some kind of moral *deus ex machina*.[71] Moral reason resolves the antinomy by reducing atonement to moral complement. This allows the possibility of Christ's moral struggle and individual victory as serving as moral complement to others' moral struggles but in

---

[70]*Religion*, 110; KgS VI:120.
[71]*Religion*, 107, 110; KgS VI:116, 119.

no wise substituting for them. Their own original fall is not erased by any action on the part of Christ. His deed becomes an additional basis for their being accorded the grace of being counted well-pleasing. This is certainly not a philosophical statement of atonement theology as it comes to expression in St. Anselm. Yet, however much trimmed by practical reason, it still contains the notion of the deeds of an other transferred to my moral account. Naturally, I cannot be required to believe in a moral grace deriving from a historical personage. Yet I can think and believe it and even find it a stimulus to action. Historical faith harbors dangers but can be practical, if it helps one to grasp the whole and if one thereby becomes more active in doing the good. For Kant, then, if I believe, *credo ut intelligam ac agam:* I believe in order to understand and, more importantly, to act.

After reinterpreting the role of a historical Christ, Kant finally concedes his actuality as a "ripe" moment that is understood as the combined product of the ills of the Jewish theocracy and the Greek sages' ethical doctrine of freedom.[72] The "envoy from heaven" is superior to the Greek philosophers.[73] After the "prince of this world" fails to deputize him, the same prince orchestrates his persecution and death, which nonetheless serve as a manifestation of the good principle and as an example for imitation. The envoy from heaven, he notes, does not conquer evil but merely breaks its hold. Most significantly, he is the first not to succumb to evil.[74]

Kant concedes historical actuality to his symbolic description of the good principle in conflict with evil when he writes, "And when [the good principle] made its appearance in an actual human being, as an example to all others. . . . ''[75] But before this admission, Kant has already taken away much of the force in his stressing the more important presence of the idea of the good principle in all of mankind:

---

[72]The Greek sages are never mentioned in the four gospels, and whether one can construe St. Paul's reference to the Greeks as meaning these sages is at best quite questionable.

[73]This section parallels Rousseau's comparison of Jesus and Socrates, with the difference that for Kant Jesus is a superphilosopher rather than a god. His remarks on Judaism as merely external and legalistic rather than moral are rather representative of the attitude toward things Jewish even in the so-called Enlightenment period, with the notable exception of Lessing.

[74]In a footnote (*Religion*, 74-75; KgS VI:80), Kant allows for the possibility of one born without the propensity to evil and offers some unintentionally amusing speculations on how such can be understood.

[75]*Religion*, 77; KgS VI:82.

> Yet the good principle has descended in mysterious fashion from heaven into humanity not at one particular time alone but from the first beginnings of the human race . . . and it rightfully has in mankind its first dwelling place.[76]

Despite all the qualifications, Kant in the end confers a special significance upon the unnamed Christ. For in him the good principle has been actualized to a new degree and he thereby becomes a source of hope and an object for imitation. Of course, Kant accords Jesus the role of moral teacher, as did Rousseau and others. On the basis of selections from the Gospel of Matthew (with the one exception of a quotation from Luke), Kant analyzes the teachings of Jesus and finds them to emphasize inner disposition and outer, moral action and to warn against passivity—teachings that reason recognizes as its own. On this basis, he adds, "Here then is a complete religion, which can be presented to all men comprehensibly and convincingly *through their own reason.*"[77] Jesus is therefore not only the "teacher of the gospel" but the teacher of religion that revolves around the moral law and not, of course, the meaning or identity of Jesus himself.

The status of Jesus allows a reappreciation of the movement he founded and thus leads to special status for Christianity. But, we observe again, Kant's repeated singling out of Christianity and Christ (even when he does not refer to them by name) are, in fact, unjustified by his method of inquiry. A philosophical consideration of religion may, of course, look at historical religion and, indeed, should do so. But Kant looks all too instinctively at Christianity, so much so that one finally recognizes that his interest in Christianity underlies his philosophical inquiry into religion. Were he evenhanded, he would have to investigate at least parallel material from other historical religions. His standpoint is clear, however, even if unsupported: he regards Christianity as the only truly moral religion. Thus his continued interest in highlighting its moral content and in transforming or eliminating less praiseworthy elements is evident throughout.

CHRISTIAN CHURCH AS MORAL ALLIANCE

While Jesus is the symbol of the good principle and while his own life symbolizes the struggle of good against evil, his life and death do not constitute triumph over it. The "envoy from heaven" is indeed credited with

---

[76]Ibid.
[77]*Religion,* 150; KgS VI:162.

breaking the sovereign hold of the evil principle, but only this. And while any who struggle to set good over evil should do no less, alas each can do no more: neither Christ nor others who imitate his moral example effect universal and final victory of the good. Moreover, neither is the evil principle decisively defeated in any single battle, nor is final defeat assured. (On these points, Kant also departs from the Zoroastrian scenario.) Simply maintaining one's ground is an arduous task, and the risk of relapse into the sovereignty of evil remains a constant danger that requires ongoing vigilance and effort. The possibility of ultimate victory, therefore, demands more: a moral alliance and supernatural aid, both at the beginning and at the end of the process.

The necessary alliance of morally struggling individuals thus required brings a social dimension to the struggle of the good against evil and constitutes an important development in Kant's thought. In elaborating his view, Kant further emphasizes his break with the naively optimistic social thought of his times. For Kant rejected the Enlightenment's romantic notion of an original state of nature that is corrupted by a bad society (as in Rousseau). The roots of human nature's corruption lie, as we have seen and as he stressed, in radical evil. Society may indeed contribute to one's moral corruption, but the individual first corrupts himself and then the society he enters. Creation of a better society thus requires more than improved social structures created by men of good will. It demands individual moral recovery and then a practical moral-social formation.

In light of the reality of radical evil then, the only hope for a good society—one that will not recorrupt the morally struggling individual—is for each to join forces with other individuals who have similarly struggled for the good and to form with them a commonwealth of persons who act individually and advance collectively toward moral perfection. Their goal, philosophically expressed, is an ethical commonwealth, for which the "Kingdom of God" is religion's expression. The idea of God now required is that "of a higher moral Being through whose universal dispensation the forces of separate individuals, insufficient in themselves, are united for a common end."[78] God's role here is to be the final guarantor of the social good.

Kant's elaboration of the formation of the ethical commonwealth leads him into the articulation of a philosophical ecclesiology. He identifies the

---

[78]*Religion*, 89; KgS VI:98.

concept of an ethical commonwealth with the religious concept of a "people of God" under ethical laws (in section III) and goes on to assert that a church is the sole form in which the idea of a people of God can be realized (section IV). The ethical commonwealth thus requires a church, at least for its beginnings, and even a scripture. For Kant will next assert (in section V) that every church has its origin in an historical, revealed faith, founded on a scripture.

Kant's philosophical inquiry into religion will now employ the language of biblical theology—of historical faith, church, people of God, revelation, and scripture. All the while, these expression are understood as synonyms provided by history for various philosophical terms; and, even while using them, practical reason always provides their content.

But it is highly significant that Kant uses them at all and that he considers them useful, since philosophy has its own terms, after all. It is additionally striking that the religious terms to be used are closely allied with Christianity, which is only one historical religion among many. Other religions—particularly Judaism and Islam—will, indeed, be mentioned, but only to suffer by comparison with a Christianity that is, for Kant, the moral standard among religions. One cannot pass over Kant's betraying cultural influences and prejudices in his discussion. But at the same time there is a self-consciously positive content that the modern secularist cannot ignore: Kant's profession of his own intellectual alliance with a Christianity understood as the moral force inspired by Christ's life and death.

Ethical commonwealth and kingdom of God have been made synonymous. And the church is recognized as the historical actuality seeking to attain the ideal expressed by both. Practical reason defines the church, of course, and notes it as an imperfect social formation and interim stage on the long road to moral perfection.

From a philosophical standpoint, what is most striking is moral reason's acceptance not only of an historical actuality but also of an historical actuality that claims to be a revealed faith. Indeed, this historical actuality and initial stage toward the formation of a moral order, initiated with divine aid, are viewed as a practical necessity.

This turn in the work presents its own problems. For, if the (idea of) morality leads inescapably to the (idea of) religion, as the First Preface observes, we must note that the idea of an ethical commonwealth does not lead to the idea of a revelation-based church. Even if we find that church is a practical step toward the eventual attainment of the ethical commonwealth and even if we deem it a practical necessity, given man's fallen state, we shall still find that the idea of an ethical commonwealth leads ultimately back only to itself. On the theoretical level, a revelation-based church is an escapable and dispensable step. On the practical level, it must be dispensed with, in due time, so that the process of moral advance may go forward, as it should and must, by human effort alone (until the limits of human power are reached).

The church's proper role—theoretically, practically, and actually—is that of intermediate stage, to be transcended in the formation of the kingdom/commonwealth. However, even when formation into an alliance of those seeking the Good comes to be viewed as a practical requirement, such a moral alliance does not finally assure attainment. In fact, Kant notes that the idea of an ethical commonwealth is "sublime . . . never wholly attainable."[79]

Moral reason requires God once again at the social level and indeed may even be said to require God in order to get beyond his church. For just as God was required to be guarantor of moral perfection, when considered an individual matter in the Second Critique, so God will be required again to achieve the consummation of the task that is now understood as social. Socialization of the struggle for the good has not done away with the final requirement of God's supplying men's want. Individuals bring about a revolution in their state of mind (*Gesinnung*) and then form themselves into a social unity. The final state of moral perfection will be attained with God's assistance and after individual striving and mutual support. It will be manifested in the transformation of their social unity into the Kingdom of God or, philosophically expressed, the ethical commonwealth. But in the meantime, their social unit is called the visible church.

Why the need for a divinely founded church? It might seem that mankind requires all too much divine assistance. Moreover, a historical church, by virtue of the particularity its very history confers upon it, can never serve as the basis of the universal kingdom/commonwealth that all aspire to. Yet, Kant tell us, while only pure religious faith can serve as the basis of a universal church, "by reason of a peculiar weakness of human nature" pure faith can never suffice alone to found a church.[80]

---

[79]*Religion*, 91; KgS VI:100.
[80]*Religion*, 94; KgS VI:103.

The "peculiar weakness" is radical evil, and once again the natural development is impeded or blocked by the consequences of an original moral deed and requires temporary, divine intervention. The historical Christian church is thus the product of such a need and of such intervention. It is the beginning of the movement toward a universal church, but still cannot serve as its basis unless and until it is transformed. For this to happen, the historical element will have to be dissolved. Moreover, as if to emphasize this, Kant states that the actual and historical church can only be regarded as the "true church" to the extent that it recognizes itself as transitional and as the imperfect vehicle of pure religion.[81]

Kant has really conceded little to the church. He philosophically validates only its past, or only its beginnings. It is not an eternal formation. It is still a great distance from the goal. Nor is it the embodiment of pure religious faith which will be attained only in the commonwealth. But, since it is not pure religious faith, it cannot, according to Kant, serve as the basis of a universal church. It is very much a circumscribed and interim formation. But it is, all the same, a necessary one.

Having conceded so little, Kant is vigilant in pointing out the dangers to which the interim church can give rise (and has given rise). The essential danger of a historical religion that provides something sensibly tenable is that its adherents think that the sensibly tenable might render them well-pleasing to God. Kant has in mind the danger of worship. And he speaks of a "propensity to the religion of divine worship" (*Hang zur gottesdienstlichen Religion*)[82] and contrasts it to the "predisposition to moral religion" (*Anlage zur moralischen Religion*).[83] The terminology suggestively parallels the "propensity to evil" and the "predisposition to Good" that Kant employed in the discussion of radical evil. (Kant also mentions the "propensity to passive faith" [*Hang zum passiven Glauben*].[84])

Division two of Book III follows out the theme already suggested above: the historical church's fall into its own kind of radical evil and hence its failings as a moral alliance. Kant rehearses a short history of the Christian church's episodic abuses and unfaithfulness to the good principle in succumbing to the propensity to divine worship. Worship, for Kant, means

---

[81]*Religion*, 106; KgS VI:115.
[82]*Religion*, 97; KgS VI:106.
[83]*Religion*, 102; KgS VI:111.
[84]*Religion*, 123; KgS VI:132.

not only the sensible church service but any attempt to win divine favor outside of strictly moral action. But the Christian church's propensity to evil has taken other forms as well: mystical fanaticism on the part of hermits and monks, the glorification of celibacy, concern with miracles (a problem to which Kant returns), dogmatic squabbles and despotic teachers turned ecclesiastical rulers with earthly ambitions. He sums up his characteristic Enlightenment critique of historical faith with the oft-quoted remark from Lucretius's *De Rerum Natura* (I, 101), "tantum religio potuit suadere malorum"—such are the evil deeds that ecclesiastical faith has prompted. Early Christianity does not stand under such judgment, but only because it had no learned public to give a full record of its deeds. While it is really not known to what extent moral improvement can be attributed to earliest Christians, the greater part of Christian history stands under severe judgment:

> . . . the history of Christendom, from the time it became a learned public itself, or at least part of the universal learned public, has served in no way to recommend it on the score of the beneficent effect which can justly be expected of a moral religion.[85]

The Christian church is thus certainly not the vehicle of salvation history but simply a distinguished passenger. Although the formation of the Christian church is a decisive event in setting the vehicle in motion, the Christian church itself eventually needs to be saved. The time for this is now at hand, in the restoration of the predisposition to moral religion and the dissolution of historically grounded (and limited) faith. The moment is ripe, and Kant proclaims that

> If now one asks, What period in the entire known history of the church up to now is the best? I have no scruple in answering, *the present*.[86]

It is the best because its original predisposition to moral faith can now be recovered in the present and by human effort alone. Philosophy is the agent of this recovery, and particularly the chastened moral reason that Kant himself has articulated. Hence modern philosophers are implicitly the priests of the pure moral religion to come, and they usher it in after having helped Christianity to self-understanding and recovery in its role in the formation of pure religion. This is a revalidation of the Christian church on

---

[85]*Religion*, 121; KgS VI:130.
[86]*Religion*, 122; KgS VI:131.

the part of philosophy, but also for philosophy itself a far-reaching self-ascription, however modestly expressed by Kant. (It will find its most extreme expression in the next century in Hegel's philosophy of religion.)

Despite the indictment of Christian history, Kant has nonetheless defined a place for Christianity in relation to moral religion, and it is, in the final analysis, still a positive place. This is self-consciously in contrast to the Enlightenment in general and proceeds along lines begun by Rousseau. Kant has carefully eliminated any overvaluation of Christianity by insisting on its circumscribed role in the process of establishing moral religion and he keeps Christianity humble by reminding all of its limitations and failings. Yet Christianity remains an important phase because it is the moral assembly that arises from the life and death of the moral teacher of the gospel. It has been historically indispensable and still serves to quicken moral sensibility until the age is ready to move beyond it. On this point, Kant's own rationalist optimism precludes his speculating on the role of Christianity in an age that might refuse to rise to universal moral faith.

CHRISTIANITY AS RELIGION

The Christian church, we have seen, is a stage on the way to the attainment of the pure religious faith of moral reason. Christianity is a historical religion, and it is in its history that Christianity has served as both a catalyst in marshaling the struggle for the good and also as an obstacle to it. In the end, it is Christianity's very historicity that stands in the way of attaining the pure religious faith and ethical commonwealth to which it has made its praiseworthy but surpassed contribution.

But Christianity is not, for that, simply one historical religion among others. For Kant, it is emphatically the only moral religion and it thus has a unique status. Kant alludes to Christianity's relation to other historical religious configurations, particularly Judaism and Greek paganism. His philosophical account of the history of religions is minimal at best and is characteristic of his century in its prejudiced view of the religion of the Jews and its romantic treatment of the religion of the Greeks. Christianity, he even asserts, has no essential tie to Judaism. For Judaism, in his view, was a political commonwealth that did not allow itself to become truly religious, that emphasized its own exclusivity as a chosen people, thereby rejecting any possible universal role, and that revolved around legal rather than moral commandments. Kant rejects the Old Testament on the whole and thus would seem to have ceased his reading of the Hebrew Scriptures before he came to the Prophets (as well as to have begun his study of Greek religion with the Age of Pericles). For the Prophets' was a moral deity that we would expect Kant above all to view positively. Even Judaism's monotheism does not redeem it in his eyes and he goes blindly on to suggest the inferiority of a monotheistic, legalistic Judaism to polytheism with a moral core.

Kant still grants that Christianity arose from Judaism and thus must account for its moral orientation vis-à-vis the legalistic orientation of Judaism. Greek paganism provides the point of transition. For Greek paganism and philosophy influenced Judaism and prepared it for the moral revolution that Judaism itself did not experience but that then broke out in Christianity. "Thus Christianity arose suddenly, though not unprepared for, from Judaism."[87] The historical significance of Judaism, then, is its having been the agent of transmitting Greek moral and philosophical content to Christianity.[88] Kant would assert that Christianity and moral paganism have more essentially in common than Christianity and Judaism, yet he cannot entirely sever from Judaism a revealed and historical faith that claims continuity not with Socrates, Plato, and Aristotle but with Abraham, Isaac, and Jacob.

But if the Christian religion stands more essentially indebted to the morality of the Greeks than to the legalism of the Jews, Christianity is not for that reason simply morality. It is moral theism. In Kant's *Vorlesungen über die philosophische Religionslehre* or *Lectures on Philosophical Theology*, moral reason led to the concept of God as moral ruler of the world (*Weltbeherrscher*), which Kant then termed moral theism. Religion, which Kant defines as "(subjectively regarded) the recognition of all duties as divine commands,"[89] has the standpoint of moral theism. The "recognition of all duties as divine commands" is beyond both the plain theism of natural theology and the deism of transcendental theology. If this definition reduces

---

[87]*Religion*, 118; KgS VI:127.

[88]This historically untenable view gives a new twist to the Christian Apologist vs. Enlightenment controversy on the relationship between Greek wisdom and the Old Testament. For just as the 2nd- and 3rd-century Christian Apologists were prima facie convinced that the wisdom of the Greeks must have been plagiarized from the Scriptures, so were the antireligious *Aufklärer* and *philosophes* certain that any wisdom in the Old Testament must have been taken from the Greeks. In his insistence on the cleft between Judaism and Christianity, Kant is a kind of "philosophical Marcionite."

[89]*Religion*, 142; KgS VI:153.

the life of religion to morality, it does not make religion thereby merely equivalent to morality. Recognition of the moral ruler who issues the moral commands makes an essential difference and elevates Christianity above morality to moral religion.

But Christianity's moral theism does not remove it from the natural plane. It is still a natural religion when it remains faithful to itself. For a natural religion is one in which (moral) reason has primacy. Of course, Kant admits Christianity's claims to revelation and even concedes Christianity's additional status as a revealed religion, or one in which divine command has primacy. Can it have two primacies—divine command and moral reason? It cannot have both simultaneously but only sequentially. Christianity, which began with the primacy of divine command, can—and should—detach itself from its historical, revealed content in order to emerge as natural religion in which moral reason is primary.

The Christian religion is called upon to become natural religion as morality united with the concept of God as moral author of the world.[90] The rest is husk that protected a once fragile seed and that now must be stripped away. As a natural religion, Christianity can also be separated from its holy books. And only a religion which could *only* be revealed religion could not be so separated.[91] In fact, once its teachings are acknowledged by reason, their supernatural revelation may be forgotten without loss.

There is, then, natural religion and revealed religion. And a historical faith may be both. If it is, it is called upon to establish the proper hierarchy. The ordering is clear: naturaral over revealed and historical. Right ordering means subjugation of revealed and historical elements to purer natural religious elements in a historical faith until such time as the revealed and historical can be dispensed with. The right ordering is reminiscent of the right order of the moral incentives (moral law above self-love), and reversal of the right order suggests fall and corruption and the need for recovery. The parallels are too obvious in Kant not to be deliberate. And Kant takes pains to point out Christianity's failings. Yet with its acknowledged predisposition to moral religion—something that it alone among historical religions possesses—it has the hope of recovery and thus of taking its proper self-effacing place in the formation of pure religion.

---

[90]*Religion*, 145; KgS VI:157.
[91]*Religion*, 144; KgS VI:156.

PROBLEMATIC CHRISTIAN NOTIONS

The text of *Religion within the Limits of Reason Alone* documents moral reason's difficulties with traditional Christian teachings. Enlightenment religious thought, on the whole, had generally dismissed the Christianity and Christ for whom Kant's moral religion carves out distinctive places. But Kant could not include certain traditional teachings and doctrines that had grown up around Jesus without essential modification. Moral reason is wary of them altogether and, as if to reflect this wariness, Kant relegates discussion of most of them to special parerga appended to each of the four books that comprise *Religion within the Limits of Reason Alone*. Among the problematic subjects are grace, miracles, mysteries (including the doctrine of the trinity), and means of grace. Also included are prayer, pilgrimage, ascesis, and mystical experience claims. Such ideas are held to be inherently dangerous, even if they arise in order to supplement our recognized moral insufficiency. For the notion of works of grace leads all too frequently to fanaticism, the notion of miracles to superstition, the notion of mysteries to illumination, and the notion of means of grace to thaumaturgy.[92] And a notion such as vicarious atonement brings with it the serious danger of moral passivity.

The possibility of grace was discussed above, immediately following radical evil (and in Kant's own order), since those two subjects are so intimately linked. There we saw that moral reason tightly controls what is intellectually and morally allowable. The same model is followed whenever a doctrinal problem is mentioned.

Miracles

Miracles were a frequent subject of eighteenth-century discourse on religion and Kant deliberately gives them only minor consideration. From the standpoint of intellectual reason, miracles are highly troublesome since they would amount to violations of the laws of nature by nature's own God. From the standpoint of moral reason, they are largely superfluous, while not without a tolerable role in story and symbol. Kant avoids outright dismissal of miracles, not in order to abet traditional religion but rather in order not to give aid to the new enemies of religion.

---

[92]*Religion*, 48; KgS VI:53.

Kant's discussion is not unambiguous, but his meaning can be gleaned. Since miracle claims are part of almost all historical religions, he feels compelled to say something about them. But, we recall, his only interest in historical religion really revolves around that one historical religion that is directly involved with the attainment of pure moral religion, and so it is only Christian miracle claims that figure directly.

Kant grants the role of miracles in the Scriptures:

> . . . it is wholly comfortable to man's ordinary ways of thought, though not strictly necessary, for the historical introduction of [a religion based on the moral disposition] to be accompanied and, as it were, adorned by miracles, in order to announce the termination of the earlier religion, which without miracles would never have had any authority.[93]

Yet Kant here grants the place of miracles only in *narrative,* not in fact. They are the trappings (*Hülle*) that have brought into currency a doctrine engraved in reason and in need of miracles. They have some practical usefulness—in the narrative—but cannot be a tenet of faith.

Kant's real position, interestingly, is expressed in a footnote, where not a few of his most important points are to be found:

> Thus, miracles must be admitted as [occuring] *daily* (though hidden under the guise of natural events) or else *never* . . . and since the former alternative is not at all compatible with reason, nothing remains but to adopt the latter maxim.[94]

In sum, there may have been some practical usefulness in the miracle stories of old, among the people of old, but there can be no such miracles today, nor is there any possible use for them. Kant's thrust is to dismiss all miracles, including those believed to have had practical historical effect. But there is nothing practical to be gained in dismissing the miracle stories themselves and so they are allowed. The only real ''miracle'' that Kant is prepared to accept, without terming it such, is the marvelous event of one's being accounted well-pleasing to God—a wonder that is safely supersensible and that does not disturb any law of nature.

Mysteries

Mysteries too were a stock subject of eighteenth-century philosophy of religion. They seem quite unimportant to Kant, and he takes them up largely

---

[93]*Religion,* 79; KgS VI:84.
[94]*Religion,* 84n; KgS VI:89n.

because of their stock nature. Nevertheless, he effectively dissolves them as a category of religion as he subjects them to moral reason's scrutiny.

According to Kant, we can never come to any knowledge of God as he is in himself but only as he is for us as moral beings. Hence, when we come to a church doctrine such as the trinity that purports to teach something of the mysterious nature of God in himself, we cannot really have in it what the church has traditionally believed. Nonetheless, it is not a useless teaching. For it can be pared down and rendered practical. God as holy legislator, good governor, and righteous judge is a triune notion but no mystery, since it presents itself spontaneously everywhere. The distinctiveness of Christianity in relation to it is that Christian revelation first made public the threefold quality of the moral ruler.

Practical reason is capable of coming to this idea alone but recognizes the fact that it has come initially to expression of the idea through historical revelation. But practical reason develops the revealed notion by arriving as the *true* understanding, which it recognizes as having nothing to do with the mysterious nature of God but rather with God's meaning for moral beings.

Historically or scripturally revealed "mysteries" are thus not mysteries after all. And the three "mysteries of reason," or transcendent concepts, are not really mysteries either. For the mystery of divine call to the ethical state is demystified by Kant's noumenal/phenomenal distinction: man remains noumenally free and can aspire to recovered moral standing. For moral reason, this is wondrous and evident. The mystery of vicarious atonement is only apparent, for "vicarious" cannot and therefore does not mean "substitute" but only "complementary." and the mystery of election is unreal because it would be unjust.

Only one genuine holy mystery remains: the individual and moral community's relationship to the moral ruler of the world, revealed in historical faith and now correctly understood by practical reason which thereby restores faith to its proper end, viz. preparing the pure religion of reason.

Means of Grace

For Kant, there is only one genuine grace (the moral supplement of being accounted well-pleasing to God) and only one means of meriting it (moral struggle and self-recovery). All else is illusion.

Whatever, over and above good life-conduct, man fancies he can do to become well-pleasing to God is mere religious illusion and pseudo-service of God.[95]

Ascesis, prayer, pilgrimage, and so forth are all worthless in making one well-pleasing to God. Nor could direct communion with God substitute for moral action. In addition, any such claims are fanatical since sensuous human nature has no faculty for receiving intuitions of the supersensible Supreme Being.[96]

In the parergon to Book Four, Kant even argues that "means of grace" is a self-contradictory term. For "means" are "all the intermediate causes, which man has in his power,"[97] while a "means of grace" is precisely what is not in man's power. Religious rituals can also be such an illusion of obtaining grace but they can be useful means of sensuously awakening and sustaining attention to true service of God. Likewise, prayer can awaken the disposition to goodness, while it cannot obtain grace. Churchgoing may validly spread goodness because of the practical social effect. Baptism and the Lord's Supper, the two sacraments of Kant's own Lutheranism, are valuable for fostering the community but neither wash away sin, in the first instance, nor bring one into direct community with the deity, in the second.

ASSESSING KANT'S MORAL PHILOSOPHY OF RELIGION

ESSENTIALS OF HIS MORAL RELIGION

The links between reason and morality, morality and religion and moral religion and God will have become clearly established. But any identifications would be rash. Each maintains its distinctiveness and is not absorbed by the other.

Reason and Morality

The movement in Kant's writing is clearly from morality to religion and not vice versa. But even if "Religion is an idea which belongs to mo-

---

[95]*Religion*, 158; KgS VI:170.

[96]Cf. *Dreams of a Spirit-Seer*, trans. Emanuel Goertwitz, ed. with introduction and notes by Frank Sewall (London and New York: Macmillan, 1900). Kant's moral point is plain here, but his facile assertion that human nature has no faculty for intuiting or communing with the divine is contested, not by arguments but by claims to self-validating mystical experience. Those who assert such experiences frequently have no interest in arguing with those they view as dismissing an experience which they insist on denying to themselves.

[97]*Religion*, 180; KgS VI:192.

rality," as Kant wrote in a *Vorarbeit* to *Religion within the Limits of Reason Alone,*[98] not only are the two not identical in Kant's mind but neither is religion in the end totally reduced to morality, despite suspected tendencies to such in his writings.

Kant's own definition of religion as "the recognition of all duties as divine commands" might at first seem inadequate to all that he included in the pages of *Religion within the Limits of Reason Alone.* For religion is there more than a list of duties and even more than a *prise de conscience* about moral obligation. It remains distinct and distinguishes itself from morality first by the recognition of the fallenness of man and of the presence of an enduring propensity to evil, as well as by the hope of being found well-pleasing to God that is introduced through historical faith. None of these comes about through reason a priori, as can the discernment of the moral law. But regarded more carefully, his definition of religion as "the recognition of all duties as divine commands" itself points beyond morality to include the recognition of the connection between duty discerned by moral reason alone and the divine being postulated by moral reason as necessary to guarantee the eventual fulfillment of the moral law. The God-postulate of moral reason is not in any sense apodictic, that is, necessary to the idea of morality, but is a necessary postulate, given the human condition. Thus Kant's definition of religion really points to an essential difference between morality and religion, namely, God-consciousness, including the process of coming to it.

Religion distinguishes itself from morality, then, by virtue of God, the consciousness of whom is essential to religion, while of course not essential either to discerning the moral law or acting upon it. "God" also provides the hope that the moral law can be fulfilled and that happiness can be realized. For Kant, these are essential aspects of religion, but not essential facets of morality.

Religion and morality, while distinct, remain united, the former an extension of the latter, but not identical to it. If religion is more than morality, morality is very much its core. Religion depends on the concept of morality derived from practical reason. It is the base without which the edifice of religion cannot stand. And if someday morality should be shown to be no more than an instrument of social self-preservation, as some hold,

---

[98] KgS XXIII: 96.

rather than a law inscribed in every human heart, then Kant's concept of religion would fall together with his concept of morality. In sum, morality without religion is theoretically possible, while religion without morality is unthinkable. And despite Kant's conceding the apparent practical necessity of a historical faith in order to set the moral process underway, he would always argue for the sufficiency of reason at least in attaining recognition of the moral law.

Religion and Reason

Religion and reason are also distinct, despite certain expression in Kant's *Nachlass* and *Opus Posthumum* in particular. When Kant wrote that "Reason for itself is the whole of religion,"[99] he was not identifying the two but rather expressing the teleology of reason, in which religion is included.

Practical reason and the moral law that it discovers are at the core of religion and also its source. The moral end of all things—the actualization of the purposefulness (*Zweckmässigkeit*) that reason discerns in the world—is also the final end of religion. The "Kingdom of God" is religion's expression for the attainment of the kingdom of purposes. But religion is distinct from historical faith too (and historical faith is of course not a product of reason).

Moral Reason and God

If religion is not reason, it remains to be asked if God is reason. When Kant wrote in the *Streit der Fakultäten* concerning biblical interpretation that "the God in us is himself the interpreter,"[100] he was not identifying reason and God but expressing God's immanence in human reason. *Religion within the Limits of Reason Alone* at times appears to echo the puzzling remarks of the *Opus Posthumum* in which we read that God is identical to the moral law. Moreover, one might come back to an interpretation of *Religion within the Limits of Reason Alone* from the *Opus Posthumum* and idealism and see in Kant's earlier work the dissolution of the God-concept, or at least identification of God and reason that there seems clearer. In *Religion within the Limits of Reason Alone* and despite Kant's careful lan-

---

[99]Quoted by Josef Bohatec, *Die Religionsphilosophie Kants in der "Religion innerhalb der Grenzen der bloßen Vernunft"* (Hamburg, 1938) 39, from Rudolph Reicke, ed., *Lose Blätter aus Kants Nachlass* III (1899):90.

[100]KgS VII: 48, 67.

guage, mystery has dissolved into symbols, miracles into narrative embellishments, the historical Jesus into moral teacher, and the Christ into a metaphysical principle, while his church has become destined to dissolve into the ethical commonwealth. Can the God-concept withstand this mighty course of dissolutions?

Leaving aside for the moment the difficult and perhaps finally indecipherable *Opus Posthumum,* one can reply that indeed God escapes dissolution. For he is conceived as the *subject* of the moral law and as author of creation's final purpose, and not merely as personification of the moral law or as a name for the cosmos itself ("pantheos").[101]

But the God of *Religion within the Limits of Reason Alone* and of Kant's moral religion is not the traditional God of Christian theologians or of philosophers. For, as Jean-Louis Bruch remarks,[102] unlike the "God of the philosophers" he is a living God, the judge of human hearts and not merely a God of ends. But unlike the traditional Christian God, his providence consists in willing creation's moral goodness and not intervening in the process. For the Kantian deity is a practically necessary postulate, the guarantor of the potential attainment of the kingdom, not the decisively and abidingly active Father who promises its final attainment. Bruch concludes that

> The God of Kant is neither the God of the philosophers and of the learned—for his presence is interior and his function eschatological—nor the God of Christians, since one does not at all call upon him. He is at one and the same time near and distant. Near, since he is the author of the moral law: the God in us. Distant, since he is an implacable judge. . . He is the God of Moses rather than the God of Jesus.[103]

But if one wishes to place an Old Testament emphasis on the anthropomorphic qualities of this god, one must also note an essential difference for Kant between the lawgiver of Sinai and his own. For Kant, the law given Moses was purely statutory and external, while the moral law issued by the God of reason, revealed in moral reason and echoed in the teaching of Christ, concerns the individual in the most personal way.[104]

---

[101]Cf. also KgS XX:22.

[102]*Religion,* 217.

[103]*Religion,* 264.

[104]It may, in the end, be more correct to locate the Old-Testament-styled deity of Kant in the Book of Job than in the Pentateuch. For the God of "Job" is more symbol of the religious man. Not only is Job a morally good man but he is also firmly against all currying

Because the closest one comes in Kant to experiencing God is in his moral law, the temptation arises to identify God and the moral law, which would be incorrect. Experience of a personal God as the Holy seems absent altogether and this raises a final subject that defines Kant's concept of religion by its very exclusion.

Religious Experience: Its Absence

Kant expresses awe and astonishment, as at the end of the *Critique of Practical Reason* ("Two things fill the mind with ever new and increasing admiration and awe, the oftener and more steadily we reflect on them: the starry heavens above me and the moral law within me"). Yet Kant is no forerunner of Rudolph Otto. One may suspect or believe that religious sentiments underlie Kant's writings and his moral theism. If this is so, Kant did not find them important enough to give them place in his discussion of religion.

The most that one may conclude from Kant's restrained expression is that the moral law uplifts man, that reflection upon it uplifts the soul, and that the moral law is the nearest one comes to encountering the divine. But it is certainly not to be construed as a direct experience of God. To be sure, Kant took pains to deny any kind of such experience, particularly emphasizing the lack of any faculty for direct perception of God.

The absence of a genuine discussion of religious experience is a serious shortcoming in Kant's philosophy of religion. He had his reasons, of course. Beyond personal reticence was his fear of any opening to fanaticism and superstition. But Kant's understanding of religion also emphatically excludes it. For religious experience, beyond edifying reflection upon the starry heavens, moral law and immortality, is simply not practical.[105] It is likely to lead to quietism and passive absorption in place of striving to fulfill the moral law. Kant is firmly within that group of Western think-

---

of favor with the divine, i.e., all corruption of religion, as he reveals in rebuffing his friends' suggestions about appeasing the God purportedly punishing him. In addition, Job is a person of sincerity and of reason, and, on this basis, he goes so far as to challenge the deity's incomprehensible conduct. The sequence to this challenge illustrates, however, a fundamental difference between Job's Lord and Kant's. For in the Book of Job, when Job challenges God to a debate, God uncharacteristically obliges, to Job's own surprise. Kant's God could not appear, even unexpectedly, for there would be no way to recognize him.

[105]Allen Wood (*Kant's Moral Religion*, 201-202) would defend Kant in this, arguing that Kant was only interested in feelings that gave rise to belief or action. But Wood also thereby takes Kant's view of religion.

ers—indeed is leader among them—who insist that religion must foster morality and intensify moral commitment. Thus religious experience that fills or thrills the soul, even if possible, is a danger that is likely to distract from moral effort. Kant never entertains the possibility of religious experience that does not lead to passivity, that might calm the striving Faust and still his struggling ego and thereby even play some role in the restoration of the right order of the moral incentives.

ESSENTIALS OF KANT'S MORAL CHRISTOLOGY AND CHRISTIANITY

Jean-Louis Bruch observed that historical religion for Kant is really an ensemble of institutions and beliefs for which reason can illustrate the rational kernel and a grasp of how corruptions came about. As such, it is not a body of doctrines.[106] Had Kant viewed religion as in any essential sense doctrinal, he would have felt obliged to point out, fully and severely, nonrational and absurd elements. But because he viewed doctrine as unessential to the true meaning of religion—and thus unessential to the one historical religion that can be true religion—he is able to be less harsh than his age would expect, and he is indeed even able to be sympathetic in his treatment of Christianity. Certain intellectually troublesome elements are indeed dealt with, and the parerga to *Religion within the Limits of Reason Alone* treat them in particular.

Yet however much the emphasis is not upon doctrines, Kant engages topics that are traditional doctrinal matters even if, as Bohatec notes, he uses theological formulations in a meaning tailored to reason.[107] To be sure, grace, revelation, and trinity are central points of Christianity theology which moral reason appropriates. Grace is greatly circumscribed and the trinity is philosophically transformed into symbol, as one might expect of an Enlightenment philospher. Kant found the idea of revelation less a threat to man's dignity—and pride—than the Enlightenment did and so accords it a significant practical role, albeit in the distant religious past. He allows at most for one revelation, safely limited to antiquity, recorded in the Christian Bible and interpreted by moral reason. Kant thereby makes biblical theology clearly subservient to rational theology (or the philosophical inquiry into religion) as he understood and practiced it. Kant's handling of the doctrine of the trinity and reduction of it to the symbolic expression of

---

[106]*Religion*, 35.
[107]*Religion*, 30.

a triple personhood is a reinterpretation with soon-seen implications. For the reworking of this central Christian teaching means the dismissal of Christocentricity as traditionally understood. Yet the example of Christ will be at the epicenter of moral-religious thought.

Kant's treatment of Christ comes in the aftermath of the publication of the epoch-making Reimarus *Fragments,* edited by Lessing, in which Jesus and his disciples were depicted as schemers and deceivers. Thus, as Despland notes, "Kant was at the beginning of a series of thinkers for whom it became clear that Jesus must either be reinterpreted or lost."[108] In part, Kant tried to save Jesus from the *Auklärer,* much as Rousseau had done from the *philosophes.* Practical reason has use for a moral teacher, for a model of humanity well-pleasing to God. But in order to serve in the practical role assigned him, Jesus must be human and exclusively so (that is, of one nature only). A divine nature would render him "useless" in that he would then be beyond the scope of imitation. But as a human model, Kant's Jesus is nonetheless beyond the deism that saw in him most positively the moral teacher. For Jesus wins a victory over evil and becomes the inspiring symbol of the battle of good against evil and, as such, remains an active force among us still. Kant's Jesus is thus also beyond Rousseau's, notwithstanding the Savoyard Vicar's sentimental talk of the "death of a god." For Jesus incarnates a humanity risen above radical evil. His godlike life is more than an example and more than a story. Kant concedes to Jesus a practically indispensable role when, in his darker moments, he seems to doubt that reason alone can muster the will for the uphill struggle against radical evil. For if any symbol can supply the moral supplement and inspiration that the will requires, it is that of Jesus the moral Christ.

Despite his dismissals of rationally untenable Christian teachings, his criticism of historical Christian excesses and deviations, and his reduction of Christianity and its Christ to the horizon of practical reason, Kant carefully and deliberately presents a positive view of Christianity and its Christ—even if they are no longer easily recognizable as the community and founder of "New Testament faith." Kant declares Christianity an objectively natural, while subjectively revealed, religion. He is not thereby engaged in a ploy to exalt it only while undermining it. Indeed, he could

---

[108]*Religion,* 259. This is true of Kant in the German-speaking world. In the French-speaking world, Rousseau is first, even if for different reasons.

be paraphrased to say that Christian faith is indispensable in the attainment of the triumph of the good. Kant would be able to accept this, we imagine, and most of the orthodox of his time could have been satisfied—if Kant had said no more. But for Kant, Christianity is not the culmination of religion; it is only its historical beginning. True, Kant affirms the superiority of Christianity to other historical faiths and goes beyond the provocative neutrality of Lessing's *Nathan the Wise*. But, while affirming Christianity, he makes it clear that Christianity must be overcome, indeed that it is part of the very dynamic of the authentic Christian religion to evolve toward a purer, higher form that can dispense with the historical. In this, Kant breaks with any view that accounts the historical indispensable, in the past as well as in a future in which the Christ still has a role to play in fact and not merely in symbol.

What remains is a Christianity that has been a morally useful stage on the road to pure religion. And Christianity emerges as not only *a* but *the* historical moral religion. Additionally noteworthy in an eighteenth century given to romanticizing primitive peoples and their ways is that Kant never assigned this place of honor to some pure religion of reason supposed originally to have existed among noble savages or other peoples of the past and now lost. Instead, it is given to the historical (and historically blemished) religion of European culture. But the one directly useful historical faith is plainly subordinated to the pure moral religion that has not yet been and that is to come about, as men recover themselves from fall into evil and as historical religion recovers itself from fall into superstition, fanaticism and passive faith, both with the help of reason come into its own.

CONCLUSION

If *Religion within the Limits of Reason Alone* had been published anonymously, one might well ask if it would have been attributed to Professor Kant of Königsberg in the way Fichte's work of 1792 had been. We may well suppose that it would not have been, since it breaks with Enlightenment thought in a way that his other writings do not and even as Fichte does not. Moreover, it may even seem not to be the work one would have expected from the author of the three Critiques. Its true authorship becomes, therefore, a call to review interpretations of his other writings. *Religion within the Limits of Reason Alone* is, nonetheless, very much an Enlightenment document, even if Kant does not take the usual *Aufklärer* position on religion. For the central role of reason is never to be doubted within it and it evidences a sure confidence in the power of a reason come into its own. In addition, the themes of progress and hope; the combat of superstition and fanaticism; the central, more humanistic orientation, where man is the measure, and reason the judge of all—these mark Kant's work as a product of its time.

That Kant is in the end part of his times is itself only a commonsense observation, but one not to be taken for granted as long as some intellectual historians still pluck thinkers out of time. Kant, along with Lessing and Rousseau, is rightly seen as standing at the intellectual turning point of his age,[109] particularly with regard to religion. But he is in advance of all, and especially in his interest in rehabilitating the moral religion of history.[110] He is more positive than Lessing, more thorough and systematic— and diplomatic—than Rousseau. With the not unimportant exception of the Prussian king, Kant's *Religion within the Limits of Reason Alone* and his philosophy of religion with it were not perceived in high places as a threat, either by the church, the state or the philosophers, to anything near the degree Rousseau's *Profession* was, and no "great conspiracy" followed in this instance. Yet Kant's work is far more radical.

Kant is in some senses less a man of his century in *Religion within the Limits of Reason Alone* than in the Critiques, where he makes radical innovations in philosophy. The reintroduction of radical evil into discourse on religion would itself have to be characterized as radical—even were it merely in the radical conservative sense understood by Goethe and Herder. But radical evil transforms, and deepens, the grasp of both morality and religion.

While his treatment of Christianity is positive in intent, he makes no attempt to conceal objectionable, unacceptable aspects. And his "reconciliation" of philosophy and theology may be said to be more of a "dictated peace."[111] The usefulness he discerned in Christianity foreshadowed Hegel's subsequent contentions about Christianity and religion—assertions so loud and resounding as to be perhaps temporarily deafening in Berlin, but audible in Kierkegaard's distant Copenhagen. While some would claim that he supported religion in the only way he could and that

---

[109]Cf. Barth, *Protestant Theology in the Nineteenth Century*, 266.
[110]Some, of course, would consider his position reactionary or backsliding.
[111]Cf. Barth, *Protestant Theology in the Nineteenth Century*, 278.

such may be "the best independent support" the religious man can get,[112] one cannot forget that Kant in *Religion within the Limits of Reason Alone* was still writing as a professional philosopher, as he attempted to analyze religion with the fine tool of reason.

In the execution, Kant's effort is not without its limitations, and not all of these can be attributed to his times. His concept of God, for example, is limited by the practical reason that postulates it. There is no knowing what or how God works and very limited tolerance of any revealed data in this regard. The postulates finally provide very limited information indeed. They see no way toward the complete conquest of evil in time, and the eternity/immortality further postulated to complete the process remain vague and distant at best. God is so totally tied to the moral law that if the moral law should prove to be the product of other hands, then the implications for religion and God would be clear. To say that Kant's God-concept is like the God of Moses or even the God of Job is to employ simile and perhaps to obscure differences. For theirs was a "living God," as was the moral God of the prophets, whom Kant simply ignores. So too was the God of Abraham, Isaac, and Jacob, to whom the Jesus of the gospels links himself but whom Kant passes over altogether. By his own definitions, his concept corresponds to moral theism, but the *theos* is remote, transcendent, and impersonal.

Kant's silence on religious experience is in itself significant, as has been observed. For whatever the reasons for his exclusive emphasis on the moral core of religion and for effective silence about the experience of the divine (except for references to fanaticism), the failure to discuss religious experience is a serious flaw in any philosophy of religion, an absence that necessarily distorts the treatment of religion, theoretical and historical, as seen from the standpoint of any critic who concedes it a place of importance in religion and religious claims.

Opposing currents in Kant's thought expressed in *Religion within the Limits of Reason Alone* are never fully reconciled and lead one to understand how various interpretations of his position on religion have arisen. Jean-Louis Bruch notes some of them:[113]

---

[112]W. H. Walsh, "Kant's Moral Theology," *Proceedings of the British Academy* 49 (1963): 262-89.

[113]*Religion*, 247.

autonomy of will	vs.	radical evil
individualism of the 2nd Critique	vs.	theory of ethical community
theory of church as institution necessary for establishing the invisible church	vs.	progress toward disappearing of dogmas and institutions

His account of human alienation and reconciliation is a significant accomplishment of human reason. Equally, his attempt to reconcile theoretical religion with historical faith, working exclusively with the tool of reason, is of a high order. In particular, his symbolic interpretation of the language of historical faith is a breakthrough in this direction.[114] The harmony toward which they seem to move for some, however, remains more apparent than real.

In this attempted reconciliation, Kant stresses the teleology of historical faith—the destiny of faith to become religion—and the identification of religion with the moral perfection of humanity. In the process, and despite his claim of independence from them, *Religion within the Limits of Reason Alone* and his philosophy of religion reveal themselves as a pediment supported by all three pillars of the Critical Philosophy.[115]

That Kant's religious thought is perceived generally as having more influence upon theology than upon philosophy is not in itself either praise or criticism of his achivement. In philosophy of religion, in which *Religion within the Limits of Reason Alone* is a pioneering work, his influence has been enormous and, to the extent that philosophers admit its legitimate place, Kant's significance in philosophy increases. The critical question is not whether Kant's effort has been influential upon or pleasing to either philosophers or theologians but, as in the work of any serious thinker, whether he handled the particular problematic intelligently, consistently and adequately. The judgment upon Kant's philosophy of religion is not unmixed, but his accomplishment remains great for its times and, its limitations corrected, a model for modern philosophy of religion as well. In Kant, reason and religion meet without threat and without acrimony. In

---

[114]Cf. also Eberhard Jüngel, *Gott als Geheimnis der Welt* (Tübingen: Mohr, 1977) Abschnitt 17: "Das Problem analoger Rede von Gott."

[115]The ties to the Third Critique remains an area worthy of more extended study.

him, reason regards historical religion, with its stories and symbols and underlying reality, as a valid part of human life and a legitimate subject for critical, reflective inquiry. And as a man of his times and ahead of them, he betrays neither the haughtiness of eighteenth-century philosophy with regard to religion nor the contended blindness of so much of twentieth-century philosophy.

PART TWO

THE JESUS
OF SPECULATIVE REASON

3

HEGEL AND THE JESUS OF CONSUMMATE RELIGION

INTRODUCTION

The claims of philosophy and theology had been so decisively reduced by Kant that the matter might have seemed settled. However, Hegel and his contemporaries soon made major efforts to reclaim the very ground that Kant had ceded not long before. Moreover, the transition from Kant's position is, interestingly, first via the late Kant himself, who seemed to open the door in his later writings to the idealism that would follow, and then via Fichte, the early Schelling, and finally Hegel. Idealist philosophy set out to prove and demonstrate the kind of knowledge that Kant had held to be impossible. With traditional territories reclaimed and restored, philosophy of religion could expand beyond the confines of morality, plow old fields once again, and reap a hitherto unimagined harvest. Hegel's Berlin *Lectures on the Philosophy of Religion*[1] (1821-1831) are the late and ripe product of just such a restoration.

Although Hegel's *Lectures on the Philosophy of Religion* did not formally require full knowledge of the Hegelian system of philosophy on the part of the initial Berlin audience, the present-day reader can hardly grasp what Hegel set forth in this lecture series without some understanding of the larger system. For the Lectures (delivered in 1821, 1824, 1827, and 1831)

---

[1] *Vorlesungen über die Philosophie der Religion;* for the specific German and English editions referred to herein, and for an explanation of the method of citation, see note 6, below.

belong in substance and form to the system. One might even say that they restate the system,[2] or at least its essence, from the chosen standpoint of the Lectures. Thus Hegel's philosophy of religion has a relationship to the larger authorship that is quite different from those that Rousseau, Kant, or even Schelling had to their own. In reading Rousseau and Kant, for example, one finds a philosophy of religion that is an extension of the thinker's program. Thus, their philosophies of religion are, to an extent, attempts to complete a systematic survey of philosophical problems and themes, as well as to pursue special individual interests. While this is partially true of Hegel as well, Hegel in a very real sense did not erect his system piece by piece. For he began his philosophical program with the demands and conception of a whole system,[3] and after several trial runs arrived relatively early at the outlines of his system. Before one comes to the 1821-1831 philosophy of religion, the system had been fully conceived and was in a sense already in place. Moreover, religion had already been assigned its part and been defined in the *Phenomenology of Spirit* and in the *Encyclopedia*.[4]

But whatever the force of the system, Hegel did not begin his early philosophical reflections without religious interest, as the *Early Theological Writings* make amply clear.[5] There he traced a course which, under the influence of modern French Enlightenment and of ancient enlightened Greece, began with a view of Christianity worthy of a *philosophe,* moved on to discover in Jesus the teacher of Kantian morality, gave voice to some puzzling mystical elements, and seemed to turn ultimately secular—to some, atheistic. But in all this, there was also an "existential" motivation,

---

[2]Michael Theunissen, *Hegels Lehre vom absoluten Geist als theologisch-politisches Traktat* (Berlin: de Gruyter, 1970) 79.

[3]The *Systemfragment von 1800* is a witness from a very early period to the systematic character and emphasis in Hegel's thoughts about doing philosophy.

[4]*Die Phänomenologie des Geistes* (Würzburg and Bamberg, 1807); and *Encyklopadie der philosophischen Wissenschaften im Grundrisse* (Heidelberg, 1817; 2nd enlarged ed., Berlin, 1827). It is a truism of Hegel interpretation that the system constitutes a circle, and a most carefully constructed one, such that there is no proper point of entry. One enters where one will—or where one can—and must follow the circle at least one full round in order to understand any one major topic.

[5]Several interpreters have cited the inaccuracy of the adjective "theological" in the editor-selected title. Georg Lukács, for example, views these writings as antitheological (*The Young Hegel,* trans. Rodney Livingstone [Cambridge MA: MIT Pess, 1976] 4). *Hegels theologische Jugendschriften,* ed. Hermann Nohl, were first published in 1907; English translation by T. M. Knox (Chicago: University of Chicago Press, 1948; reprinted by University of Pennsylvania Press, 1971).

namely, to describe the religion or God-idea that should serve as basis for the proper modern state, a concern that is present in the Lectures as well.[6]

Hegel struggled with and tried out several views of religion and of Christianity in his early career, and Christianity was by turns both villain and hero. But once the system came together, the view of religion and of Christianity was also set, at least in its outlines.[7]

Since the essential view of religion had been sketched in previously published works, the Lectures sought to describe in greater detail religion's defined place in the philosophy of spirit, first abstractly (Part I) and then historically illustrated. Hegel's philosophy claimed to have conceived a form and unifying principle according to which *all* of reality could be explained. The oneness of all as spirit was to be the insight, formula and foundation that would allow the construction of the aimed-at system.[8] In his conception of absolute spirit, he sought to overcome limits imposed by Kant in his bifurcation of noumenal and phenomenal realms but also to correct the failed attempts of Fichte and the early Schelling to create an idealist system. The *Lectures on the Philosophy of Religion* in a sense apply to religion the claim to have discerned and articulated a philosophical, unifying principle. In the Lectures, Hegel then illustrates the connection between that dynamism of spirit and the history of religions as he proceeds to demonstrate the role of religion, theology, and, of course, philosophy in

---

[6]Cf. especially "The Relationship of Religion to the State According to the Lectures of 1831," *Lectures on the Philosophy of Religion*, ed. Peter C. Hodgson, trans. R. F. Brown, P. C. Hodgson, and J. M. Stewart (Berkeley: University of California Press, 1984-) I:451-60; *Vorlesungen über die Philosophie der Religion*, ed. Walter Jaeschke (Hamburg: Felix Meiner Verlag, 1983-) Teil I:339-47. All citations of Hegel's *Lectures on the Philosophy of Religion* will be from the new Brown-Hodgson-Stewart translation, with the pagination of the new German edition following. Thus, for the above: Lectures of 1831: LPR I:451-60; VPR I:339-47. On the State, cf. also Lectures of 1821: LPR I:200; VPR I:109 *et al.* Citations will normally be to the Hodgson and Jaeschke editions unless noted.

[7]This is not, however, to suggest that Hegel had his system entirely set either at the beginning or at the end. The present writer subscribes to the "loose ends" theory of intellectual history, according to which great thinkers remain great even in their incompleteness and without the posthumous tidying up that so many disciples later undertake. It is one thing to claim that a thinker had everything in place by the end of his career, quite another to maintain that all was settled in detail from the start. In Hegel's case, such a view would fly in the face of extant drafts and frequent revisions of details.

[8]Cf. James Collins, *The Emergence of Philosophy of Religion* (New Haven: Yale University Press, 1967) 199ff., where Collins discusses the adjustment of God and religion to the demands of the system.

the life of spirit. In the process, the Christian religion and its Jesus find a place not only of prominence but of decisive import.

There is the danger that Hegel's philosophy of religion appear merely as the logical elaboration of the place that religion *must* occupy in order for the system to be what it claims to be. Part I would then be seen as situating the concept of religion *in abstracto* in his system, Parts II and III merely demonstrating how historical religions *in concreto* illustrate the "concept."[9] But his philosophy of religion is far more than a mechanical explicitation. For, while it is a powerful affirmation of the shared dynamism binding God and world together, it is a profound insight into and tracing of humankind's coming to knowledge of God and of itself in the history of religions. And it culminates in a brilliant speculative meditation on Christianity, the absolute or consummate religion that arose from the deed of a Promethean Jesus who brought to humanity the fiery consciousness of divine-human unity.

HEGEL INTERPRETATIONS

Hegel's philosophy of religion has by turns been interpreted as pantheism, atheism, and even orthodox theism, and Hegel interpretation has seen these views boldly maintained and presented in various hues, despite Hegel's efforts to protect himself against at least the first two.[10] The present study has profited from and struggled against many of these interpretations and found several to be enduringly vigorous contestants. That has not, however, in the end halted rejection of such positions one and all. But the

---

[9]Such is the view of Søren Kierkegaard, for example. In light of the importance of the system to an understanding of any part, one can appreciate the perceptiveness of Kierkegaard—whether or not one subscribes to his judgment—when he identified the system itself as the primary "enemy," as the agent with a logic of its own that necessarily led to a radical new view of Christianity and its Christ. For his part, Kierkegaard regarded Hegel's achievement as a perversion of the Gospel rather than the philosophical elevation of religious representation and doctrine. But Kierkegaard's protest was not the final word and historians of religious thought have come increasingly to admire Hegel's accomplishment.

[10]Not only was Hegel's position disputed and variously interpreted after his death, but Hegel was aware of controversy during the years when he delivered the Lectures. He had tried as early as June 1821 to defend himself against charges of pantheism and atheism. In his letter to Niethammer (*Briefe*, ed. J. Hoffmeister, Band II, 217-72), aware of an order of the Prussian king against any university lectures which might lead to atheism, he wrote that he planned to lecture on the philosophy of religion and had a "good conscience" about it.

plethora of Hegel interpretations, and of the most contrary sorts, must lead one to ask if the lecturer himself does not bear some responsibility. Certain statements would simply seem to lend themselves to various and contradictory interpretations and even the new German edition that restores the original texts from various dubious conflations will not entirely change this. Serious interpreters naturally cite the text, and most are accused of proof-texting by those who cite other texts and differing contexts. Unfortunately, both sides are often well founded. In addition, Hegel's "intention" is sometimes invoked, as if this should settle the matter—and as if his intention could be definitively established. But even if his intentions were indisputable, one should not preclude the possibility that a thought-system may develop a momentum of its own. Indeed Hegel himself, in his philosophical unfolding of the Christian religion, would never have been deterred by any talk of the "intentions" of Jesus and of early church fathers in setting forth doctrines. This is not to argue for license and irresponsible interpretation but rather to undercut the dogmatism that characterizes so much Hegel interpretation.[11] For the *Lectures on the Philosophy of Religion* have been a particularly contested piece in Hegel scholarship, constituting as they do the shibboleth between right- and left-wing Hegelians from Hegel's death down to the present. Hegel perhaps may even be credited with inspiring such a range of interpretations, for he is quoted in his 1824 Lectures as saying of scriptural interpretation:

But where interpretation is not merely explanation of the words but dis-

---

[11]Given the passionate nature of Hegel interpretation, the present writer perhaps must beg indulgence for his tolerant spirit in this matter.

Hegel's "intention" is invoked most recently by Peter C. Hodgson in various publications attending his editing of the newly released English-language translations of Hegel's Lectures. In his editorial introduction to volume 1 of the new English translation of the Lectures, Hodgson writes: "Left- and right-wing interpretations would have been alien to his central intention of overcoming unproductive antitheses between tradition and criticism, faith and knowledge, revelation and reason, infinite and finite, theism and atheism. But for those who could think only in such alternatives, Hegel must have appeared (and still does appear) to be a bundle of conflicting tendencies and contradictions" (30; cf. also Peter C. Hodgson, "Hegel's Christology: Shifting Nuances in the Berlin Lectures," *Journal of the American Academy of Religion* 53:1 [March 1985]: 25. This is really a kind of *pro homine* defense of Hegel. If one wishes to invoke Hegel the man in interpreting Hegel texts, one might finally do better to cite his clear example in treating a subject rather than his sometimes inscrutable intentions.

cussion of the content and elucidation of the sense, it must introduce its own thoughts into the word.[12]

Hegel knew that Scripture had been made into a "wax-nose."[13] Little perhaps did he realize how pliant his own lectures would be to twists toward right, left, and center.

This study finds all interpretations of Hegel as pantheist and atheist—as well as orthodox theist—equally incorrect but at the same time worthy of continued attention. For, as others have noted, the extreme Hegel interpretations are often the most suggestive.[14] Left- and right-wing Hegelians continue to publish and to spar. "Centrist" Hegel interpretations also emerge but inevitably seem to tilt to either the right or the left.[15] For our part, we have attempted to avoid membership in any established school, whether "right" "left" or "middle," but will not be so presumptuous as to think that we have entirely succeeded. At the same time, this interpreter (who suspects himself of inclining to the left) also sees Hegel as a "monist." This designation requires qualification, and perhaps the least misleading qualification would be "monist sui specie"—a monist with theistic as well as mystical inclinations, and one that paradoxically leaves place for divine transcendence.

In interpreting Hegel, much depends upon seriously accepting Hegel's thesis of the indentity of identity and difference.[16] The phrase strains the mind, now as then, but only if it is held to can one follow his course, unhampered by the sirens of pantheism, atheism, and theism.[17] Views of He-

---

[12]Lectures of 1824; LPR I:123; VPR I:39.

[13]Lectures of 1824; LPR I:123; VPR I:40.

[14]Cf. Emil Fackenheim, e.g., on Iljin's and Kojève's interpretations, in: *The Religious Dimension of Hegel's Thought* (Boston: Beacon Press, 1970; original edition, Indiana University Press, 1967) 76n.

[15]This is the case, e.g., with Peter Hodgson and his self-definition as a centrist. Hodgson does hold commendably to the center, except in his interpretation of the incarnation. And there his one-sided emphasis on God's action in Jesus pushes him to the right—and despite his intentions in the matter. Thus the anthropological meaning of Jesus' achievement does not receive its proper weight.

[16]Hegel embraced Schelling's Philosophy of Identity early on, but by the publication of the *Phenomenology of Spirit* he had set out on his own distinctive path.

[17]For those Hegel interpreters who look only to the "architectonic," to the neglect or indulgence of content, and particularly so in the philosophy of religion, the present study will appear a trivial exercise. But it proceeds in the (perhaps quaint) conviction that philosophical authors mean something by their words and that a philosophical work consists of both form and content. The form is of course important to Hegel as even such a critic as Kierkegaard noted in satirizing Hegel for constructing a fine philosophical castle only to take up residence outside. Some modern Hegelians would seem no longer interested even in the castle but only in the drawing plans that they reconstruct and savor in abstraction.

gel as mystic deserve a few words also. There is of course no denying the presence in the Lectures of such well-known and much-cited mystical remarks as that of Meister Eckhart: "The eye with which God sees me is the eye with which I see him; my eye and his eye are one."[18] The skeptical reader might suggest that Hegel employed such a quotation merely because he found it expressive, and indeed the Lectures not infrequently engage in poetic-religious flourishes and edifying quasi-sermonettes on religious themes. However, the oneness of which Eckhart wrote was *for Hegel* an intellectual requirement necessary for the construction of a system of philosophy that was to avoid Schelling's errors. Thus, for Hegel, Eckhart's remark expressed a sine qua non for his system. But it is the second part of the Eckhart quotation that is really more in the spirit of Hegel, if one reads it with Hegel's own definition of such terms as "knowledge" and "thought":

> In righteousness I am weighed in God and he in me. If God did not exist nor would I; if I did not exist nor would he. But there is no need to know this, for there are things that are easily misunderstood (and that can be grasped only in the concept).[19]

The identity of identity and difference, as well as the unity of the divine and the human, and expressions of the total immanence and transcendence of God are formulae with which Hegel attempted to surmount antithetical thought categories and bring off a unifying thought system. They in no wise appear to be reflections of any private devotional life. Moreover, it is ultimately one of the shortcomings of Hegel's philosophy of religion that it nowhere engages in analysis of the meaning of the private religious experiences of *individuals* (despite several general references to religious feeling and intuition and their relation to consciousness). His philosophical interpretation of religion is social, collective, cultural, and world-historical. Herein lies its merit and even its greatness, but also its limitation.

Hegel did not think himself a mystic or a theist in a conventional sense. But he did esteem himself a theologian, that is, one who pursues and attains knowledge of God. Nevertheless, while Hegel is not to be taken necessarily at his word on being a theologian, he is to be taken seriously. For he did view himself as taking on the properly (but not exclusively) theo-

---

[18]Lectures of 1824: LPR I:347; VPR I:248. The new English translation renders the German *eins* here by "the same."

[19]Ibid.

logical task of knowing the deity and viewed himself as reinaugurating true theology in the wake of Kant's having undermined knowledge of God. And in this, he understood himself as rescuing theology from Kant and Kantian theologians, but always for the sake of philosophy.[20] The predicate ''theologian'' to some extent still applies, whether one finally views Hegel as antitheologian effecting a perversion of Christianity (as Kierkegaard and Barth saw him), or sees his theological preoccupation as a cultural conditioning that he had not yet overcome and that masked his true atheism (as viewed by Feuerbach and Kojève, for whom he was the ''atheist theologian''), or holds him to be a profound Christian thinker (as he is understood by Marheineke, E. Schmidt, and, in a different sense, M. Theunissen). But more than a theologian, and more importantly, he was a philosopher of religion, as his Lectures might suggest. For, while interested in knowledge of God, Hegel sought it not in the mode of biblical or natural theology but of speculative reason, and not only in Christianity but in the history of religions. However, it can perhaps not be emphasized enough that insofar as Hegel does theology, he always does so as *philosopher*.

THE "TEXT" OF THE LECTURES ON THE PHILOSOPHY OF RELIGION

While the *Lectures on the Philosophy of Religion* constitute Hegel's last public word on religion and the philosophy of religion, there is in the strictest sense no text, and even the most recent edition of the Lectures does not alter this fact. *For Hegel neither authored nor authorized a published philosophy of religion.* (Hegel had, however, edited the *Lectures on the Proofs of the Existence of God* just prior to his death.) Yet there is a philosophy of religion and there are several texts for it. The existing texts include Hegel's 1821 lecture manuscript and various surviving student transcriptions from later lecture years. While Hegel generally read from a manuscript in his lecture course, he did not read verbatim and student lecture notes (from all series but that of 1821) attest to additions that Hegel made. Hegel's *Kollegheft* or lecture manuscript of 1821 is itself full of

---

[20]Cf. in this connection Karl Löwith's comment: ''Hegel was, from the very beginning, a theologian—for the sake of philosophy,'' in Reinhard Heede and Joachim Ritter, eds., *Hegel-Bilanz: Zur Aktualität und Inaktualität der Philosophie Hegels* (Frankfurt: Klostermann, 1973) 16.

deletions, additions, and emendations, and the margins contain a modified ordering of the material. It is unclear when many of these editorial notes were made, even when the difficult handwriting can be deciphered. (Compare both Lasson's and Ilting's account of this.[21]) Thus, for the 1821 Lectures, we have the *Kollegheft,* with materials from later than 1821, without any extant student transcriptions or notes. For the 1824 and 1827 Lectures, on the other hand, there are reliable transcriptions. For the 1831 Lectures, excerpts have been recently discovered. The fullest and most recent discussion of the state-of-the-texts is in the editorial introductions by Walter Jaeschke in the new German edition and by Peter C. Hodgson in the English translation. Given the passionate nature of Hegel interpretation, it is not surprising that there has been heated controversy about the editing of the texts as well. Such controversy began at least as early as Bruno Bauer's 1840 edition, for which edition Bauer was attacked by both left and right. Even the most recent German edition was contested before its publication by K.-H. Ilting, who began his own new edition. However, with the completion of the Jaeschke edition and English translation based upon it, as well as a forthcoming and related critical edition from the Hegel-Archiv, the state of the text seems fairly settled, barring important new text discoveries.[22]

Hegel delivered the lectures in 1921 to forty-nine students; in 1824 to sixty-three students; in 1927 to 119 students; and in 1831, it is thought, to 200 students.[23] Several editions of the Lectures have since appeared. The first edition was published in 1832 after hasty editing by the theologian and Hegel-disciple Philipp Marheineke, then also serving as the rector of the University of Berlin. This edition was a compilation of student transcriptions with some limited use of the 1821 *Heft,* according to Ilting. In 1840 Bruno Bauer brought out a second edition in which he made greater use of

---

[21]Karl-Heinz Ilting, "Zur Edition" in G. W. F. Hegel, *Religionsphilosophie,* Band I: *Die Vorlesung von 1821* K.-H. Ilting, ed., (Naples: Bibliopolis, 1978) 735ff. Lasson has a section "Zur Feststellung des Textes" at the end of each of the four volumes of his edition: G. W. F. Hegel, *Vorlesungen über die Philosophie der Religion,* Georg Lasson, ed., 4 vol. in 2 (Hamburg: Meiner Verlag, 1974; reprint of 1925 original).

[22]The recent death of K.-H. Ilting would seem to seal this episode. The background of the Jaeschke project is related in: Walter Jaeschke, "Hegel's Philosophy of Religion: The Quest for a Critical Edition," *The Owl of Minerva,* Vol. 11:3 (March 1980): 4-8. Part Two of the article is contained in 11:4.

[23]Figures cited by Albert Chapelle in his *Hegel et la religion,* 3 Volumes (Paris: Editions universitaires, 1964-1971) 1:229.

the 1821 Hegel manuscript (although he did not quote directly from it) and additional materials. Bauer's subsequent move toward atheism made this edition suspect for many, although he seems to stand acquitted of charges of falsification.[24]

In 1925, Georg Lasson, also a theologian, published a second edition in the "Philosophische Bibliotek" (reprinted 1966, Felix Meiner Verlag, Hamburg), based on Hegel's manuscript of 1821 and student transcriptions of the 1824 and 1827 lectures. Lasson distinguished between the quality of the various *Nachschriften,* citing cases of greater and lesser reliability. In some cases, the student had faithfully recorded the lecture, in other cases had interpreted it. The Lasson edition was, until relatively recently, accepted almost uncritically, and many modern studies of Hegel's philosophy of religion are based upon it.[25] Reinhard Heede made the strongest case against the Lasson edition, whose residual worth is viewed as deriving from its deciphering of Hegel's manuscript. Ilting's new edition gives the Hegel 1821 edition and restores it to the original order violated by Lasson.

The Jaeschke edition dismembers the editorially conflated lecture texts published in Hegel's *Werke* and by Georg Lasson. In their place it publishes, by lecture year, the available text for each major division of the lectures. This restoration of the Lectures renders the 1895 Speirs-Sanderson English translation out of date. An English-language translation team under the direction of Peter Hodgson has brought out a new translation. Jaeschke in German and Hodgson in English will undoubtedly become the standard editions in their respective language spheres. These editions both allow and compel a more careful reading of Hegel's "texts" than has been possible up to now. But the scholarship of the past need not, and will not, be erased on that account. The old "conflated" texts may have made "shifting nuances" (Hodgson's term) imperceptible, but the main themes of Hegel's lectures will not have changed.

---

[24]The Marheineke-Bauer edition of 1840 is the text upon which the Speirs-Sanderson English-language translation of 1895 was based; it is also the text reprinted in the Moldenhauer-Michel *Hegel Theorie Werkausbage,* 20 vols. (Suhrkamp Verlag, 1969ff.).

[25]Emanuel Hirsch, however, refused it from the outset. Cf. Reinhard Heede, "Hegel-Bilanz: Hegels Religionsphilosphie als Aufgabe und Problem der Forshung" in Heede and Ritter, eds., *Hegel-Bilanz,* 81.

PHILOSOPHY OF RELIGION AND THE HEGELIAN SYSTEM

Hegel's frequent references to religion throughout his writings are never an analysis of religion alone. His attention to religion is always as part of philosophy and to it as manifestation of the life of spirit. This is as true for the *Lectures on the Philosophy of Religion* as it is for any other Hegelian work. Yet the analysis conducted in the Lectures is distinct in scope and focus. Detailed comparison of all Hegel's writings on religion goes beyond the limits of this study but some indications of interrelationships are warranted.

The *Lectures on the Philosophy of Religion* view the consciousness of religion in its concrete and abstract representations and do so from the standpoint of Hegelian philosophy. Hegel traces the course of religious consciousness through (essentially Western) history, but by no means strictly chronologically. In the Lectures he repeats much that is to be found elsewhere but in them he brings in particular his indictment of the philosophies of Kant and Fichte which, in his view, had excluded knowledge of the absolute and reduced religion to mere morality. He also included criticisms of such contemporaries as Schelling, Jacobi, and Schleiermacher, the latter being singled out in the 1824 and 1827 versions for reducing religion to feeling. Both the opening and closing polemics of the Lectures are thereby aimed at late Enlightenment and successive philosophies. For they had given rise to the various kinds of subjective idealism against which Hegel had to struggle to clear the way for his own objective idealism and its unique grasp of religion.

The theological point of departure for the Lectures had already been expressed in the *Logic, Phenomenology of Spirit,* and *Encyclopedia.* In the *Phenomenology of Spirit,* religion's place was shown in the history of spirit's coming to knowledge of itself. His phenomenology of spirit was thus the "noumenology" of God, the study of the becoming of God in human consciousness.[26] It articulated the absolute standpoint that made possible the explication of the process illustrated in his history of religions. The *Logic* had set forth Hegel's definition of theology: "theo-logy" as the "logic" of God's life, as knowledge of God in his essence, as idea. The *Logic* knew God as eternally absolute and transcendent and concluded with

---

[26]Cf. Jean Hyppolite, *Genèse et structure de la Phénoménologie de l'esprit de Hegel* (Paris: Aubier Montaigne, 1946) 518-22.

the idea of determining itself upon infinite appearance, the study of which found (finite) expression precisely in the Lectures. The *Logic* thus presented God in his ideality and left it to the Lectures to depict him in his truly realized appearance of the divine idea.[27] The Lectures reflect not only the God of the *Logic* but the structure as well, for in them one finds *Begriff-Urteil-Schluß* as (Part I) the Concept of Religion, (Part II) Determinate Religion, and (Part III) the Consummate Religion, and the subdivisions follow the same sequence of universality-particularity-singularity.[28] In addition, the Lectures share the architectonic of the *Philosophy of Right* and of the *Lectures on Aesthetics* with their threefold division into (1) abstract, universal part, (2) differentiating, definite part; and (3) absolute, triumphing part.[29]

The *Lectures on the Philosophy of Religion* are in effect Hegel's "last" word on religion, due to his sudden death in 1831. But they are correctly regarded as his culminating work on the subject, the fruit of efforts that go back through the entire Hegelian corpus. As Karl Löwith wrote,

> The Lectures on the Philosophy of Religion, held four times between 1821 and 1831, are the ripe product of the early intention to make clear for himself what it would mean to "draw near to God" and to ground in thought "the Kingdom of God."[30]

The concern with religion and religious themes went at least as far back as the *Early Theological Writings,* that is, to the earliest philosophical writings by the graduate of the Tübingen theological seminary. Their reading contributes to an understanding of Hegel's intellectual development, but Hegel himself considered them surpassed.[31] The changing views of religion in these early writings arose partly from the influence of Kant's moral religion, partly from an even-earlier-formed romantic view of Greek religion, and from an equally romantic search for a *Volksreligion* or folk re-

---

[27]Heede, "Hegel-Bilanz," 42. He also writes, "Ist Hegels Logik eine Onto-Theo-Logie, so ist die Religionsphilosophie eine Phänomen-Theo-Logie" ("If Hegel's Logic is an onto-theo-logy, then the philosophy of religion is a phenomenal-theo-logy").

[28]Cf. Falk Wagner, *Der Gedanke der Persönlichkeit Gottes bei Fichte und Hegel* (Gütersloh: Mohn, 1971) 204-205.

[29]Cf. Ernst Bloch, *Subjekt-Objekt: Erläterungen zu Hegel* (Frankfurt: Suhrkamp, 1977; original edition, 1962) 314.

[30]"Hegels Aufhebung der christlichen Religion," in *Hegel-Studien,* Beiheft I (1964) 194.

[31]Reinhard Heede, "Hegel-Bilanz," 43.

ligion. Noteworthy in this connection is that the often negative view of Christianity in the earliest writings quickly disappeared. And, for example, whereas a Socrates-Jesus comparison in the *Early Theological Writings* favored Socrates, the 1831 Lectures clearly place Jesus in a superior position.[32]*Volksreligion* of a more spiritual kind is found in the Lectures, as is veneration of the Hellenic age, but Christianity is no longer on the defensive. It has overcome the harsh indictment of the Enlightenment and emerges in Hegel's thinking as the consummate religion that provides the final meaning and perspective—as fulfilled religion—to its spiritual predecessors. (It is still left for philosophy, however, to provide the final meaning of religion.)

HEGEL'S CONCEPT OF PHILOSOPHY OF RELIGION

In the Lectures, Hegel initially defined philosophy of religion simply as the consideration of religion by philosophy. But religion is relationship and consciousness, as is philosophy. And the meaning of philosophy of religion will turn on the common content of consciousness and the relation of the two modes of consciousness to it and to each other. Since philosophy and religion both have the same essential content, namely, spirit, they might seem identical:

> The object of religion, like that of philosophy, is the eternal truth, God and nothing but God and the explication of God. Philosophy is only explicating itself when it explicates religion, and when it explicates itself it is explicating religion.[33]

But they are also importantly different—in *form,* and the *Lectures on the Philosophy of Religion* aim to reconcile the differences. Philosophy of religion thus becomes redefined as the philosophical consideration of a form of consciousness and knowledge (namely, religion's) that has the same content as philosophy itself. It will be a consideration of religion's consciousness with the consciousness of philosophy and also a consideration of the relation of religion's mode of cognizing God to philosophy's mode. From the standpoint of philosophy, the two forms of consciousness will be quite distinct and one must beware of confusing the one with the other, or

---

[32]LPR III:321, n. 196, quoting the Lasson edition and *Werke;* VPR III:244, line-note 893-95. Jesus and Socrates are more equal in earlier lecture versions.

[33]Lectures of 1827; LPR I:152-53; VPR I:63.

stopping short of full philosophical penetration of a religious representation.[34]

The difference between philosophy and religion, as two forms of knowledge dealing with an identical content, turns on the *Art und Weise,* the "kind and manner" of consideration that each is. For religion deals in representations (*Vorstellungen*), while philosophy deals in concepts (*Begriffe*). Religion and philosophy are each the result of a different kind of, but interconnected, mental activity. In the first instance, feeling and intuition produce representations; in the second, speculative thought produces concepts from the representations of religion (that is, from story and, in the higher forms of the Christian religion, from doctrine).[35] In connection with types of mental activity, Hegel defines philosophy of religion as a "thinking, comprehending cognition of religion" ("denkende, begriefende Erkenntnis der Religion").[36] That is, speculative thought grasps and conceptualizes that which religion has grasped in intuition and expressed in representations. Intuition grasps objects as a whole; reflection, as a middle activity, distinguishes and recognizes diversity and in the process loses sight of unity. On the pre-conceptual level then, either diversity or unity is lost sight of. Speculative thought, however, holds the two together. Speculative philosophy, in doing philosophy of religion, will thus look to religious representations and seek to grasp and then philosophically articulate the idea intuitively expressed in them.

Philosophy of religion is, moreover, intellectually necessary. For without philosophy, the connection between the consciousness represented in religion and the rest of consciousness would be missed.[37] But, in addition, the mind, according to Hegel, is not satisfied merely with a representation of God. It naturally wishes to penetrate to logical knowledge of the nature of God, as grasped by thought. This carries it naturally beyond religious representation and past the renunciation, complacency and

---

[34]This seems to be the error of the right wing and of those who would take Hegel's philosophical reformulations of Christian doctrines as a new "theology" in the conventional sense of the term rather than in Hegel's philosophical sense.

[35]*Vorstellung* and *Begriff,* cardinal terms in Hegel's philosophical vocabulary, are troublesome even for the German-language reader. For the English-language reader they are more difficult still, since Hegel employs these substantives in various senses and uses verb forms (e.g., *vorstellen* and *begreifen*) as well.

[36]Lectures of 1821: LPR I:109; VPR I:27.

[37]Lectures of 1821: LPR I:92; VPR I:11.

despair of the early nineteenth century regarding knowledge of God.[38] In the Hegelian system, God was already grasped by thought in the *Logic,* where speculative thought described God in his eternal life, before creation of the world. But in the *Logic* God was comprehended exclusively as idea, not in manifestation (although manifestation is known as one of the necessary moments in God's life). Philosophy of religion, therefore, seeks to view the God known to thought as he is manifest in representation, and reviews his self-manifestations in the history of religions judged relevant. In doing so, philosophy contributes to the life of spirit. For the idea that is spirit and that has manifested itself in the life of religion seeks completion that is higher than the universal, nonphilosophical consciousness of religion and strives toward self-consciousness, as concept. "[O]nly in philosophy is spirit an object as concept."[39]

Thus the *Lectures on the Philosophy of Religion* are the study of the evolution of content in the special form of religion up to the point of transformation and sublation (*Aufhebung*)[40] into the higher-form philosophy where form and content are at last adequate to each other. Philosophy of religion as such leads to the culminating moment when religious representations can be elevated to philosophical concepts and be fully grasped in relation to the unfolding life of spirit, the "concept" itself. This can only happen because Hegelian philosophy has attained true content in true form and can thus review the history of philosophy's self-actualization with a particular view to religion's indispensable contribution.

> Philosophy of religion does, of course, have to develop and represent the necessity of religion in and for itself, to comprehend that spirit advances and must advance from the other modes of its willing, imagining, and feeling to this its absolute mode.[41]

It would be a mistake to think that this means the end of religion, or of religious feeling and intuition. It means, instead, the unveiling of the whole

---

[38]Lectures of 1821: LPR I:86-87; VPR I:6-7.

[39]Lectures of 1824: LPR I:147; VPR I:60.

[40]Cancellation/preservation, transcending. As is frequently remarked, there is no adequate English translation for this ambiguous German term.

[41]Lectures of 1821; LPR I:90; VRP I:8-9. Cf. also Alexandre Kojève, *Introduction à la lecture de Hegel. Leçons sur la Phénoménologie de l'esprit* (Paris: Gallimard, 1947) 514, where Kojève calls religion the anticipation of philosophical thought and lays emphasis upon negation in the moment of *Aufhebung*. However, Hegel does not believe that the old form can be totally discarded even after achievement of true form, except perhaps by the philosophical elite.

truth struggling to expression in religion, but it will be seen only by those who can see.[42] Thus, counter to the interpretation of left-wing Hegelians, Hegel does not, by engaging in philosophy of religion that seeks to elevate the content of religious consciousness to philosophical clarity, intend the end of religion. Religion will continue as a valid form of knowing God. And even those philosophers who are able to elevate religion's representations to concepts will not seek its demise, any more than they will seek the abolition of art and other manifestations of the life and consciousness of spirit. Hegel remarks in this connection that

> Religion is for everyone. It is not philosophy, which is not for everyone. Religion is the manner or mode by which all human beings become conscious of truth for themselves.[43]

The goal of philosophy of religion (as Hegelian philosophy) is to raise the manifestation of God in the history of religions to the level of thought. It is to discover the God of the *Logic* in the history of religions and to discern the necessary moments of the triune God in the apparent contingencies of history. This is also ultimately to discover the transcendent God of the *Logic* in the immanent trinity of the Christian religion and then to trace his explicit trinitarian life. Hegelian philosophy of religion, in sum, begins with a clear conception of what philosophy is and has achieved, what religion is in relation to philosophy, and what philosophy is to do with the materials of religion, namely, elevate them to philosophy. In Hegel one thus finds for the first time in modern philosophy a clear and self-conscious notion of philosophy of religion as well as of the exact relation between philosophy and religion. The meaning of religion is at last totally clear of philosophy, precisely because philosophy has become transparent to itself.

Philosophy of religion is, of course, *philosophy;* but it is *not* religion, nor is it religious. Hegel calls it, however, ''service of God'' (*Gottesdienst*)[44] for it is relationship to the divine. And the relation of finite spirit and of finite reason to the divine takes place in true philosophy of religion.

---

[42]Hegel's way of describing the relationship between religious and philosophical seeing recalls the myth of the cave in Plato's *Republic*. But however heroic philosophical seers may be, Hegel is really rather tolerant and sympathetic toward those who cannot break free to a higher mode of knowing.

[43]Lectures of 1827: LPR I:180; VPR I:88.

[44]Lectures of 1821: LPR I:84; VPR I:4.

Hegelian philosophy of religion is thus a very different enterprise from any Enlightenment effort. Hegel had polemicized against the whittling down of religion to narrowly rational elements, particularly in *Faith and Knowledge* where he attacked those who confined themselves to religion "within the limits of reason" and then in the Lectures where he lamented contemporary philosophy's almost perverse pride in knowing nothing of God and in confessing itself unable to know him. Hegel acknowledged no such limits and Hegelian philosophy of religion, rather than reducing religion to reflective reason (*Verstand*), esteems itself to be elevating all of religion to speculative reason (*Vernunft*).

For Hegel, philosophy of religion is true theology. The *Logic* was also "theo-logy," in the sense of giving essential knowledge of God as idea. The philosophical theology of the Lectures has the task of advancing beyond both the self-imposed darkness of Enlightenment natural theology and the poverty of mere historical church theology. And Hegel returns to such doctrines as the trinity, the resurrection of the body and the divinity of Christ because he discerns in them the unfolding of the concept of spirit.[45] Doctrine, important to theology, is of great significance in and to Hegel's enterprise. For this hybrid of idea and representation distinguishes the consummate religion, Christianity, which he takes as the culmination of the history of religions. ("Hence the Christian religion is essentially doctrine; it offers representations and thoughts."[46]) As the religion of doctrine, it is religion on the threshold of philosophy. The consummate religion's founder and central figure of doctrine—its Christ—consequently occupies a distinctive and unique position in religious history and his philosophical meaning merits and receives careful attention.

The philosophical history of religions within Hegel's philosophy of religion is, in effect, a prehistory of Christianity, more important in its sweep than in some of its details, and the record of triadic movement in religion: being-in-itself, division and reconciliation, until it culminates in Christianity as the absolute or consummate religion around which the Lectures revolve.[47]

---

[45]Lectures of 1827: LPR I:164; VPR I:73.
[46]Lectures of 1821: LPR I:106; VPR I:24.
[47]Cf. Chapelle, *Hegel et la religion*, 1:198.

THE "CONCEPT" OF RELIGION

Part I of the *Lectures on the Philosophy of Religion* is an abstract and theoretical statement about the dynamic of religion and a sustained argument for speculative thought's appropriation of religion into philosophy's higher form. Religion is the life of the absolute from eternity to the present and the history of religions is a series of evolving religious representations of this life. Philosophy, as a higher form of mental activity, seeks to elevate the religious representations and thereby express the life of the absolute in concepts and finally to express it as "the concept." This is, in Hegel's view, to bring the absolute full circle and in so doing is a contribution to that life.

For, while Hegel speaks of "concepts," he emphasizes their fundamental unity when he notes that there is but one concept (*Begriff*). And the concept is the absolute, the universality toward which the thinking mind strives, even in articulating intermediate concepts. Indeed, all conceptualizing is conceptualizing of the absolute and whenever there is true grasping, it is the one same object—the absolute—that is grasped.

The "concept of religion" therefore means the conceptualizing of religion. But as such it means the elevation of religion to philosophy and of the concept of religion itself to the concept. It is in a sense the very task of philosophy of religion to give religion the form of concept.

Hegel states in the 1827 Lectures that "the beginning of religion, more precisely its content, is the concept of religion itself."[48] This is the absolute in its primordial state of unity with itself, and it is here that religion begins, before history and time. This implies that the concept of religion must also include a grasp of that moment in the life of the absolute before time. And this is precisely what Hegel's philosophy claims to have articulated in the *Logic*. The concept of religion thus requires philosophical movement backward and forward: backward, to recreate and grasp the life of absolute in its primordial state by means of speculative thought; forward, through the history of religions and the elevation/transformation of religion into philosophy. The *Lectures on the Philosophy of Religion* can move forward through the philosophy of religion because the *Logic* has done the preparatory work.

---

[48]Lectures of 1827: LPR I:366; VPR I:266.

The life of the absolute proceeds through the moments of universality, particularity, and *Aufhebung* or reconciliation. These moments are manifest in every historical religion,[49] although not to the same extent. The criteria for distinguishing among them and hierarchically arranging the moments of religion exist because the concept is now known in its totality. God who "*is* essentially in thought . . . [who] is only for thought, through thought, and in thought"[50] is totally known, (1) before the history of religions, (2) in the history of religions, and (3) beyond it in philosophical conceptualization.

The concept of religion reveals that religion is relationship. At first, it is the relationship of infinite spirit to itself. Subsequently, it is the relationship of finite spirit to infinite spirit and of infinite spirit to finite. Relation presupposes difference. Yet what is explicitly different is implicitly identical.[51]

For religion, we recall, is consciousness. It begins when God is other, but most truly when he is other for consciousness—when God is consciously recognized as other. In the highest moment of consciousness—in Christianity—religion is "the self-consciousness of absolute spirit, its self-consciousness of being for itself as spirit,"[52] the moment when God knows himself in human consciousness and when man knows himself in and as God. Hegel puts it most expressly in the Lectures of 1831:

> Thus God knows himself in humanity, and human beings, to the extent that they know themselves as spirit and, in their truth, know themselves in God. This is the concept of religion, that God knows himself in spirit and spirit knows itself in God.[53]

The very same consciousness in which God has come to know himself in human consciousness and a human consciousness has come to know itself as God is, we shall see, the consciousness in which Jesus declared, "I and the Father are one."

Religion is the result of God's need:

> In the loneliness of his being-for-itself he feels himself needy and negated,

---

[49]Lectures of 1824: LPR I:142; VPR I:56.
[50]Lectures of 1824: LPR I:273; VPR I:179. Cf. also Lectures of 1827; LPR I:394; VPR I:290.
[51]Recall Hegel's formula on the identity of identity and difference.
[52]Lectures of 1824: LPR I:325; VPR I:227.
[53]Lectures of 1831: LPR I:465; VPR I:354.

and this deficiency is first overcome when he knows himself in the other. This concept of God and of religion is first attained in the revelatory religion.[54]

It is also God's activity and essentially so, although not exclusively. For in religion God returns to himself and man returns to God simultaneously when finite spirit comes to know that only infinite spirit really is. But this moment of consciousness is a moment in the infinite's own life and can thus be truly called the activity of the infinite which alone truly is: "[R]eligion is self-knowing of divine spirit though the mediation of finite spirit."[55] The philosophy of the history of religions, therefore, traces man's religious grasp of spirit's evolving self-disclosure, until the moment of full disclosure in the God-man Jesus, when God comes to man and man comes to God, when God actively discloses himself in man and man actively discovers God in himself. But the God-man is a representation, not yet free of the sensuous and particularity and not yet elevated to universality. Hence the special significance of the moment when the God-man casts off the sensuous and particular and is elevated to the universal in death on a cross.[56]

THE CONSUMMATE RELIGION AND ITS CHRIST

CHRISTIANITY AS CONSUMMATE, ULTIMATE, AND ABSOLUTE

For Hegel, Christianity is unquestionably religion's attainment of purest form *as religion*. And it is such because it is the religion in which God

---

[54]Ibid.

[55]Lectures of 1824: Hotho transcript. Cited LPR I:318, n. 120; VPR I:222, linenote 663-72.

[56]But not everything is done on God's side. Cultus, or worship, is the overcoming of divine-human separation by man's action and God's grace. "In the cultus, on the contrary, God is on one side, I am on the other, and the determination is the including, within my own self, of myself with God, the knowing of myself within God and of God within me" (Lectures of 1827; LPR I:443; VPR I:331). For the individual subject, this means that worship is the stripping off of subjectivity and achieving knowledge of one's true spiritual substance. It is self-spiritualization through thought. "The goal, God, is to be attained by me and in me, and that toward which the action (which is my own action) tends is just this surrender of myself, with me no longer clinging possessively to the self as personal property existing on its own account" (Lectures of 1824: LPR I:349; VPR I:249).

This work may also appear, from God's side, to be his work, since infinite spirit is the source of all substance, but the human input here is recognized and emphasized. Worship, or cultus, might appear to be practical in contrast to thought as theoretical. But, for Hegel, thought effects and overcomes the distinction between theoretical and practical. And the final overcoming of the separation between God and man is effected by thought's grasping the divine-human relationship as it already is. In this sense, thought is also worship.

is fully manifest—in sensuous human form—and finally known as spirit. Religion is thus consummate (*vollendet*) in Christianity, and yet in another sense not so. For Christianity is not static and is not complete. It is moving toward absoluteness, in a dynamic evolution that will eventually mean transcending the form of religion for the purer form of philosophy. In a real sense then, referring to the Christian religion as the "absolute religion" is misleading (even if Hegel does use the term in passing). Hegel posits Christianity as the final historical religion and a better term might have been the "ultimate religion." For Christianity is not really "absolute religion" until it has become *aufgehoben* into philosophical religion.[57] Yet the very recognition that "absolute religion" is really "philosophical religion" would suggest that the ultimate religion is really penultimate, that in a sense it is really not consummate until transformed. Hegel means Christianity as consummate in the sense of the completion of the historical procession of sensuously-bound religions and their manifest fulfillment.

But precisely as religion, Christian religion is God's life and therefore not finished. For God is a living God. In the process of moving toward absoluteness, Christianity passes through two decisive post-New Testament figures: Luther, to purify it of medieval Catholicism; and Hegel himself, to spiritualize it further and finally elevate it to philosophy. When it has reached absoluteness, Christianity maintains the same content but a different form, namely, philosophy. It will then at last be "absolute religion": *religio a religione absoluta* or (the content of) religion absolved from the form of religion. This is, of course, Hegel's meaning of *philosophy* and the goal of philosophy of religion.

HISTORY OF RELIGIONS AS PREHISTORY OF CHRISTIANITY

The religions surveyed by Hegel in Part II of the *Lectures on the Philosophy of Religion* are so ordered as to represent consummate religion's prehistory.[58] Hegel's knowledge of world religions is impressive by the standards of his day, but he treats them with some arbitrariness. Even if he waivers about a detail or two, their role and meaning is determined and clear on the same basis as those of Christianity. Their role, in sum, is prep-

---

[57]On this point passionate debates have emerged as regards what has been cancelled and what preserved, and the split into right-and left-wing Hegelians turns on the interpretation of Hegel's view of religion.

[58]Cf. Chapelle, *Hegel et la religion*, 1:148. This assertion holds even in the face of the fact of the different ordering of the decisive non-Christian religions in the four-lecture series.

aration and subordination. For each historical religion considered is regarded as a moment in the formation of the consummate religion, as part of a developmental process. Although Hegel speaks of religions, he might have spoken of a single religion and then distinguished among the moments of religion (much as he did distinguish among the moments of the Christian religion). In that way, he would have emphasized the life of spirit that binds them together. But this point comes through nonetheless. Never are they portrayed as isolated or even independent movements, for the life of spirit is one. Nor are they viewed as trial-runs or failed attempts. Instead they play a coordinated part in the attainment of fulfilled religion. Hegel regarded them all as part of a single developmental process, namely, the coming to consciousness of implicit divine-human unity. And when some of the facts disturbed his theory, he pressed forward, with his grand vision relativizing inconvenient details. Thus it is possible for him to have varied the order of the pre-Christian religions in his lecture series—with Roman religion even appearing as a clear devolution in the Lectures of 1827—and yet make the same point.

Hegel can be partially excused for his historical blind spots since the Lectures are no phenomenology of religion or strict history of religions but rather a philosophical history of religions. At the same time, his sometimes arbitrariness with the facts of religious history cannot be overlooked. It is most evident in his handling of Islam, a development that simply does not fit in with his determined order. For Islam is the only major religion that appeared *after* the consummate religion. Hegel finds no place for it in his schematization, not even as a spur to spirit in Christian Europe. Thus it is virtually ignored.[59] His regarding Lamaism and Buddhism as identical is as peculiar as it is incorrect and he seems unaware of Shinto, as well as of important developments of Buddhism in China and Japan. He never considers sects or heresies, not even in Christianity, although much could be learned from them. And, in Christianity, no post-Reformation movements are cited. For Hegel, religion came into its own in Christianity and reached its prephilosophic culmination in Lutheranism.

---

[59]The only significant mention of Islam in volume III is found in the Lectures of 1824: LPR III:242-43; VPR III:172. There it is described as standing in antithesis to Christianity, a spiritual religion but one in which God remains abstract. Very brief mentions of Islam are found in the Lectures of 1821 and 1827, and in volume II Judaism and Islam are compared.

In the prehistory of Christianity, the most important religions are the three religions of subjectivity immediately preceding Christianity: Jewish, Greek, and Roman religion. Hegel varied the ordering of the three in different lecture years. In each case, they follow upon an original primitive or natural religion and they precede Christianity. As a result, Jesus might seem at least as much the Son of Zeus and Jupiter as of Elohim. But his placing Christianity after the teleological Roman religion presents a clue to his understanding of the consummate religion and even of his own philosophy. For Hegel held that the proper view of religion was to serve as the basis for the state. The Christian religion's notion of human freedom is important in this connection. For the growing human self-consciousness represented in the history of religion revolves around freedom and finds its culmination in Christianity. Every state is based on the ideas expressed in religion and hence Christianity's human self-consciousness, including its notion of freedom, is at last adequate for the construction of a higher state.

"REVEALED" VERSUS "MANIFEST" RELIGION

Religious history is the historical, pictorially and sensuously represented life of spirit moving to fulfillment. Christianity is this fulfilled religion because in it God has become fully "manifest" (*offenbar*) not just in the sensuous, pictorial representations of a historical religion but in the flesh of Jesus of Nazareth. Christianity is thus "manifest religion." This is also to say that in the consummate religion, God has become more than revealed (*geoffenbart*). He has been known as spirit and, most decisively, in consciousness.

Hegel distinguishes between *geoffenbarte* ("manifested" or "revealed") and *offenbare* ("manifest") religion. The terms are based on a single German root (*offen*) and are without easy English equivalents.[60] God is manifested (*geoffenbart*) in varying degrees in all religions, but there is only one in which God is fully manifest (*offenbar*).

---

[60]The distinction is not unique to the Lectures. The *Phenomenology of Spirit* discussed the *offenbare Religion*, while the *Encyclopedia* devoted attention to the *geoffenbarte Religion*. The emphasis upon God's becoming totally manifest, beyond formal revelation, contains a scarcely disguised and ongoing polemic in the Lectures against Kant. In the *offenbare Religion*, in which God is known to *Vernunft* (speculative reason), there is no mystery or secret left, as there is in the theology and philosophy à la Kant that limit themselves to *Verstand* (understanding). Cf. Michael Theunissen, *Hegels Lehre vom absoluten Geist als theologisch-politisches Traktat* (Berlin: de Gruyter, 1970) 216ff.; also Bloch, *Subjekt-Objekt,* 321.

Geoffenbarte Religion is religion with its source outside human consciousness. In it one has only the religiously inessential—the exterior and foreign, the sensuously grasped element, even if that inessential element remains indispensable until its deeper content comes to consciousness. In such revealed religions, God is known but not as he reveals himself, that is, as spirit: "In the other religions, God is still something other than what he reveals himself to be."[61]

In contrast, religion is *offenbar* when the concept of religion is fully realized in it, when the idea or spirit has been exteriorized and returned fully to itself. For Hegel, this occurs uniquely in Christianity and culminates within Christianity in the moment of Christ's death as a result of which God is known as he reveals himself, that is, as spirit, and no longer as something else. But, as has been observed, even this culmination is in a very real sense itself completed only when it is understood and articulated by Hegelian philosophy. For in philosophy the full meaning of religion is apprehended in consciousness as it recognizes that absolute spirit is in unity with finite spirit. While this already occurs in the *offenbare Religion,* it is fulfilled in philosophy. And in this sense, the consummate religion becomes truly *offenbar* when it becomes philosophy—that is, paradoxically, in the very moment that it transcends religion.[62]

The Jesus of the consummate religion is himself an example of an indispensable inessential in *historical* religion, eventually dispensed with for the sake of *spiritual* religion. In Jesus, spirit evidenced the extreme of exteriorization or alienation (*Entäußerung*) and reconciliation (*Versöhnung*). But eventually the flesh-and-blood Jesus, who plays a heroic role in the life of spirit, must himself vanish, for the sake of completing the process in which he is decisive but not final. His death began it; with that, the deed of Jesus became a memory (*Erinnerung*), the stuff of interiorization (*Er-Innerung*). Thus, as Jean Hyppolite writes,

> The God immediately present must disappear. He is no longer, but he has been. And this "having been" must become, in the *Erinnerung,* the interiority of the common memory, a spiritual presence.[63]

But beyond that, the memories and representations of historical religion must themselves be overcome and elevated, by grasping their interior

---

[61]Lectures of 1821: LPR III:64, VPR III:4.
[62]If this is the *Aufhebung* of religion, it is (to repeat) not the annihilation of religion.
[63]Hyppolite, *Genèse et structure,* 542.

meaning and then by the community's appropriating or interiorizing that meaning.

Given Hegel's interests, his account of Christianity as the "manifest religion" does not turn on its "revealed" aspects and attendant matters in the manner of the Enlightenment and even of Kant. Instead, he seeks to discern and portray in Christianity the necessary life of spirit in its final movement to completion in history. Christianity as the "manifest religion" is thus the philosophical reconstruction of what appeared in history. But the reconstruction is also a philosophical construct. For in grasping the innermost truth of religion, philosophy adds to it.

Geoffenbarte, or historically manifested religion, is religion to-be-spiritualized. Christianity is also a manifested, revealed religion, but is more, and is therefore able to rise above the historical so that spirit may be manifest. But even *offenbare*—revelatory, manifest—religion must be purified to spirit. This involves spiritualizing the reality represented in Jesus but also in other aspects of the Christian religion: Bible as writings containing spiritual truths and doctrine as the first steps toward a more spiritual expression of biblical truths. The Bible, in general, can be read "spiritually" (in Hegel's sense) by penetrating behind its words first to feelings, then to thoughts and to the philosophical examination of its forms of thought. At the same time, miracle stories contained therein are simply dismissed as incapable of witnessing to the spirit, hence as nonrational. For true, or philosophical, faith has no interest in miracle stories as such, in what the guests at Cana drank or whose wine it really was.

> What is supposed to be attested by them is the idea; but that has no need of them, and therefore no need to attest to them.[64]

The only true miracle is the miracle of spirit itself, the absolute intervention (*Eingreifen*) of the divine into human affairs. And this miracle alone bears witness to Jesus and verifies him even as it points beyond him.

DOCTRINAL CONTEXT OF HEGEL'S CHRISTOLOGY: TRINITY AND FALL

For Hegel, Christian doctrine contains important content for philosophical scrutiny. It is not scriptural or revealed, even while based on scripture and revelation. And, while not freed from the repesentational mode of religion, it is yet already on the way toward clearer restatement

---

[64]Lectures of 1821; LPR III:147; VPR III:83.

of the truths expressed in scriptural story. Hence Hegel devotes considerable attention to doctrines of the consummate religion and seeks to bring out their final truth that in doctrinal form is already breaking through. In the process, he attains new heights as he discerns the history of ideas—and of the idea—working itself out in the history of doctrine. At the same time and beyond his own intention, he also underlines for the modern reader the extent to which even early Christian doctrine is already a hybrid of religion and philosophy. His treatment of the doctrines of trinity and fall, in particular, is essential to his larger philosophical reinterpretation of Christianity but also to his articulating the meaning of the consummate religion's Christ. And his trinitarian vision of the mediation of God and world reinforces the central place of Christology in his understanding of Christian religion.[65]

Trinity

Hegel's sees in the Christian doctrine of the trinity such importance that it structures the presentation of the Christian religion. But the full meaning of the doctrine of the trinity goes beyond structure to content. For it is the doctrine par excellence that manifests God as he is and that makes Christianity consummate as religion.

The importance of trinity in all religions is appreciated with philosophical hindsight. Not only have triads been frequent in the history of religions as the true understanding of God moves toward crystallization and full manifestation, but the concept of religion itself has been manifest in triadic form, as Hegel's varying articulation of determinate religion (Part II of the Lectures) illustrates. Hegel is fully aware that Christianity is not the sole religion to have arrived at a notion of a triune God. The trimurti of Indian religion is cited as the first and crudest form, after which Hegel sketches the history of the notion from Pythagoras to Kant, who brought it back to currency in modern philosophy.[66] Hegel is not concerned that the notion is not unique or original in Christianity or that it is not explicit in the New Testament itself. While the Enlightenment took pause at such facts, Hegel regards them as inconsequential. For the real concern is the inner truth of a notion, and this comes to clearest prephilosopical expression in the doctrine of Christian theology. (That modern Christian theology had

---

[65]Cf. Hodgson, "Hegel's Christology," 39.
[66]Lectures of 1821: LPR III:80-81; VPR III:18-19.

become forgetful of the truth of the doctrine was but another argument for philosophy as the genuine vessel of modern "science of God.") The Christian religion witnesses the fulfillment of immanent trinity and the achievement of explicit trinitarianism. Moreover, for Hegel, it is clear that the truth of the doctrine of the trinity also organizes his presentation of the moments of the Christian religion. For it is a truth that his encyclopedic system has itself at last made visible in its philosophical clarity.[67]

The doctrine of the trinity is the expression of the triune God, of the eternal idea as found in Christian religion.[68] The picture images, or *Vorstellungen,* of "Father," "Son" and "Holy Spirit" express God as he is for the other, that is, for finite spirit, and as conceived by finite spirit in a finite mode. The same holds true of all predicate images of God as omnipresent, omniscient, merciful, and so forth.[69] But the same representation speaks about the life of God as immanent and explicit trinity in the Christian religion, partially known in Christian doctrine and fully known as spirit in the philosophy of spirit. For the true nature of God and of his three-in-one-ness can be grasped, according to Hegel, only in philosophical thought that knows spirit as spirit, that is, as self-relating, hence not just as other or created world but other relating back to spirit and in union with it. The dialectic of self-relationality "underlines all of Hegel's mature systematic thought, including his reconceptualization of trinitarian divine subjectivity."[70]

---

[67]For a discussion of the changes that Hegel made in his presentation of the triune life of God in the *Lectures on the Philosophy of Religion,* cf. Hodgson's editorial introduction to vol. 3 of the English-language translation (11ff.). In particular, he observes the shift away from the 1821 presentation of an outer triad (abstract concept, concrete representation, practices of cultus) and inner triad (idea of God, idea of diremption, appearance of the idea in finite spirit)—in which the Son occupies the third moment of the inner triad and the third trinitarian moment, Spirit, is placed in the outer triad—to the subsequent versions of 1824, 1827, and 1831, in which the inner triad clearly corresponds to Christian trinitarian representation, so much so that the 1831 Lectures refer to the divisions as the Kingdoms of Father, Son, and Spirit.

[68]Lectures of 1827: LPR III:275-76; VPR III:201-202.

[69]Lectures of 1827: LPR III:277-78; VPR III:202-203. There Hegel states: "Predicates as particular characteristics are not appropriate to the nature of God. . . . the predicates do not comprise the true relation of God to himself, but rather his relation to an other, the world. So they are limited and come into contradiction with each other."

[70]Dale M. Schlitt, "The Whole Truth: Hegel's Reconceptualization of Trinity," *Owl of Minerva* 15:2 (Spring 1984): 177. Cf. also, by the same author, *Hegel's Trinitarian Claim—A Critical Reflection* (Leiden: Brill, 1983).

For religion, the trinity was a mystery expressed in terms and representations of Father, Son, and Holy Spirit. But for speculative thought, God is fully *offenbar,* manifest as he truly is. It knows the life of spirit and, for it, the threeness of God's life is not mystery but the essence and dynamism of spirit reflected in all living spirit and thus very naturally and centrally found in Christianity, the religion of spirit. The Christian doctrine is not so much incorrect as it is incomplete. For it is still a hybrid of picture and thought. Philosophy must overcome for Christian doctrine the limitation of portraying "three independently represented subjects in an inadequately purified parental and filial relationship."[71]

Hegel's philosophy does this by means of its fundamental grasp of the life of spirit as universality-particularity-individuality and then by discerning this triune life of spirit in religion. In doing so, it recognizes not one but two trinities, an immanent trinity that describes distinction within the divine itself and an explicit or "economic" trinity that describes the externalization of this distinction in human history.

The two trinities are integrally related; one embraces the other. And the immanent trinitarian life of God, outside of human history, is the first moment of the life of God as it moves into explicitation. The religious representation, and traditional Christian theological term, for this moment is God as Father, God as he is originally in-and-for-himself. "Father" expresses the moment of God's implicit identity with himself before the creation of nature and of finite spirit but, as understood by philosophy, also his implicit otherness and implicit return to himself.[72] God's being in-and-for-himself *before* creation means the *implicit* reality of an other over against God and an other who is also in implicit unity with God. Thus, from the beginning, God is in unity with himself. But his self-unity is implicit, potential, and imperfect. The other must stand over against God and then achieve reconciliation and explicit, actualized unity. At this point, God will be in-and-for-himself in the fullest sense. This happens as the life of God naturally and necessarily passes out of the moment of the Father into that of the Son (Other) and Spirit (reconciliation and final, explicit self-unity).

---

[71]Schlitt, "The Whole Truth," 176.

[72]One might qualify Hegel's predicate here and say that God is "in-and-for-himself" in the mode of "in-itself." For his being for-himself, or explicitness, is *implicitly* contained in his being, but he is not yet *explicitly* for-himself. This is to suggest a distinction between being "in-and-for-itself" in the mode of *in*-itself and being "in-and-for-itself" in the mode of *for*-itself.

"Father" is thus the expression of God's life in its potentiality rather than in its actuality.

God's life in movement from abstract universality into particularization and into space and time is the moment of the Son. It begins in the necessary act of creation, in which other-being becomes actual over against God. The world is the otherness first created, a world in which man as the being qualified by spirit emerges as a more distant and hence higher form of otherness and as such has a distinctive role to play in the necessary self-emptying of God. And in living God's life into alienation and then self-conscious alienation, Adam and Jesus have unique roles to play.

Holy Spirit as the third moment of God's life is the moment of reconciliation and of the attainment of explicit self-unity. It is also the present moment of God's life. God's life as Holy Spirit is found in all movements that go in the direction of explicitating God's self-unity and divine-human unity. Thus both religious community and philosophical brotherhood reflect it.

Despite Hegel's best attempts to elevate the Christian trinity to a purer, philosophical one, there are problems. For one thing, this is not the God to whom one could say "Our Father." One cannot pray to him but only think him. He does not exist, for he represents God's life as potential. As such, he does not correspond to Jesus' representation of him. Jesus' and Christian theology's conception of the fatherhood of God plainly suggests existence. This would cause Hegel difficulties, if he conceded the point. For in his schematization, the only place for an *existing* Father would be in the moment of the Son. Hegel's reconceptualization of the Christian trinity, while a purification and elevation, is also a partial negation. For his reconceptualization has implications for the Christian doctrine of atonement. As Dale Schlitt observes, it negates

> . . . the continuing projection of reconciliation as achieved in a divine subjectivity over against the self. The true content of the religious reconciliation is preserved, according to Hegel, in the move to philosophical thought as the full mediation of subject and object, self and concept in self-determining conceptual thought.[73]

Hegel's schematization has other points of conflict with Christian theological views of the trinity as well. For Hegel places alienation from God

---

[73]Schlitt, "The Whole Truth," 177.

(understood as God's movement out from himself) in the moment of the Son and reconciliation in the moment of the Spirit. This is in contrast to and disregard of theological views that not only understand alienation in quite different terms but deem reconciliation with God to have begun in the moment of Jesus' incarnation. Hence Christian theology would dispute Hegel that it simply sees the same truth darkly. It claims to see something quite different and Hegel, in his disagreement, ought to—but does not—go beyond his declaration of its incompleteness to the bolder proclamation of its incorrectness.

Evil and "Fall"

Trinity is a doctrine without equal and is so important to philosophy as finally to organize its exposition of Christian religion. But other doctrines too have a deeper philosophical truth which is already breaking through in doctrine and requires philosophical elevation for its full truth to be manifest. The second principal doctrine that figures thus in Hegel's exposition is that of the fall—the fall of other-being into evil.

To be sure, this is no event to be regretted. Even Christian theology had seen the *felix culpa*. But philosophy sees in the biblical story/representation of Adam's fall the expression of a necessary event: the externalized diremption in God's life that precedes achievement of the externalized unity that comes about in the God-man. Thus what Bible represented as evil and Christian liturgy called "happy fault," philosophy sees as a manifestly necessary good.

> The story is the eternal history of humanity. The deep insight of this story is that the eternal history of humanity, to be consciousness, is contained in it: (a) the original divine idea, the image of God; (b) the emergence of consciousness, knowledge of good and evil, (and at the same time responsibility;) (c) the knowledge of good and evil emerges as something that both ought to be, i.e., it ought not to remain as knowledge, and also as the means by which humanity is divine.[74]

Hegel's discussion evokes Kant's treatment of evil in *Religion within the Limits of Reason Alone,* but Hegel certainly had Kant in mind when he wrote:

> It is false to ask whether humanity is only good by nature or only evil. That

---

[74]Lectures of 1821: LPR III:106; VPR III:42.

is a false way of posing the question. In the same way, it is superficial to say that humanity is both good and evil equally.[75]

For Kant, in the question whether man is good or evil by nature, "nature" constituted the ultimate ground of the adoption of maxims and man formed his own nature in the choice of the ground of maxims. As a result, he was either good or evil. For Hegel, in contrast, man is *both* good *and* evil by "nature," but in a quite different sense from Kant's.

"Humanity is good by nature" refers to his potential, not his actual condition.

> When humanity exists only according to nature, it is evil. The way humanity is implicitly, or according to its concept, is of course what we refer to abstractly as humanity "according to nature"; but concretely the person who follows passions and instinct, and remains within the sphere of desire, the one whose law is that of natural immediacy, is the natural immediacy, is the natural human being. At the same time, a human being in the natural state is one who wills, and since the content of the natural will is only instinct and inclination, this person is evil.[76]

In his actual condition (before reflection), he is in a sense already evil, for he is not good in his actual nature. He is not yet what he should be, even if he is innocent and unconscious of the fact. He is good in-itself but not good for-itself; that is, he is potentially and implicitly good but not yet actually and explicitly good. Insofar as he is separated from his spiritual, rational destiny and is divided within himself, "humanity is evil by nature." Man's not being what he ought to be constitutes the cleavage in his being and his self-alienation. In order to overcome it, he must advance from evil to "guilt" (*Schuld*), a term that Hegel uses in the sense of "accountability" (*Imputabilität*), hence responsibility for evil.

> Humanity ought not to be innocent . . . it ought not to be brutish; insofar as human being is good, it ought not to be so in the sense that a natural thing is good. Rather it is up to its responsibility (*Schuld*), its will, to be good—it ought to be *imputable*. Responsibility (*Imputabilität*) means, in a general sense, the possibility of imputation.[77]

---

[75]Lectures of 1827: LPR III:299-300; VPR III:224.

[76]Lectures of 1827: LPR III:298; VPR III:222.

[77]Lectures of 1827: LPR III:298; VPR III:223: "Der Mensch soll nicht unschuldig, nicht tierisch sein; sofern er gut is, soll er nicht sein, wie ein natürliches Ding gut ist, sondern es soll seine Schuld, sein Wille, er soll imputabel sein. Schuld heißt überhaupt Imputabilität."

And, he adds, "humanity has dignity only through the acceptance of guilt."[78]

It is paradoxical that in order to become actually good he must first become guilty (by becoming conscious of not being actually good), discovering in reflection that he is really evil insofar as he is not yet what he should be. In the moment of reflection, he achieves knowledge of good and evil, and knowledge of himself as good and evil. For it is his nature to pass out of the immediate and natural state. He begins as *good,* but not *actually good.* Only in the attainment of actualized good does he fully merit the predicate "good." The transition is accomplished by an act of the will, the very faculty that sets man higher than the animals. At first, his higher status is one of mere form. For the content of man's will does not distinguish him from the animals until he rises above instinct and natural animal desires. To be guiltless like the animals is merely to be will-less; and man is destined to rise above the natural, animal level in order to fulfill himself as spirit by giving rational content to the will. Hence the path of self-actualization includes becoming first consciously evil and self-alienated, then guilty and accountable in freedom, and finally self-reconciled as spirit. This is the road that each and all must follow. Adam was the decisive first who began the process; Jesus was the heroic, paradigmatic second who completed it.

The Adam-story is a representation of the universal human condition, for which the prephilosophic expression is the doctrine of original sin. Hegel emphasizes the tree in the Genesis tale: the tree of the knowledge of good and evil. The biblical story recounts cleavage, recognition of the separation of man's being from what he ought to be *and* the origin of knowledge of good and evil. For the serpent does not deceive: knowledge *does* come from eating the fruit. The fall story *recounts* but does not *account for* the development that is symbolically represented. For it is the limitation of *Vorstellung* not to be able to express the necessary connection between elements depicted.

Hegel flatly rejects the notion that without the deed of Adam evil would not have arisen. Since there is no true knowledge without knowledge of both good and evil and since knowledge was Adam's and humankind's destiny, there had to be evil and in the strict sense there already was. Eat-

---

[78]Lectures of 1821: LPR III:102; VPR III:39.

ing of the fruit of the tree brings Adam to *knowledge* of good and evil, to consciousness and thus toward the overcoming of evil. Evil and knowledge enter together, as the story suggests. But the two are one, since philosophy understands that the evil represented really means consciousness of evil. Furthermore, man's determination as evil is eventually overcome by heightening it and thereby overcoming self-estrangement. Knowledge is thus both the wound and the cure.[79]

The fall story is not without its problems, and this is expectable when deep speculative content is presented in picture images.[80] The principal contradiction of the story is that physical need and mortality follow as a *punishment* for the knowledge attained in eating of the fruit of the tree, as if to suggest that what occurred somehow should not have occurred. But God's command not to eat of the fruit of the tree is equally illogical, since the forbidden deed was necessary (and to that extent good). Thus the merit of the biblical fall story is not that it accounts for the true relationship between the various story elements but simply that it recounts them.[81]

Philosophy provides the true accounting. Man began as the image of God in an implicit fashion. As a being qualified by spirit, he had the destiny of becoming in actuality what he was at first only potentially: the explicit image of God. The knowledge attained in eating of the fruit of the tree of the knowledge of good and evil set the process in motion. In the story, God himself observes, "Behold, Adam has become like one of us, knowing good and evil."

> Here it is placed on the lips of God himself that precisely knowledge—the specific knowledge of good and evil in general, that is—constitutes the divine in humanity.[82]

Hegel repeats the verse of Genesis a second time and comments:

> This "has become" gives expression to the particular moment: not that of the first and original likeness of God, but of the likeness that is to be regained. It is represented as something that has already come to be, expressing generally this other aspect of knowledge, namely, that it is in itself the turning point.[83]

---

[79]Lectures of 1821: LPR III:106; VPR III:42.
[80]Lectures of 1821: LPR III:104; VPR III:40.
[81]It deserves some note that Christ, the second Adam, is also represented as punished. But the higher religion recognizes his "evil deed"—declaration of divine sonship—as good.
[82]Lectures of 1821: LPR III:105; VPR III:41.
[83]Lectures of 1821: LPR III:108; VPR III:43-44.

The story expresses separation, knowledge of good and evil and, above all, the attainment of consciousness. The evil in the tale consists of the consciousness of being merely at the level of potential (*an-sich* or in-itself) and thus of not being what one ought to be. Thus Adam's deed is not the true evil. It is necessary and good and brings him to knowledge/consciousness of the good and evil that already are. And in coming to knowledge of evil he is able to effect the good: in becoming conscious that he is an implicit image of God separated from God he is able to advance toward becoming an explicit image and overcoming separation.

For Kant, we recall, man was inexplicably but surely responsible for his being morally good or evil, while for Hegel man is both good and evil but at first not responsible. For Kant, being good or evil was the result of a choice of the ultimate ground of maxims, and for Kant man was created good (predisposed to good) but succumbed to evil. Why one chooses evil was never clarified by Kant (nor was it by Kierkegaard). However, it was emphatically clear that man recognizes himself as having chosen evil and thus as being guilty. There was no alleviating or altering guilt by construing the deed as anything less than totally free.

Kierkegaard's point of view contains elements of both the Kantian and Hegelian views. As in Kant's work, so in Kierkegaard-Haufniensis's *Concept of Anxiety* evil enters mysteriously but surely; and man emerges, after a primoridal instant of goodness, as both evil and guilty. But for Kierkegaard, as for Hegel, the initial goodness is naive (or, in Haufniensis's term "innocent") and the way toward overcoming evil is to become conscious of evil ("guilt-conscious" for Haufniensis). But finally, beyond Hegel, overcoming evil means intensifying the guilt-consciousness of self-estrangement into sin-consciousness[84] that is the prelude to a forgiveness to be granted according to the promise and free grace of a transcendent, personal God. Just as decisively different from Hegel is the fact that this is understood as carried out on the individual rather than the collective or universal plane. Kierkegaard's interpretation of fall stresses the fall of the individual qua individual: mankind does not "sin in Adam" as a race taken as a whole, but sins as Adam did, as individual, just as he later "rises in Christ" as individual. And for this deed each individual is accountable before a personal God, not the world-process.

---

[84]Certainly the category that constitutes one of the major points of the Hegel-Kierkegaard divide.

For Hegel, the myth of the fall is the *Vorstellung* of the appearance of separation and knowledge—wound and ultimate cure—in the universal Adam. The *why* is explained—in contrast to Kant and Kierkegaard—not by the story but by the inner necessity of man's being as spirit, destined to pass beyond primordial unity into separation and ultimately into higher unity. Thus the admission of evil that for Kant and Kierkegaard is a cause for penitence is for Hegel a boast of freedom and a call to self-liberation.

Hegel's philosophical account of the fall sets the stage for the philosophical account of Christ as the second Adam. The positive account of evil suggests in advance that any doctrinal linkage of the two Adam stories into a "theology of atonement" is for philosophy not only superfluous but a distortion of the true meaning contained in the *Vorstellung*. In addition, the source of reunion is already universally present in *every* Adam so that in a real sense the "second Adam" is merely the first in the human family to achieve the goal: the actualized divine potential of everyman.

But while Hegel is principally concerned with the *universal* meaning of the fall, his analysis does pertain to the individual and does so on the psychological level. To this extent, Kierkegaard's *Sickness Unto Death* is not the first modern philosophical investigation of the effects of sin. Separation in the fall of Adam and of everyman is characterized by pain and anguish (*Schmerz*) and by unhappiness (*Unglück*) as the reflections of internal and external separation respectively. The source of anguish is the growing consciousness of the inner contradiction that must be overcome, while the source of unhappiness is the fact that he cannot find happiness in the world. But the root of both is separation from God, which originates in God's self-separation. For the process by which God becomes exteriorized began in creation of a world that was other and separate. It wins a new dimension when man emerges incipiently as self-conscious other in the knowledge of good and evil and in his first moment of self-affirmation chooses himself in separation from God. Hegel terms this moment of subjectivity "*Selbstsucht*," self-seeking or selfishness, the choice of the self without its proper ground and substance. Hence, selfishness is paradoxically self-lessness. For, divided within himself, cut off from his proper ground, he does not possess true selfhood. His division within himself, which is also division from God, is the source of his anguish; and his estrangement from the world, which is also estrangement externally from God, is his unhappiness. As consciousness develops, opposition is intensified. Growing self-consciousness raises one to consciousness of implicit unity with God and of explicit separation.[85] And the process gives rise to infinite anguish from which one yearns to be delivered.

Consciousness, knowledge, and anguish are phases of exteriorization before the moment of reconciliation. Historically and in biblical story, the first moment of reconciliation is found in the consciousness of the dying Christ, in whom God's self-emptying is first completed. The Jesus of New Testament story is he in whom God's self-emptying is manifested and fulfilled. Thus understood, the Christ of philosophy is the hero and model of universal reconciliation.

PHILOSOPHICAL CHRISTOLOGY

Hegel, in the manner of his Enlightenment predecessors, makes Jesus a spokesman for and representative of his own philosophical standpoint. Philosophy's evolution beyond the moral reason of Rousseau and Kant meant that the Christ of philosophy also evolved—from moral teacher to the representative of divine-human unity.[86] However, as a representative of Hegel's philosophical position, Jesus is not to be taken as a philosopher, not even as an implicit Hegelian. For he is a representative within a representation.

Jesus of Nazareth and his story are the central event of the consummate religion. As such they receive the extended philosophical consideration that they merit on religion's road to philosophy. That Hegel finds Jesus central and decisive by no means suggests that Hegel's interpretation is a traditional one, although right-wing Hegelians would find in him a modern-day St. Thomas revitalizing orthodoxy with a new philosophy-theology. Indeed, in light of Hegel's early (unpublished) "Life of Jesus" and its dismissal of the Christ of orthodox Christianity, it would be difficult to construe him as having come back to traditional theological teaching on the incarnation: God *fully* present in Jesus of Nazareth from the moment of his conception, as the *free*, unique, and vertical descent of God into the affairs of men. And even though Hegel finds great significance in Christ's death on a cross, his Speculative Good Friday remains far removed from atonement theology. Nevertheless, what one finds in Hegel's Christology

---

[85]Because the potential for explicit unity is not yet fulfilled. Lectures of 1827: LPR III: 304-307; VPR III: 228-31.

[86]For Karl Löwith this represented a new "gnostic Christology," in which Hegelian philosophy supplied the gnosis. Cf. Löwith, "Hegels Aufhebung der christlichen Religion," *Hegel-Studien* 1 (1964):198.

is a kind of modern *Cur Deus Homo,* but equally a speculative *Quomodo Homo Divus.* For in the end Jesus' status is as much *divus* as *deus.* Indeed, Hegel's proclamation that *Deus fit homo* ("God becomes man") in Jesus of Nazareth translates, from the human side, *Homo fit divus* ("man becomes divine," that is, rises to divine consciousness).

Teachings of Jesus

Hegel's philosophical thinking about Jesus had evolved from the Kantian moral teacher in the early writings to the Prometheus of consciousness in the *Lectures on the Philosophy of Religion.* In the latter, Jesus is again a teacher but with a markedly higher teaching. His life and his teaching are in fact joined. And his life and death, taken together, constitute the meaning of his teaching. As Hegel remarks, his death is "the seal of his teaching."[87] In exploring Jesus' teaching, Hegel focuses on the consciousness reflected in them: "His teaching . . . belongs to his appearance as a free relationship of spiritual consciousness to spiritual consciousness."[88] But if there is a teaching of Jesus that is decisive for Hegel it is that "I and the Father are one." The truth of this teaching, and the beauty of the Christian religion, is that Jesus is God manifested in humanity but also the heroic first man to come to consciousness of his unity with God. This latter aspect is fully appreciated only with the insight of philosophy. For, "All are one stem, not this or that single individual . . . and thus one man is humanity as such."[89] Jesus represents at one and the same time the extreme of exteriorization in God's life, as he dies forsaken on a cross, and the beginning of God's reconciliation with himself as finite spirit is reconciled with infinite spirit. As the *first* he is unique in that the idea is realized in his individuality. And thus it is that *his* death represents the fullness of God's self-emptying and the beginning of God's new self-unity.

Jesus, is, however, a clear instance of a man made by the times. For Jesus of Nazareth appears and does what he does at the kairotic moment when spirit is ready. In other words, Jesus is the man on the scene when it is time for the consummate religion. And one may imagine that, if Jesus of Nazareth had not been there, another would have risen to the task. But, in fact, Jesus was there. Thus for the past he was necessary. But in another

---

[87]Lectures of 1821: LPR III, 124; VPR III, 59.
[88]Lectures of 1821: LPR III, 115; VPR III, 50.
[89]Lectures of 1821: LPR III, 122; VPR III, 56-57.

temporal sense, namely, the future, he is very much dispensable. For in order that true reconciliation with God be effected, divine-human unity must finally be universalized. This can only occur in the time of God's life beyond Jesus—in the third moment of God's trinitarian life that is Holy Spirit. Thus it was necessary for Jesus to disappear from the scene, just as it is necessary for the religion about Jesus to "disappear" in its turn as it is spiritualized into philosophy.

But before he vanished, he freely accomplished the necessary inbreaking of consciousness of divine-humanity. Hegel writes:

> This cognition must come to us in such a way that it actually can be empirically universal, universal for immediate consciousness. For the immediate consciousness this can only happen as the demonstration of the unity of divine and human nature to it in a wholly temporal, completely ordinary worldly appearance in a single human being—this one man who is known at the same time as the divine idea, not as a teacher, not merely as a higher being in general, but as the highest idea, as the Son of God.[90]

In Jesus, God has appeared as man in mankind, and one man, representing mankind, has been revealed as God. Christ is the representation of reconciliation as Adam was the representation of separation. And the full truth of Jesus is not apprehended by the representation any more in this instance than in that of Adam. It requires philosophy to correct religion's inadequate representation and to bring out the full truth in adequate form. Thus just as philosophy of religion moves beyond Adam it will also necessarily move beyond Jesus. For the truth of Jesus is not his being a teacher of morality, as we know, or even a martyr to the truth, but the immediate presence and certainty of the idea in him. Jesus is the model of divine-human unity, but he is not himself reconciler or redeemer of others. He is not the "man for others" so much as the man for spirit, and herein lies his usefulness.

But, as was noted above, Jesus remains in a sense unique. "In the eternal idea there is only one Son, one only exclusive of other finite beings."[91] He is the unique representation of divine sonship. And the statement quoted describes Jesus' identity from the divine side. This is only part of the truth of Jesus. And one must not be misled by the language of religious representation such as to forget the human meaning and identity of Jesus. Jesus

---

[90]Lectures of 1821: LPR III, 110; VPR III, 46.
[91]Lectures of 1821: LPR III, 115; VPR III, 49.

is truly human and not a passive shell of divine action in him. The divine and human together form the full context of Jesus' meaning. Indeed, Hegel's striking statements about the uniqueness of Jesus are somewhat relativized when one remembers his human meaning. For, from the human side, one may say that God has (and needs) only one son and that Jesus is there in time for adoption. For his sonship also arises out of his humanity and his human deeds, most importantly his attainment of divine-human consciousness. And this Promethean attainment elevates him, from the human side, to divine sonship.

God is present in Jesus and uniquely so, but not of course exclusively, nor for the first time. For the history of religions reveals that God has been present before—in a burning bush and in the tales of incarnation in Indian pantheism. In Jesus, however, God is present in a new way and for the first time in this way. But this is not unique. For as we return to contemplate Jesus' identity on the human side, we recognize that Jesus' accomplishment is everyman's spiritual destiny, and there is essentially nothing that Jesus has done that everyman might not do. Each has to strip off subjectivity and to return to his new ground. Michael Theunissen writes:

> The sole self-consciousness in which the universal substance has revealed itself is the subjectivity of Jesus. In it is presented "evil as implicitly negated" because Jesus places his will entirely in that of God.[92]

But this still leaves Jesus merely the first, even if he were, to date, still the sole exemplar. He remains the model for universal salvation, to be effected universally. As the first he is unique. But he does nothing directly for others. He is not a personal savior. His attained consciousness is important for Jesus and for the life of spirit, and the life of spirit must be completed in the repetition and extension of Jesus' consciousness in others.

Death of Jesus

The meaning of Jesus' life reaches its climax in his death and Hegel's philosophical meditation upon the death of Christ is a rhetorically rich piece appropriate to his Speculative Good Friday. The language is poetic and moving, but its meaning at the philosophical lectern is far removed from any Lutheran sermon celebrating reparation for sin.

Nonetheless, among modern theological commentators, Eberhard Jüngel, who expresses a cautious appreciation of Hegel's religious thought,

---

[92]Theunissen, *Hegels Lehre,* 527.

identifies the death of God as the theme in which, from the theological standpoint, Hegel's philosophical thought soars. He even sees in Hegel's meditation on the death of God a philosophical attempt to bring Christianity and the Enlightenment tradition together: "Philosophy had to reconcile Christianity and Enlightenment with each other. For this, it needed and made use of the dark word of the death of God."[93] But while theologians may be instructed, enlightened or even edified by Hegel, his *Lectures on the Philosophy of Religion* and their meditation upon the death of Christ remain very much philosophy, not church theology.

In death, Jesus as flesh-and-blood representation completes a necessary moment in the life of the idea, namely, total emptying. Hegel declares in a famous quote from the Lectures of 1827 that

> "God himself is dead," it says in a Lutheran hymn, expressing an awareness that the human, the finite, the fragile, the weak, the negative are themselves a moment of the divine, that they are within God himself.[94]

The meaning of the death of Christ for philosophy is that God had human nature completely, even unto death. Death is thus the most complete proof of the humanity and self-emptying of God. The death of Christ is the death of God, but this monstrous and fearful depiction is necessary and expectable. In the humanity of Christ, full even unto death, God attains total self-exteriorization and Jesus is spiritualized:

> All distinctiveness, all traits of personality, all interests and purposes toward which the natural will might direct itself, are as nothing. This is a revolutionary element to the extent that it gives the world another shape. All things great and of worldly value are as nothing; all these things are buried in the grave of spirit.[95]

Christ's death represents negation in God, but at the same time the negation of negation. For in his death, otherness, which is negation, is also obliterated; and the death of the God-man can be termed, with theology, the death of death.

As the negation of negation, the death of the Christ is also the negation of evil. For evil is simply nonunion with God. Hegel employs the language of atonement theology but gives it philosophical content. Thus he speaks

---

[93]Jüngel, *Gott als Geheimnis der Welt* (Tübingen: Mohr, 1977) 117. According to Jüngel, the culminating point in this movement is Hegel's doctrine of the trinity (p. 121).

[94]LPR III:326; VPR III:249.

[95]Lectures of 1821: LPR III:128-29; VPR III:64.

of the death of Christ making up for sin and mentions atonement (*Genugtuung*). But any notion of Christ bearing the "punishment" of sin is without place in Hegelian philosophy since it is an errant product of religious *Vorstellung*.[96] The notion of atonement is equally dismissed even as the language of atonement is preserved. Thus Hegel's 1821 manuscript notes:

> [T]his death is one that makes satisfaction for us because it presents the absolute history of the divine idea as a history that has taken place in itself and happens eternally.

And he adds:

> Besides, everyone dies on his own, and everyone must be and achieve on his own, out of his own subjectivity and obligation, what he ought to be.[97]

Thus the idea of one man doing a deed that makes up for the guilt of another or that releases the other from doing a deed is as objectionable to Hegel as it was to Kant. For the latter, juridically each must make up for deeds of his own doing. But in Hegel's presentation, the juridical context vanishes. For Hegel, Christ is not a symbol of a changed moral disposition à la Kant; he is the representation of God's completed exteriorization and of the beginning of actualized divine-human unity. He is also clearly more than symbolic. He is fully historic and necessarily so.

The meaning of the atonement representation is that God can be satisfied only through himself, that the deed is substantially God's own—just as fall was. This is in the end a matter of consciousness, just as it was in the beginning. For once one rises from finite to infinite spirit, the deed is indeed one's own in unity with the divine. The doctrine of atonement, philosophically unfolded, emphasizes the locus of substantiality in the divine. Speculative reason is thus able to preserve and give universal dimension to a doctrine that Kant's practical reason could only take as symbolic depiction of an inner, personal process between individual and

---

[96]To illustrate how far Hegel is from the theological standpoint, Hegel could say that Christ was "steeped in sin" by his death—a formulation that theologians would quickly reject—for he completes the necessary negation process to the point of the negation of negation, living out separation from God to the point of forsakenness and resolution. Thus one should not misinterpret Hegel's speaking of Christ's bearing the sins of the world since its translation and meaning for philosophy is simply that Christ took on finitude completely.

[97]Lectures of 1821: LPR III:127, 128; VPR III: 62, 63.

God. The process that Hegel speaks of is, at one and the same time, individual and universal, interior and exterior, and as essential to God's life as it is to man's.

Verification of Jesus as the Son of God

The Concept of Religion, as developed by Hegel in Part I of the *Lectures on the Philosophy of Religion* made plain that, in the necessary unfolding life of God in history, the Son was to come. With John the Baptist, we might ask: But is *Jesus* the one who is to come or shall we look for another? That is, was that individual known to history as Jesus of Nazareth, the carpenter's son and itinerant teacher, the necessary and expected concrete instantiation of God's life? Indeed he was. There have been, as Hegel observed, other divine incarnations, and others have been honored for their deeds. But in Jesus the matter was different, for the time of the full manifestation of the idea was at hand. In Jesus, the nature of spirit was perfectly expressed. Philosophy recognizes it in his spiritual teaching about the coming of the Kingdom of God. Above all, it recognizes it in his death. And it is his death, which Hegel calls "adequate to the idea," that, above all, raises Jesus above a divine hero like Hercules, for example, and makes him God's Son. The total self-emptying of the divine in Jesus reveals him as the perfect instantiation expected in the fullness of time.

> However, the infinite idea of humanity could attach itself only to Christ and see itself realized only in him, for the time had fully come, the idea was mature in its depths.[98]

Can one be sure that Jesus was the expected one? Yes. Spirit does not err.

In an unpublished *Zusatz* to paragraph 465 of the Heidelberger *Encyclopedia* (later paragraph 565), Hegel wrote that it is not the words and deeds of Christ that matter so much as his meaning for the people, the idea that for them is manifest in him.[99] That idea was God's life. His teaching, according to Hegel, was rightly perceived as a threat to a state that was based on a different—and lower—religion, and his being a threat was acknowledged by the Roman state's executing him as a criminal. The role of the state in this religious story is significant, for Jesus is the founder of that

---

[98]Lectures of 1821: LPR III:145; VPR III:81.

[99]Cited by Heede, "Hegel-Bilanz," 71. "Nicht was ihr sogennanter Stifter in prosäicher Wirklichkeit-Geschichte gewesen—darauf kommt es nicht an,—sondern auf die Religion, d.i. was er den Völkern geworden, welche Idee ihnen in ihm offenbar geworden;—er insofern nicht Stifter, sondern ihre Entwicklung ist ihre Stiftung."

new religion whose unfolded philosophical meaning Hegel seeks to set as the foundation of a reformed and fulfilled state. Indeed, Jesus' teaching about the Kingdom of God was religion's way of representing the state founded on the religion of spirit, a state in which subjects are destined to achieve for themselves both Jesus' consciousness of union with God and Jesus' freedom.

TRANSCENDING JESUS: FROM DOCTRINE TO PHILOSOPHY

Jesus' death is not, of course, the end of him. But for Hegel to say this would not be necessarily to confess a Resurrection faith. Just as, of necessity, the Son of God must come as part of God's life, so God's life must continue beyond him. This occurs in the third moment of the exteriorized trinity, in the moment of the Holy Spirit to which Jesus himself points. In God's self-revelation in Christ, religion was consummated but the religion that the Christ founded is not to be religion about him. Christianity, as a spiritual community, is to be the community of the Paraclete, philosophically defined.[100] And historical representation of divine-human reconciliation—as occurs in Jesus as the Christ—is a precondition for this spiritual community. Modern Christianity may lovingly recall the appearance of Jesus as God's Son but the real event for modern Christianity is clearly not the past event of the Christ's death. For this very death points Christianity beyond him, directed toward the future event of spirit's coming, promised indeed in the gospel story and incipiently manifest in the Acts of the Apostles, fully manifest in the philosophy of spirit. In this light, the consideration of the historical Jesus is a tribute to his role in the past life of spirit and an emphatic moving beyond him as philosophy discerns his truth and makes his consciousness its own. The community thereby advances from faith in Jesus to faith in spirit. The historical Jesus is, in fact, a stumbling block for those who need to move beyond grasping spirit's life as sensuously represented in Jesus. Thus philosophy, which has "saved" Jesus by finding a preeminent place for him in the history of religions and in the life of spirit, must now pass beyond him. For philosophy must be free to express the full truth of the concept, unhindered by the representations and formulations of the past.

---

[100]Cf. Hyppolite, *Genèse et structure*, 547. Hegel remarks that "The formation of the community comes about as [Christ's] friends are filled by the Spirit" (Lectures of 1821: LPR III:142; VPR III:78). And in the 1827 Lectures he states, "The community is made up of those single, empirical subjects who are in the Spirit of God (LPR III:329; VPR III:252).

But Christianity itself had already begun the process, in the formulation and development of doctrine. For church doctrine had gone beyond the representation of the life and death of Jesus to express his meaning for the community, namely, the reconciliation in him of the divine and the human. In this wise, the consummate religion had already started to formulate the spiritual meaning of the background events, actual deeds, and future implications of the life and death of Jesus. What remained to be accomplished was the spiritual reinterpretation of the philosophical truths contained in church doctrine. Thus doctrine, like Jesus himself, must be transcended. For doctrine is a hybrid of sensuous representation and idea. As such it needs to be purified of the former so that the philosophical truth contained in it might be grasped in its universality, no longer limited by an individual. Since the sensuous residue still present in doctrine revolves around Jesus, the spiritualization of doctrine necessarily means completing the transcending of him.

For Hegel, the central church doctrine and the richest source for philosophical transformation was the trinity. He grasped its truth in the abstractness of his *Logic* and in the Lectures sketched its ascent from concrete sensuous representation toward abstract universal idea. But Hegel did more than review. He continued on to the specific philosophical transformation of Lutheran sacramental theology (Baptism and Lord's Supper) so that the spiritualization process might be concretely advanced.[101] Thus Hegel returned to two church doctrines in particular that revolve around Jesus in order to advance the community to philosophy.

Baptism

Baptism is socialization into the spiritual community. It is a "second birth" into that fellowship for which evil is already essentially overcome (through the negation of negation, in the death of the Son of God) and for which God is reconciled. In contrast to Persian religion and to the Kantian presentation of continuing moral struggle, the battle with evil, Hegel claims,

---

[101]Since the section discussing sacraments is structurally part of "Cultus," one looks in particular for a sense of how these sacraments contribute to achieving divine-human unity. But what one perceives there is that doctrine itself is cultus—intellectual furthering of the process, and that its spiritualization into philosophy constitutes "divine service" (*Gottesdienst*).

is already over.[102] The spiritual fellowship is religiously designated "church."

In the concluding section of the Lectures, Hegel discussed attaining the "invisible church" first mentioned in a youthful letter to Schelling.[103] Both Schelling and Hegel had advanced far beyond their earliest standpoints when they tended to share the Enlightenment's negative criticism of Christianity. Hegel still sought a community that was essentially philosophical but saw its attainment as necessarily proceeding through the historical religious community that grew up around the representations of Jesus. The church, as the community which in its faith in Christ had laid hold of the truth of the unity of divine and human natures, plays its special role in an "education of the spirit" so that this truth becomes the content of the will. The church thus aids in completion of the remaining task, until the philosophical brotherhood replaces it.

That task is explicitation of divine-human unity, the overcoming of evil. Evil, we are assured, is essentially overcome. Yet we know that man is still not yet what he ought to be—and this is one of the very definitions of evil. Hegel's contention parallels the church's: the death of Christ is the decisive turning-point, victory is in a sense already won but in another sense requires completion. The wounds of the human separation from the divine still require nursing as the battleground is transformed into a field of victory. This is accomplished by the church, in education, practice, training, appropriation and in "becoming habituated to the good and the true."[104] Despite the claim of reconciliation already achieved, Hegel does not appear to be so far beyond Kant as he might like to be. But how the Hegelian differs from the Kantian presentation is significant all the same. For in the Hegelian, all the elements of final, complete victory are already at hand: one has no need of being counted well-pleasing by a divine grace which, even if one merits it, still constitutes a deed from outside. Everything, in the Hegelian presentation, actually is in the power of man—as it has al-

---

[102]Cf. Lectures of 1824: LPR III:234; VPR III:164-65. Also cf. Lectures of 1827: LPR III:337; VPR III:260. For discussion of Persian (or Parsee) and Kantian dualisms, cf. vol. II of the Lectures.

[103]*Briefe*, ed. J. Hoffmeister, 1:218. The discussion of the Church has struck many commentators as rushed on the part of the lecturer. If it was perhaps due to the semester's coming to a close, this would justify the lecturer only for the first lecture series. But in none does Hegel really adequately engage the subject.

[104]Lectures of 1827: LPR III:336; VPR III:259.

ways lain implicitly in his power—once the Son of Man has lived unto death the moment of the divine's self-emptying. Hegel does not deny an original fall. He simply removes any moral content from the event. In his philosophical reinterpretation, he parts with Kant's imagery of a battle of good against evil in favor of imagery of return. But in so doing, has Hegel really done more than shift from a mythology of Zarathustra to the more abstract mythology of Plotinus? Universal reconciliation is still far off in both representations.

The Lord's Supper

The Lord's Supper is the celebration of unity in the consummate religion; it is the enjoyment of the presence of God. Hegel notes the centrality of the sacrament of the Lord's Supper in Christian doctrine and it becomes for him the measuring rod for assessing the spiritual level of the various Christian denominations.[105] In comparing the Roman Catholic, Lutheran, and Reformed (Calvinist) theology of the Eucharist, Hegel finds the Lutheran to be superior and true because it is the most spiritual. The Roman Catholic doctrine fails because, in its teaching of transubstantiation, God is understood as *physically* present in the consecrated bread and wine, and this is the spiritual shortcoming of the doctrine. Such a doctrine would suggest the divine becoming sensuously present once again and runs counter to the ascent toward nonsensuous manifestation that philosophy knows to be true. The Roman Catholic theology thus binds itself to the sensual level. In the Calvinist teaching, on the other hand, the Lord's Supper is merely a lively remembrance of the past, in which the divine is present only in memory. This, Hegel asserts, is an unspiritual interpretation. In the Lutheran doctrine, however, God is present in the sacrament of the Lord's Supper in *spirit* and in *faith*. Its doctrine thereby expresses the truth of unity and reconciliation as spiritual.[106]

When church doctrine has been fully spiritualized, then true "theology" or God-knowledge is achieved. And this is but the religious synonym for philosophy. As Hegel remarks:

> This reconciliation [in the process of thinking] is philosophy. Philosophy is to this extent theology. It presents the reconciliation of God with himself

---

[105]This parallels the *moral* measuring-rod in Enlightenment thought for distinguishing among Judaism, Christianity, and Islam.
[106]Lectures of 1821: LPR III:155; VPR III:90–91; et al.

and with nature, showing that nature, otherness, is implicitly divine, and that the raising of itself to reconciliation is on the one hand what finite spirit implicitly is, while on the other hand it arrives at this reconciliation, or brings it forth, in world history.[107]

These observations at the end of the Lectures are but a reproclamation of the beginning and of the completed circle: proclamation of the philosophical standpoint that alone is able to grasp the absolute and then discern its life concretely in the history of religions before raising it to the abstract level. Philosophical knowledge provides the harmony to counter the discord reflected by the inner disruption in the spiritual community. For, while the gates of unreason do not prevail against it, discord is in evidence. Indeed, there are those who continue—sometimes resolutely—in the dissonance of religion, of a form whose time has passed. Hegel does not elaborate but its implications for his program are very great. For if some—or most—cannot or will not rise to the philosophical grasp of religion and to the reconciliation that it means, this would leave philosophers as isolated *initiati* alone with their higher knowledge. More importantly, it would mean that the absolute might not be able to come to total explicit reconciliation. Indeed, if philosophy cannot command universal allegiance, the absolute in its progress from separation to reunion with itself would thus seem to have frustrated its own designs by having chosen philosophy's narrow way. And if Kant's ethical commonwealth required a moral miracle of justification, Hegel's version of the Kingdom of God seems to require the even more remarkable miracle of transforming all into philosophers. The philosophical Parousia is thus indefinitely delayed as long as humankind, including some Jesus-fixated Christians, refuses to rise to absolute spirit.

ASSESSING HEGEL'S PHILOSOPHY OF CHRISTIANITY

Hegel's *Lectures on the Philosophy of Religion* offer something for nearly every intellectual interest. For systematists, there is the aesthetic satisfaction of observing Hegel's ordering of religion within his system. For religionists, there is striking execution of a set theory of religion. For theologians, there are the insights, challenge, and provocation of an interpretation of Christianity and its Christ that has both awed and scandalized. For the philosopher, there is the affirmation of philosophy of religion as

---

[107]Lectures of 1827: LPR III:347; VPR III:269.

an indispensable element in a philosophical program and the challenging assertion of its central place. In addition is the heady Hegelian claim that the true content of philosophy is the true content of religion and that philosophy can only be authentic and complete when it analyzes that content. For the philosopher of religion, there is the volatile interaction of philosophy and religion and the difficult question posed about the place of history of religions in the task.

At the same time as one seeks to assess Hegel's achievement, the question gradually and inevitably arises: *In what sense and to what extent can there be philosophy of religion after Hegel?* It is not that Hegel has achieved the unsurpassable philosophy of religion. Rather, his philosophy may have unintentionally illustrated that, while there can be philosophy of the Christian religion (and of any other) and also Christian philosophy of religion, philosophy of religion may never be able to be "pure" and unqualified because the requisite "objective" standpoint is impossible and the increase in information about historical religions is simply overwhelming.

Hegel's *Lectures on the Philosophy of Religion* may also provide grounds for concluding the impossibility of executing a philosophy of religion that preserves the integrity of both. Hegel speaks of elevating religion to philosophy, but he fails to persuade fully and many may legitimately accuse him of reducing the one to the other instead. [108] For while in Hegel's philosophy of the Christian religion—which is (at least in the cultural sense) still a kind of Christian philosophy of the Christian religion—form is as adequate as Hegelian thought or any thought system can make it, yet the content sometimes resists, stubbornly and in advance, the elevation that Hegel seeks to force upon it.

But the problem is not only his presumptiousness but his presumptions. For Hegel's philosophy of religion begins not only with his system but with Christianity presupposed as the historical fulfillment of religion and its consummation qua religion. His philosophy of the history of religions has the task not of analyzing religions for their own sakes but rather of illustrating how they lead to Christianity as the inevitable highest form of religion. He never convinces us that his view of Christianity is more than arbitrary and this points to the cultural biases of his enterprise. On the other hand, without any organizing interpretive principle there can be no "phi-

---

[108]Interestingly, the reverse charge will be heard against Schelling, namely, that he surrendered philosophy to religion. Cf. chapter 4, below.

losophy'' of religion but rather only cataloguing. Thus the dilemma of constructing a similarly a priori theory or else sifting the overwhelming mass of historical data that will allow an alternative.

Hegel is clearly bound up with the Christian tradition. Not only does his philosophy of religion end with the triumph and transcending of the Christian religion, but his concept of religion is indebted to his Christian religious heritage from which, even in the moment of *Aufhebung* into philosophy, he does not entirely free himself. But if Hegel is both the philosopher of the Christian religion and (residually) the Christian philosopher of religion, his role as the latter is not easily to be equated with any previous effort in European intellectual history. His accomplishment might find a parallel in Voltaire's famous work on Charles XII which challenged the prevalent notion of the Christian philosophy of history, according to which all events from Creation to the Last Day find their place and meaning in God's plan. After Voltaire's work, it was no longer God but the historian who declared the plan of history, while history continued, however, to be perceived as purposeful without him. Hence the meaning did not change so much as the source. In parallel fashion, Hegel would make it manifestly clear that henceforth the philosopher—and not the founders or theologians of a religion—declares the meaning of religion, including the Christian religion. For Hegel challenged the widespread Christian philosophy of religion in which Christianity had already defined religion and religion was simply seen as fulfilled in Christianity and on Christianity's own terms; and he did so both more successfully than the French *philosophes* who philosophized about religion but only negatively, and more radically than Kant who also maintained the old language but changed its content. For Hegel, philosophy first defined religion, after which it illustrated a history of religion that still culminated in Christianity, but in a redefined, sublated form. Unlike Voltaire, Hegel did not break his ties with Christianity, nor did he cease in a residual sense to be a Christian philosopher. But Christian philosophy of religion and the Christian religion irrevocably pass in Hegel's Lectures from ''divine'' to human definition. Where Rousseau had halted and Lessing had hesitated, and where Kant was ambiguous, Hegel pressed forward to subject religion to human reason definitively and thereby to secularize religion, religious history, and philosophy of religion with them.[109]

---

[109]For some, the result was also to neutralize religion, as the necessary first step toward a postreligious culture.

Hegel's philosophy sees in Jesus as the "anointed of God" the implicit God-man singled out by spirit to be the locus of spirit's unfolding. In so doing, it recognizes Jesus as the God-man on the scene at the critical moment when God can fulfill his inner necessity to be manifest in human form. Jesus thus fulfills God's life as the first to attain consciousness of divine-human unity. "God becomes man in Jesus of Nazareth," for Hegel, in the very same moment that man is ready to become—and does become—God. Hegel expresses thereby the profoundest grasp of the full humanity of Jesus, namely, that he is God. With Rousseau and Kant, Hegel rescued Jesus from an untenable notion of godhead and divinity, made him fully human and thus once again a man for others. However, in the face of an Enlightenment tradition that would accept Jesus' slightly edited teachings and nod admiringly to him as the teacher of morality, Hegel made the identity of Jesus central to the philosophical meaning of Christianity.

But certain philosophical cautions are in order. Christian faith began in Jesus and in Christianity's sense of the spiritual presence of Christ, but the faith of philosophy purifies it to the sense of spirit as spirit. For Jesus' achievement gave rise to faith but was destined to issue in a faith that had spirit and not Jesus as its focus. Hegel's Christology thus points unmistakably beyond Jesus, even as doctrine had begun to. For doctrine, beginning with St. Paul, emphasized the spiritual meaning of Jesus. Philosophy completes the process. To the dismay of those fixated on the sensuous trappings of history, Jesus can now appear to be "in the way." The sensuous Jesus must go *and has gone.*

Philosophy recognizes the spiritual meaning of Jesus in New Testament representation. The status of Jesus that emerges—sometimes despite language to the contrary—is not one of absolute uniqueness but rather one of primacy: he is the distinguished first to have attained divine-human unity. Although Hegel had no need to say it, the death of whoever had been this distinguished first would have been decisive in the life of God. But there is no reason to think that John the Baptist, had his consciousness been higher, might not have served the purposes of spirit equally well. Indeed, except for Hegel's cultural biases, there is no reason to think that Gautama Siddhartha might not have done the same (or that he did not do the same).

As philosophy, Hegel's achievement points in two directions at once. On the one hand, it looks backward and nods respectfully toward the philosophies of Greece and the Eastern theologies linked to them. On the other, it affirms philosophy in the future and situates Christianity and its Christ in relation to it in a fashion that is more than honorific. For he discerns in their story and doctrines the spiritual truth of the future: the unity of God and man and the freedom of the sons of God. Hegel may be prone to speculation that gives pause to some, but in his philosophy of religion we find stated in modern philosophy what it means for humans aspiring to be Christlike that God was present and conscious in Jesus of Nazareth.

Beyond the majesty of Hegel's achievement, the great accomplishment of the absolute philosophy may, ironically, consist in its pointing to the inevitable arbitrariness and nonabsoluteness of any kind of philosophical theology, including its own. Hegel's Lectures sensitize the listener to the relativities of historical ideas—of those claiming eternal validity and absoluteness—and awaken him from any "doctrinal slumber." The philosophy of the history of doctrine implicit in the Lectures would hold that there can be no permanently valid and intelligible statement of the meaning of Christian beliefs, either theologically or philosophically.

Hegel did not seek to create any new doctrine or new theology, but rather a philosophical statement of religion that could serve as the basis for the state. And Jesus' death as criminal on a cross points to the political significance of the religion that he founded. Hegel's Lectures are the philosophical reformation of religion that is to allow and be the impetus to political and social reformation. His elaboration of the process by which the idea of God becomes initially concrete in religion and then fully manifest in the consummate religion is in the end more in the spirit of Rousseau and the civil religion of the *Social Contract* than that of Kant and the ethical commonwealth. To the extent that one sees Hegel's treatment of religion, then, as contributing to the intellectual groundwork for the state as a "reflecting social unity" (*reflektierende Zusammengehörigkeit*), one may ask if the Lectures are not one vast digression from this fundamental point uttered in 1831 on the relation of religion to the state. For there Hegel maintained that one could not have a good state without a correct notion of God. And the notion that he found represented in the Christ of Christianity and that he himself finally articulated adequately for philosophy was the freedom of man and his attainment of self(= God)-consciousness. But the Lectures are of course more than an excursus on religion and the state. They are a philosophical history of religions, the elaboration and fulfillment of a task laid down by Hegel's system, namely, that the implicit become explicit, that the abstract life of the idea be demonstrated in the concrete life of God.

Hegel's lectures in general are considered his most accessible works, and the *Lectures on the Philosophy of Religion* are no exception. But they are a long-winded exercise, even if they end in a hurried breath. Their dizzying high point consists in the meditations upon doctrine, supplying them with new philosophical meaning, even as the old language is maintained. The meditations upon the trinity and the death of God are the richest and most important in this respect. The Lectures are, furthermore, a masterful attempt to force the history of religions into the Hegelian system and its dialectical view of reality. They constitute a thought-experiment of a very high order, but one that must also be judged unsuccessful if religion is more than thought. Hegel's religion is barren on the existential plane, and the process by which the pious religious heart might be elevated to the serene Hegelian mind in religion remains the deepest mystery. But while the religious individual may, because of his individual religious life, feel somehow left out of the all-important world-historical process of which the Lectures tell him he is part, Hegel's reflections are highly suggestive on the broader plane, namely the teleology of religion and its role in the social dimension. On this point Hegel is strongest precisely where Kierkegaard, his fiercest existential critic, is himself weakest.

But in the hurried ending to the Lectures,[110] Hegel does not develop the very relationship of religion and state that seems so important to the Lectures' view of religion. A true conception of God, we are told, is necessary for a good state, good government, and good laws, since a bad concept leads to a bad state, bad government, and bad laws.[111] But in concluding the Lectures, even with the claim of full philosophical articulation of the correct God-concept, Hegel failed to speculate about the state to arise on that basis. The "Second Coming" and fulfillment of religion, which Hegelian philosophy claims to be, proclaims an age of the "Third Testament" that ends just as apocryphally as the Second. And, waiting endlessly for dusk on this philosophical last day, the Owl of Minerva will never take to flight.

More than 150 years after Hegel's death, dusk seems as distant as it did in 1831. And the proclamations of this Third Testament in secular language have had to be reinterpreted in light of the inexplicable delay in the

---

[110]Hurried, although Hegel gave them four times.

[111]This occurs in Part I and thus quite early in the Lectures. Cf. Lectures of 1831: LPR III:452; VPR III:340.

fullness of time. Hegel's early followers realized this and rose to the task, just as the followers of Jesus did when the expected Parousia did not occur and had to be spiritualized or delayed in the thinking of the early Christian church. This very similarity may suggest that the Third Testament is every bit as much a "representation" as it claims the First and Second to be. For what is enduringly striking in Hegelian thought is its own mythic quality, even as it soars toward the abstractness that it calls concrete. And despite excesses, its mythic quality is still capable of exercising fascination. The wholistic and all-encompassing goal of Hegelian thought can still evoke a measure of awe, despite a history that has witnessed both credulity and ridicule (and that has gradually reached sober reassessment). For, on his own terms, Hegel nearly succeeds in incorporating all of reality into his thought/ myth, and one returns to the origins of philosophy itself—in "thaumadzein"—as the Hegelian program moves from one to another aspect of reality and finally to religion. In addition, the *form* of Hegel's philosophy of the history of religions is not proven inadequate merely because of the mythological excesses of his presuppositions.

In philosophy's rising above representation and in recognizing God as spirit, Hegel's philosophy sought to fulfill religion by transcending it. However, in the very moment that Hegel thought he had settled the philosophical meaning of Christianity, he profoundly unsettled it, as subsequent nineteenth-century theology bears witness.

4

SCHELLING AND THE THEOGONY OF JESUS

INTRODUCTION

In October 1840 a Prussian monarch sought once again to intervene in the course of philosophy of religion. Friedrich Wilhelm IV, grandson of the Friedrich Wilhelm II who had sought Kant's silence after publication of *Religion within the Limits of Reason Alone,* called Professor Friedrich Wilhelm Joseph Schelling out of retirement in Munich for the philosophical restoration of Christianity in Hegelian Berlin.[1] Schelling responded eagerly and the intellectual public prepared itself for a philosophical event that began in November 1841.

In his attempt to displace Hegelianism and Hegelian Christianity, Schelling was trying to be as different as possible in articulating a new philosophical meaning for the Christian religion and its Christ. Yet Schelling's Philosophy of Revelation cannot be understood only as reaction to Hegel. For it is based on a philosophical standpoint that Schelling had sketched long before Hegel had brought his own system to completion. Indeed, in attaining his 1809 position Schelling had perceptively identified the central problem of idealism before Hegel's *Logic* was set to paper and had already philosophically set the stage for the existentialism that would emerge in the next century.

---

[1]Friedrich Wilhelm had as Crown Prince and as early as 1833 become actively interested in bringing Schelling to Berlin. Friedrich Wilhelm IV succeeded Friedrich Wilhelm III in 1840.

Schelling had been one of the founding figures of idealism. But Schelling early parted company with the movement that was destined to dominate German intellectual life. In going his own way, he set off on a long philosophical career that would take him from youthful celebrity to a long obscurity and then a brief day in the Berlin sun. Throughout, he was guided by a spirit of self-criticism that led him to several new beginnings and by an intellectual openness that sometimes led him in gnostic directions. But despite his eclipse, it is now rcognized that, in his break with idealism and with the yet-to-be-completed Hegelian system, Schelling had not simply deviated but really gone beyond them.

Schelling's break had been prompted by a simple question: If philosophy can derive a logical vision of things as they are in themselves and as they ought to be, then why does the real not correspond to the ideal? The answer, Schelling recognized, was *human freedom*. Other questions arose: In the light of man's freedom, is it possible that the actual is not the ''logical'' and the ''necessary'' (as it was for Hegel) but merely the contingent? And, if so, what must philosophy be—what form and program must it adopt—in order to be adequate to this unsettling fact of freedom that shatters logical dreams? Could there be a ''philosophy of freedom''? Schelling answered yes and spent the remainder of his career seeking the form and executing a program, but never completing it.

Schelling had foreseen the inevitable shipwreck of idealism at least as early as 1809, in his treatise *Of Human Freedom* or *Freiheitsschrift*,[2] while Hegel continued his confident launching and execution of its program until his sudden death in 1831. Ten years later, in 1841, Schelling mounted Hegel's podium in Berlin. There, in what has been called the last great event in the German university,[3] Schelling read his *Lectures on the Philosophy*

---

[2]All references to Schelling's works in German are to: *Friedrich Wilhelm von Schellings sämmtliche Werke*, 14 vols. in two divisions, edited by K. F. A. Schelling (Stuttgart and Augsburg: J. G. Gotta'scher Verlag, 1856-1861); hereafter cited as SW. Except where noted, all translations are those of the author.

Über das Wesen der menschlichen Freiheit, SW VII:332-416. In English: *Schelling: Of Human Freedom*, trans. James Gutman (Chicago: Open Court, 1936). Gutman indicates the German pagination in the margin and this will be the only pagination cited.

[3]For an informative survey of the diverse reactions to Schelling in Berlin, including the ultimate widespread disappointment, cf. Xavier Tilliette, *Schelling, une philosophie en devenir* (Paris: J. Vrin, 1970), II:232-47. Cf. also C. L. Michelet, ''Schellings erste Vorlesung in Berlin,'' quoted in Manfred Frank, ed., *F. W. J. Schelling: Philosophie der Offenbarung* (Frankfurt a. Main: Suhrkamp, 1977), Anhang III: Dokumente, 434-39.

of Revelation. For Schelling, this was to be his most public statement of the positive philosophy intended to displace the negative that he in his youth had striven to perfect; for the Berlin government, it was to be the new, hoped-for philosophical theism to extract the "dragon tooth of Hegelian pantheism."[4]

The future luminaries who attended those lectures might be reason enough to direct attention to them.[5] Kierkegaard, Engels, Bakunin, and Burkhardt are among the most famous. Perhaps never was more expected of a philosophy lecturer. Disappointment was to some extent inevitable and, by the end, Schelling had only a fraction of his original overflow audience. Along the way, Kierkegaard, initially among the most enthusiastic but soon among the most critical, remarked cuttingly in a letter back to Copenhagen that Schelling's lectures, with the puffed-up doctrine of potencies, betrayed the greatest impotence.[6]

Despite the famous in attendance, the lectures have not received their due. They remain untranslated in English,[7] in part due to the submersion of Hegelianism that took Schelling's fragile bark down in the undertow, but in part due to internal problems and idiosyncratic qualities that called the entire enterprise into question. Serious and well-grounded questions about his procedure have, however, frequently been reduced by critics to rhetorical questions, with frequently nothing more than rhetorical answers. German philosophical literature of the past forty years has revived interest in and reopened assessment of the later Schelling. Yet whatever the final assessment, Schelling's philosophy of religion deserves a hearing not just for its audience and enemies and for pointing up problems in idealistic philosophy of religion and its philosophy of Christianity. For it merits our attention most positively for accentuating and giving distinctive meaning to the concept of a "living God" and doing so in a philosophy of re-

---

[4]This is the famous and oft-cited phrase in the royal summons to Berlin that Schelling received.

[5]The 1841 Lectures were not the only version of Schelling's Philosophy of Revelation. Schelling had already presented an earlier version in Munich.

[6]Letter to P. C. Kierkegaard of February 1842, in *Kierkegaard's Writings XXV: Letters and Documents,* trans. Henrick Rosenmeier (Princeton: Princeton University Press, 1978) 141.

[7]At present, all that is available in English translation is the self-described "summary translation" of excerpts in the doctoral dissertation of Victor C. Hayes: "Myth, Reason and Revelation: Prespectives on a Summary-Translation of Three Books from Schelling's Philosophy of Mythology and Revelation" (Columbia University, 1970).

ligion that wishes to be inclusive of all historical religion. It is additionally distinctive for its view of religion as the process in which God becomes fully triune and for its theogony of Jesus the Logos as a decisive moment in religion and in the life of God.

SCHELLING INTERPRETATION AND THE PROTEUS CHARGE

To say that Schelling's contemporaries were unkind with him would be understatement, to say that they were unfair only slightly less so. Given the heady self-confidence and premature success of the young Schelling, disappointment *for* him and *in* him was almost bound to come. As Hegel's star ascended, Schelling's was already in decline, and Schelling suffered further from and by the inevitable comparisons between the one-time seminary colleagues.[8] After a prolific youth, Schelling began a literary silence that began even before Hegel's triumph and that lasted the remaining forty-five years of his life. This long silence (apart from a published foreword for Victor Cousins) contributed to the difficulty of contemporaries in assessing his work and has continued to pose problems for interpreters. Why did young Schelling suddenly fall silent after 1809 (at least as regards the printed word, for he did continue to lecture)? What role did the critical reception of the treatise *Of Human Freedom* play, the death of Caroline Schlegel Schelling, and then the steady ascent of Hegel's philosophical star? Undoubtedly, all these played some part. Since Schelling published nothing in his own lifetime after the 1809 *Of Human Freedom* (when he was only 34 years old) and was therefore known only to those who had either heard him lecture or else heard about him, the sudden collapse of Hegelianism discredited Schelling along with all known as idealists. It was only long after the twentieth century "rehabilitation" of Hegel that Schelling finally received the scholarly reevaluation that he too had long deserved. But despite this, it is not inaccurate to say that Schelling still suffers from the Hegel-Schelling tie and remains overshadowed to this day.

Schelling interpretation of the nineteenth century was affected by Schelling's rivalry with Hegel, by the hostility of the triumphant Hegelians and by the sharp criticisms of anti-Hegelians who were disappointed in Schelling's long-awaited counterthrust. Not a few who comprised the stellar audience for the 1841 Berlin Lectures were writing at length about

---

[8]In a sense he still does. And even his periodic resurrections are tied to Hegel revivals.

Schelling's lecture series, and many of these writings subsequently found their way into print. Kierkegaard's lecture notes, for example, were published posthumously, as were his letters from Berlin back to Copenhagen. In a diary entry (22 November 1841), he described his initial enthusiasm for Schelling in a New Testament simile, as he related that the "babe in [his] womb" leapt for joy when he heard the word "reality" invoked in philosophy once again. His later letters indicate (without rejoining the simile) that the babe in his philosophical womb soon miscarried. No "Schellingians" were born that winter in Berlin, and there have been relatively few since then. Schelling's philosophical fortunes were ultimately greater in the Slavic East than in the West, for reasons that go beyond Schelling personally and that may argue for something capricious in the fate of philosophies. The Hegelian Marheineke published a sharp criticism, but Paulus's publication of his combination of "commentary" and pirated lecture notes brought about another dramatic philosophical event. For Schelling, against all better advice, brought lawsuits in several German states against the publishing of unapproved lecture texts as a way to suppress Paulus's damning commentary. When he lost his case in Berlin (he won in Hamburg), he took the occasion to retire from academic lecturing in 1851 and withdrew to Munich in some bitterness. Emmanuel Hirsch, in his well-known *Geschichte der neuern Evangelischen Theologie,* issued an early twentieth-century judgment of Schelling that is typical of the nineteenth as well in its perspective and harshness:

> For the general intellectual life of Germany, the theosophy of the late Schelling can, with complete justification, be viewed as nothing other than a once-famous mind's old-age crotchet that is not to be taken seriously as philosophy. As a sort of caricature of Hegelian philosophy, it contributed much to idealistic speculation's being dismissed as mere fantasy and so had an effect exactly opposite to the intention of its founder.[9]

But Hirsch's judgment is both inaccurate and unfair. Schelling's late philosophy did fail to displace Hegelianism. And Hegelian idealism failed soon thereafter, but for other reasons. Schelling was dismissed mostly for his own early idealism and association with Hegel, while his later position was more often ignored.

Intellectual historians have been of different views about Schelling's relationship to idealism. Left- and right-wing Hegelians have developed

---

[9] 5:274.

their own Schelling interpretations and have dominated the discussion until relatively recently. In the middle of the present century, Schelling's sorry fate began to change. Two names deserve special mention in this regard: Horst Fuhrmans and Walter Schulz. Both are sympathetic critics and, while on some points their interpretations are antithetical, they are in substantial agreement about the seriousness and worth of Schelling's contribution to modern philosophy. Their studies have contributed to a Schelling revival that is modest but quite real nonetheless. The points of conflict between Fuhrmans and Schulz have given rise to subsequent "synthetic" reevaluations, and here the names Walter Kasper and Xavier Tilliette deserve mention.

Beginning with his 1940 Berlin dissertation, Horst Fuhrmans has argued for a reappreciation of the Schelling who broke with the idealism that he had helped found. Subsequent works emphasize and document how very early Schelling's break had come, and Fuhrmans locates the first signs as early as 1806. By this second Munich period of 1827-1841, Schelling is viewed as in full break with idealism and opposing it from a base in Christianity.[10] Fuhrmans argues that Schelling was always a theist—at first "immanent theist," later a "transcendent theist."[11] While elements in his view pose problems, it is overall persuasive. The thesis of immanent theism, however, seems to stretch the term theism to meaninglessness. For Schelling's so-called immanent theism still has the ring of pantheism, despite Fuhrmans's best efforts to make it sound otherwise. His emphasis on theism thus seems excessive. But there are other points as well where Fuhrmans would see clearly what strikes others as plain ambiguity.[12] And his date of Schelling's break with idealism seems earlier than is warranted. But however much one argues with Fuhrmans about the details of his thesis, overall it is sound and important for discrediting the "Proteus charge" (see below) and for illustrating the presence of the so-called late philosophy at a far earlier date in Schelling's thinking.

---

[10]Cf. Walter Kasper, *Das Absolute in der Geschichte. Philosophie und Theologie der Geschichte in der Spätphilosophie Schellings* (Mainz: Matthias-Grünewald Verlag, 1965) 10-16, for a useful discussion and overview of the Fuhrmans and Schulz theses.

[11]Horst Fuhrmans, *Schellings Philosophie der Weltalter* (Düsseldorf: Schwann, 1954) 288.

[12]Jürgen Habermas has called attention to this as a "Verlegenheitslösung" in *Das Absolute und die Geschichte* (Bonn Dissertation, 1954) 10-11.

Walter Schulz also argues effectively against the Proteus charge and identifies lasting motifs and themes in Schelling's earlier writings. His rich reading of Schelling argues, as the title of his work indicates, that German idealism had its logical fulfillment in the late philosophy of Schelling. Especially compelling is the thesis that in Schelling the modern problematic self bursts forth onto the philosophical stage, even if the event went largely unnoticed at the time. Such a thesis might be construed as making Schelling a proto-existentialist, but this is not Schulz's view. In the end, however, Schulz's reading is rather an oddly Hegelian interpretation of the idealist movement in which the dynamism of the idealist problematic—namely, overcoming subject-object—*necessarily* fulfills itself in the subject's recognition of its incomprehensibility to itself[13] and ultimately demands radical alterations in the program of philosophy. In this interpretation, reason, which wishes to grasp itself in the possibility of positing itself, shatters as it comes to recognize its own incomprehensibility to itself, owing to the brute fact that its pure existence (*Daß*) always precedes its thought.[14] Schulz's reading infuses Schelling's efforts with a sense of purpose and intellectual high drama that is finally not persuasive. For to conceive of Schelling's accomplishment as the fulfillment of idealism amounts to redefining idealism to include a phase that is better viewed as a break and hence already postidealism. Schulz's reading too confers upon Schelling's early philosophy an unjustified clarity of purpose and direction that amount to tidying up posthumously what the living man seems to have left vague.[15] As Walter Kasper insightfully observes, while Fuhrmans underplays the negative philosophy in his stress on the early establishment of a positive philosophy, Schulz would seem to underplay the positive in his stress on the completion of idealism or what Schelling called "negative philosophy."[16] Schulz maintains that negative philosophy triumphs when fulfilled in the positive,[17] but in this he fails to do justice to Schelling's express desire to have positive replace negative philosophy. In sum, Schulz tends to emphasize the positive aspects of negative philosophy at the expense of the positive philosophy proper.[18]

---

[13]This happens in Schelling nearly a century before Freud.

[14]Walter Schulz, *Die Vollendung des deutschen Idealismus in der Spätphilosophie Schellings* (Pfullingen: Neske, 1975) 7.

[15]The same charge applies to Fuhrmans as well, only on different points.

[16]Kasper, *Das Absolute in der Geschichte*, 15.

[17]Schulz, *Vollendung*, 83.

[18]Fuhrmans makes the same point as Kasper in his preface to H. Fuhrmans, ed., *Die Grundlegung der positiven Philosophie* (Torino, 1972).

The Fuhrmans-Schulz debate revolves around an assessment of what Schelling really accomplished, what his ultimate intentions were and how clear the process was. Xavier Tilliette, meantime, sees in Schelling the missing link between Hegel and his critic-heirs, as well as the precursor of postidealist philosophy.[19] In the Tilliette reading, Schelling, even if he would break with idealism, is still more tied to it than he would wish. In this view, Schelling is a compelling internal critic of idealism who saw through to the fundamental flaw in objective idealism even before Hegel's major statement of idealist metaphysics in his *Logic*. And while it may be viewed as logical, inevitable, or necessary that such a flaw should come to light, once it has done so, Schelling is to some extent beyond idealism— in intention, in problematic, in presuppositions and in starting point—even if in another sense he satisfies its inner dynamism.

THE PROTEUS CHARGE

Schelling has been frequently criticized and caricatured as the Proteus of German idealism, who moved on from his early Philosophy of Identity to a Philosophy of Freedom and later to a Philosophy of Mythology and Revelation, with other phases along the way. He is seen in this view as abandoning each system as soon as it had begun. The implication is that his philosophizing is unstable and that no phase is worthy of sustained attention, all the more so since the philosopher himself rejects each one. This characterization and caricature are to be rejected and dismissed.[20]

This is not to deny the phenomenon of change in Schelling but only to seek a more sober and balanced standpoint for viewing his development. Those who look for consistency in the *themes* of his philosophical activity[21] afford one avenue for overcoming the Proteus charge. But Schelling, it can be argued, had his general philosophical program in place as early as 1796. Certainly his program evolved. But can one dismiss a philosopher out of hand as fickle and philosophically unstable who, over the course of an ap-

---

[19]Tilliette, *Schelling, une philosophie en devenir*, II: 72-73.

[20]One might, however, wish to retain a Proteus simile but in that case fully apply the meaning given the minor sea god Proteus in Homer's *Odyssey* (4.385ff.), viz., that, no matter the form of appearance, he can be held on to until he resumes his *true* shape, whereupon he will answer all questions put to him.

[21]Such as Frederick Copleston who emphasized the relation of finite and infinite as continuous theme. Cf. Copleston, *A History of Philosophy*, vol.7, part I (Fichte to Hegel) (Garden City: Doubleday, 1965) 126.

proximately sixty-year career, abided by the themes and program outlined at the age of twenty-one and articulated by age thirty-four? Walter Schulz, in his rejection of the charge, stresses a Schelling who moved in a straight line from beginning to end.[22] This may be to say too much. For, while the line is a continuum, to suggest that it is always straight would not seem warranted. Indeed, there are major changes along the way that ought not to be downplayed in refuting the Schelling caricature. The Philosophy of Freedom and the Philosophy of Mythology and Revelation are, for their part, integrally related. But the Philosophy of Freedom, set out in *Of Human Freedom*, is Schelling's sudden and formal break with his own previous idealism and Philosophy of Identity. It seems correct to say that Schelling had two major phases, the first spanning his youthful writings up to but not including the 1809 treatise *Of Human Freedom*, the latter beginning with the treatise and spanning the forty-five years of his literary silence.

Schelling thus had two philosophies—a Philosophy of Identity and a Philosophy of Freedom. The Philosophy of Mythology and Revelation are part of the Philosophy of Freedom and constitute the farthest point Schelling reached in developing a new and alternative philosophy. This is to argue for considerable continuity between the "early" and the "late" Schelling since the Philosophy of Freedom issued from the pen of a relatively young philosopher.[23] But there was a rupture, a decisive break in his sense of the form and presuppositions of the philosophical system adequate to an exploration of the life of the absolute. His consciousness of human and divine freedom required Schelling to recast his philosophical system before the first cast had itself been completed.

But, in dismissing the Proteus charge, one must also recognize the second philosophy for what it was and what it was not. Like the earlier philosophy, it was not finished, but not because Schelling abandoned it. One might try to maintain that he died before the task was completed. However, as Xavier Tilliette has observed, Schelling had had adequate time to complete it and he never made final revisions even in the lecture manuscripts that he finally designated as his posthumous last word.[24] The *Spätphilosophie* or Late Philosophy was the final installment because of his death. But it was not the logically final piece. His system required and left

---

[22]*Vollendung*, 9.
[23]In 1809 Schelling was 34 years old.
[24]*Schelling: Une philosophie en devenir*, II:17.

unexecuted a ''Philosophy of Existence.'' And it is in no small measure the incompleteness of both the early and the later philosophy that has led critics to view him merely as a transitional figure, in the first instance preparing the way for Hegel, in the second for the existentialists. The ''late philosophy'' was thus only chronologically, but not logically, his ''last'' philosophy, the posthumously published lecture manuscripts that are the only drafted parts of an incompleted system. But the ''late philosophy'' really dates from quite early in Schelling's life. His thinking underwent radical change and the 1809 *Of Human Freedom* is testimony to it. All that followed were not new philosophies but partial drafts of the one same Philosophy of Freedom.

Schelling began his philosophy of religion with the theological presupposition of divine revelation, and by treating it as a historical reality he proposed to develop a historically grounded philosophy. But in so doing, Schelling provided the first instance of a post-Enlightenment philosophy returning to the role of ''handmaiden to theology''—in the very mode that Kant had deplored[25] and in a fashion that theology, for its own reasons, would not welcome. Indeed, in his flight from Hegelian philosophy, Schelling may even be considered unfaithful to modern philosophy, as he changed its fundament from autonomous reason to heteronomous faith. Moreover, just as he claims to have bridged the gap between faith and knowledge, he incurred the displeasure of both ''faithful'' and philosophers and awakened for some the unwelcome suspicion that the ancient span between the shores of faith and reason had only been further widened by his efforts and that the stream that courses between them might have become finally too wide to leap, too deep to wade and too swift to swim.

Curiously, Schelling insisted on being viewed as *philosophical* in his adherence to the *theological* meaning of events revolving around the life of the Son of God from creation to his ascension. Schelling added his own interpretations to such events, as shall be noted, and these interpretations are properly neither theological nor philosophical. Whatever the reasons for adopting theological presuppositions, their inclusion in his philosophy of religion means that Schelling's cannot be philosophy of religion *ac-*

---

[25]Cf. Immanuel Kant, *Der Streit der Fakultäten* (KgS VII), where Kant defines the *ancilla theologiae* role of philosophy as lighting the way rather than holding the train for the ''queen of the sciences.''

cording to the canons of the Age of Reason, and this fact is only underlined by the blend of logic and legends that he frequently employs in argument.

Nevertheless, his Philosophy of Revelation is always more than a catalogue of instructive errors and fanciful excesses. It is a philosophy of religion that tries to build upon the conviction that man is a free being in a free universe that has been created by and is ruled over by a free, personal and living God with whom he is in relation; and that the relation of free man and free God is found not merely in thought but in experience and most centrally in God's free revelation. Freedom is thus the determining ground of what Schelling hoped would be an entirely new philosophy and one in which philosophy of religion would have a culminating role. The freedom of the living God and God's creatures constitutes a radical antithesis to Hegel's philosophy and his philosophy of religion. Yet the emphasis on a living God and evolving humanity that collaborate in fulfilling themselves and each other is one that both Hegel and Schelling share and will to future philosophical attempts to grasp and articulate the meeting of the divine and human.

FREEDOM

The reflection that things are not as they ought to be came early to Schelling, with important professional implications.[26] His idealism and its logic of being can only have rendered his consciousness all the more acute. Moreover, the untimely death of Caroline Schlegel Schelling must have intensified his realization. Once he recognized and accepted that the actual world was not the world that thought would have had him expect,[27] Schelling was driven to seek the reason and, as a result, was soon driven beyond his original Philosophy of Identity and its point of departure in the identity of thought and being. His intention and goal were to confront the problem of human freedom, something that idealism, in his view, had not solved but merely subsumed into necessity. Schelling pursued freedom back to the deity himself and there, out of the hazy sequence: Eternal God—Creation—Fall, derived a new philosophical doctrine of creation. According to it, creation did not issue from pure nothingness (οὐκ ὄν) but from non-

---

[26]For a full discussion of Schelling's path to the Philosophy of Freedom, cf. Alan White, *Schelling: An Introduction to the System of Freedom* (New Haven, Yale University Press, 1983).

[27]This realization was heightened by Hegel's subsequent efforts to incorporate untidy facts of history into his grand teleology.

being (μὴ ὄν). Moreover, he elaborated his theory of creation from non-being in a doctrine of potencies that had important consequences in his theogony and Logos-theology.

The principle of freedom that distinguished and shaped Schelling's philosophy after 1809 is thus not restricted to the human plane. For human freedom is grounded in the radical divine freedom that underlies, sustains and guides creation. The Philosophy of Revelation claims that the same divine freedom is responsible for God's self-revelation. But, he adds, the content of this revelation could never have been known or determined by reason alone; a concept and philosophy of revelation are possible only after the fact of God's free self-disclosure.[28] And in the Philosophy of Revelation, so Schelling claimed, philosophy has expanded to grasp the fact and meaning of God's free, unthinkable *(unvordenklich)* self-manifestation.

That the freedom principle had become fundamental in Schelling's thought as early as the 1809 *Of Human Freedom* constitutes persuasive evidence against the Proteus charge invoked to dismiss and ignore Schelling. Indeed, while it can hardly be argued that all was in place or fully clear by 1809, the case can be forcefully made that by then Schelling already had at least the basis for what would be his "last system" and that he abided by it.[29] *Of Human Freedom* represented the outlines of this system, with the mainlines becoming clear by the time of the unpublished *Lectures on the Ages of the World* or *Weltalter* (1811-1815).[30]

While unremarkable from the theological side, Schelling's assertion of both divine and human freedom was philosophical rebellion against the dawning Age of Idealism. And because of it, Heidegger deemed *Of Human Freedom* "the treatise that undermined Hegel's *Logic* before the *Logic* appeared."[31] Heidegger defines Schelling's freedom as in effect a "non-sensuous feeling"[32] and terms the feeling of human freedom "the original

---

[28]This is as antithetical to Hegel's notion of God's necessary self-manifestation as it is to Heidegger's notion of the poet's forcing Being into unconcealedness.

[29]This is the argument of Horst Fuhrmans, although Fuhrmans ascribes a clarity to Schelling's vision that strikes this writer as unwarranted.

[30]*Schelling: The Ages of the World*, trans. Frederick de Wolfe Bowman, Jr. (New York: Columbia University Press, 1942).

[31]Martin Heidegger, *Schellings Abhandlug über das Wesen der menschlichen Freiheit*, ed. Hildegard Feich (Tübingen: Niemayer Verlag, 1971) 117.

[32]*Schellings Abhandlung*, 18. This is akin to the definition of *prajna* in Buddhist thought, although Heidegger makes no reference to it.

feeling for the unity of all being in and out of its ground."[33] But Schelling, Heidegger observes, describes it as the capacity for good and evil.[34] Heidegger stresses the conjunction "and," observing that the recognition of the role of evil alters the definition of freedom at its base.[35] In order to preserve his fledgling concept of freedom from being reabsorbed by idealism, Schelling had refused to view freedom as standing in dialectical relationship with an antithetical concept of necessity. Instead, for Schelling, freedom is viewed as consisting of necessity and necessity consisting of freedom.[36] As Fuhrmans observes, Schelling's struggle is with the dialectical method of idealist philosophy itself and Schelling wished to point to a form of being with an undialectical structure. This form is freedom.[37]

The separation between freedom and necessity remained the most fundamental category distinction for Schelling's philosophy. It was more fundamental than the difference between essence and existence that, because it is not fundamental enough, led only to error in a philosophy based upon it. Here Schelling of course had Hegelianism in mind. It is also more fundamental than the difference between possibility and actuality. For Schelling, only a philosophy that built from the deepest fundament and that recognized the non-dialectical relationship between fundamental categories could issue in a correct philosophical system. His point is two-sided: Hegelian philosophy—dialectical, built on the logical relationship between being and nonbeing—is not fundamental enough; his own new philosophy builds on a fundamental, non-dialectical relationship as manifested in the phenomenon/feeling of freedom, rather than in an idea. The consequences of this position soon become clear: all philosophy, including philosophy of religion, must be rearticulated in light of this new perspective. And religion must be understood as the "unthinkable" story of God's freedom in restoring mankind from fall.

The content and presuppositions of philosophy are to change, but not the form. For, if Schelling rejected idealism's fundament, he never rejected the idea of system and so pursued a "system of freedom." But this goal, explicitly stated in the Munich lectures[38] and partially executed in the

[33]Ibid., 82-83.
[34]SW VII:352.
[35]Heidegger, *Schellings Abhandlung,* 120.
[36]Cf. Kasper, *Das Absolute in der Geschichte,* 212.
[37]Horst Fuhrmans, *Schellings letzte Philosophie* (Berlin, 1940) 175.
[38]SW X:36.

Lectures on the Philosophy of Revelation, was never fully attained—perhaps because, as Heidegger observed on this point, "system" and "freedom" are so incompatible that a "system of freedom" is tantamount to a square circle.[39]

Since human existence is free, a mere science of reason is ipso facto incapable of grasping the realities of existence. Free existence is a form of being that is outside of thought, one that can be grasped by a mode of knowledge *(Erkennen)* that is in concourse with reality and not merely with ideas.[40] Hence a new kind of philosophy is demanded—not a philosophy of logical necessity (= Hegel) but a historical philosophy of actualized freedom.[41]

But the new philosophy demanded by the fact of human freedom must also give account of the freedom of God at its base. And Schelling's final philosophy had the task of accounting for and reconciling God's essentially in-itself completed being with the freedom that he exercises.[42] His philosophy also has to account for the source, which is revelation. Schelling reads it as a record of God's freedom (rather than of Hegelian necessity). Hegel's philosophy knew what God's life must be and reinterpreted historical revelation to reflect it. Schelling claimed that we can come to no knowledge of God's life without God's own revelation. Accepting God's self-revelation and its contents is to rescue philosophy from otherwise ignorance of God's life, but doing so proves philosophically a costly leap of faith. For it takes place on the basis of theological claims and testimony about revelation rather than on any strictly philosophical basis.

Freedom and Fall

Of Human Freedom's agenda includes why man is free, how God is free and is the basis of human freedom, and how there is evil in the world. Schelling is heir to the Zoroastrian heritage of the West in his themes of good vs. evil and in the familiar imagery of light and darkness. The darkness-evil linkage, while not new, is novel nonetheless. For Schelling posits a darkness as the source of all potential and hence as the source of both good and evil. Out of darkness came both good and evil. "For the process

---

[39]Heidegger, *Schellings Abhandlung,* 25.

[40]Fuhrmans, *Schellings letzte Philosophie,* 140.

[41]Cf. Lecture Twenty-Four. The anti-Hegelian tone is apparent here and throughout the *Lectures on the Philosophy of Revelation.*

[42]Cf. Fuhrmans, *Schellings letzte Philosophie,* 64.

of creation consists only in an inner transmutation, or revelation in light of what was originally the principle of darkness.''[43]

In sum, freedom has its base in the dark ground of God in which the possibility of both good and evil is contained. God creates what is good. But within his creation is a creature endowed with freedom and hence with the potential to choose or actualize good and/or evil. The history of human freedom includes the choice of actualizing evil and the original order of creation was thereby perverted. The aboriginal unity was shattered and evil, which ought not to have been, was actualized. Certain emphases are plain even in this brief sketch. Above all, humankind itself is responsible for evil. No evil spirit tempts in Schelling's account; the blame cannot be shifted or shared. God created a good world that mankind corrupted. God is thereby absolved from responsibility for evil—even while the possibility of evil is located in the dark ground of God's own being, not in some outside source. Schelling will avoid all Manicheanism here, and even the Zoroastrian elevation of intermediary spirits who share responsibility. In the theodicy that results, Schelling avoids all radical dualisms and locates evil within God himself while preserving the goodness of God. But God himself seems to have become dualistic in the process. He is not, to be sure, a God of good and evil. But he is a God of light and darkness —the latter being his dark ground that contains all potentiality. Evil arose from this dark ground, but not immediately. The world and humankind, themselves products of the dark ground, contain potential and, alas, actualize evil. For it was not necessary that evil be actualized (unlike Hegel's account). To underline this point, Schelling stressed the fact that God does not need the world (without which there would have been no actualization of evil).[44]

SCHELLING'S PHILOSOPHICAL RETURN TO CHRISTIANITY

Schelling's earliest philosophical standpoint had been unmistakably critical of Christianity. In this he shared in the Enlightenment mood toward historical religion, as well as in the "spell" that Ancient Greece held

---

[43]SW VII:362.

[44]He does not thereby entirely escape the rebukes of his French Enlightenment predecessors for philosophical attempts to justify God, and one might well imagine a Voltaire reacting to the account of a God who does not need a world but then creates one anyway and, alas, one that manifests so many evils. The *philosophe* might well have observed that, perhaps if God *had* needed the world, he might have created a better one.

over nineteenth-century Germany.[45] Schelling ultimately reconciled "Athens" and "Jerusalem," but in his own fashion. For the youthful Schelling, however, Athens held a clear prestige advantage. How negatively Schelling actually felt about Christianity is still debated. Even his 1802 *Lectures on University Studies,* while more theologically interested than anything from the period of his formal theological studies, still mirrors the biases of Enlightenment writers toward traditional Christianity. Thus Schelling remarked that a true understanding of Christianity was hampered by the Bible and he thus praised Roman Catholic discouragement of Scripture reading. Moreover, he went on to call for a "rebirth of esoteric Christianity and the Gospel of the Absolute."[46] The spectre of German idealism is still evident in such a phrase. The philosophical orientation toward religion is clear, along with a skeptical attitude toward the traditional, biblical view. Philosophical ideas constitute access to the highest truths at this early point in Schelling's thought, and this includes the truths contained in Christianity, nor does this standpoint change, even as he develops new respect for the content of Christianity.

His sharing the inclinations of the *philosophes* raises questions about him too being a modern day pagan at this point in his development. In this connection, one thinks of his youthful (and characteristically 18th century) Epicurean Profession of Faith of 1779, with its simple identification of nature and the divine. In addition, there is the more explicit remark:

> Everything divine is human, and everything human divine. This phrase of the ancient Hippocrates, taken from the depths of life, was and still is the key to the greatest discoveries in the realm of God and nature.[47]

Was Schelling a pantheist? Horst Fuhrmans argues forcefully, if not convincingly, for a clearly *theistic* position on Schelling's part from earliest on and distinguishes only between an initial phase of "immanent theism" and a later "transcendent theism" in Schelling's development. Thus while conceding the emphasis upon the immanence of the divine in the early Schelling, Fuhrmans contends that this did not constitute panthe-

---

[45]Cf. E. M. Butler, *The Tyranny of Greece over Germany* (Cambridge, 1935) for a very rich exploration of this cultural phenomenon.

[46]SW V:301, 305; *On University Studies,* trans. E. S. Morgan (Athens OH: Ohio University Press, 1966) 102.

[47]This remark dates from the 1813 manuscript of the *Weltalter* or *Ages of the World;* SW VIII:292; quoted and translated by Robert F. Brown in *The Later Philosophy of Schelling* (Lewisburg PA: Bucknell University Press, 1977) 231 n.11.

ism as such, despite the look of it. He maintains, furthermore, that the shift toward transcendent theism is observable as early as 1809, under the influence of Baader, Böhme, Oetinger and Hamann, and that it crystallizes into a full transcendent theism in the late philosophy.[48] Furhmans'construing apparent pantheism as imminent theism seems strained, but his main point is more important: that Schelling shifts and that the final standpoint is theism.

What is clear is that the youthful Schelling, like his seminary classmates Hegel and Hölderlin but also like so many others in the dawning Romantic period, had moved away from a paltry Christianity to the robust polytheism/pantheism of an idealized Greek world. In this, however, Schelling trod the whole path, in advance of the Romantics. For, finding the sublime creations of Greek art to be in time cold and lifeless, he made his way once again toward Christianity. Schelling thus avoided a rupture with Christianity. He also avoided the Romantic embrace of Roman Catholicism, despite accusations of inclining toward Rome and this being reflected in his long residence in Catholic Munich. His important interest in mysticism and flirtation with theosophy lend a gnostic tone to this standpoint. But even if his final standpoint were deemed gnostic, it would have to be seen as a new Christian gnosticism and not a revived pagan form. For Schelling finally returned from his intellectual interlude in an idealized Athens, without thereby ending up in either Second Temple Jerusalem or Renaissance Rome.

The return was accomplished by 1815,[49] while evidence for its being underway is present as early as the 1802 *Lectures on University Studies* that in places otherwise seem so arch-critical of traditional Christianity. The 1802 Lectures present the notion of Christianity as a *living* religion that, precisely because living, cannot be restricted to the frozen words and concepts of the Bible. Its special truth is held to be speculative rather than historical.[50] Moreover, the historicity of the New Testament is not important for understanding the real truth of Christianity. Indeed, it is more important to know about other world religions in order to grasp Christianity properly as religion. For, in religions such as that of India, central ideas of Christianity, such as incarnation, already existed. And trinity is found there

---

[48]Fuhrmans, *Schellings Philosophie der Weltalter*, 288, 301-302.
[49]Fuhrmans, *Schellings letzte Philosophie*, 51.
[50]SW V:301, 304; *On University Studies*, 97 and 100-101.

as well, observes Schelling in his own revival of the "logos spermatikos" argument of early Christian apologetics.[51] As early as 1802 then, Schelling spoke of transcending scriptures and reconstructing Christianity based on a broad notion of religion and a philosophical reinterpretation of its content. His emphasis was upon its esoteric, inner truth that he saw value in preserving. The exoteric form, for its part, was only secondary and was regarded as incapable of permanent form, in doctrine or otherwise. Thus the esoteric is stressed, and hence the call for the "rebirth of esoteric Christianity and the Gospel of the Absolute."

This early program statement was both highly idealistic and genuinely Schellingian. For on Schelling's part it indicated the desire to find an accommodation with Christianity, while the method—grasp of its inner truth—was characteristic of idealism. Other important thinkers of the period acted similarly. The content of the "inner" truth simply varied from one to another: morality for Rousseau and Kant, the idea for Hegel and the youthful Schelling.

Schelling's concern with a recoverable Christianity intensified after his 1802 program statement, even as the program itself changed. He went on to an ever deeper confrontation with Christian belief that ultimately led to a "weeding out" of his pantheistic inclinations.[52] The notion of access to the truth of Christianity through the idea was ultimately discarded when he broke with idealism, and his final position, as expressed in the Philosophy of Revelation, is perhaps best termed "speculative theism"—theism, because it centers on a living God; speculative, because speculative reason is assigned the role of filling out the meaning of the truths historically and inchoately revealed in the Christian religion.[53]

The return to Christianity was, however, not an embrace of orthodoxy. And even as late as the Philosophy of Revelation, Schelling had no hesitancy in maintaining his distance from it. And so he says,

> For me it is not a matter of agreeing with any one church teaching. I have no interest in being orthodox, as it is called, just as I would have no difficulty in being the opposite. For me, Christianity is merely a phenomenon that I seek to *explain*. What the sense or proper meaning of Christianity

---

[51]SW V:299; Schelling, *On University Studies,* trans. E. S. Morgan (Athens OH: Ohio University Press, 1966) 95.

[52]Fuhrmans, *Schellings letzte Philosophie,* 27.

[53]Tilliette, *Schelling, une philosophie en devenir,* II:103, and Fuhrmans, *Schellings letzte Philosophie,* 189.

may be, however, must be judged according to its own authentic records.[54]

At one point in the lectures, Schelling went as far as to say that he could not possibly aim to be orthodox and carry out the Philosophy of Revelation authentically at the same time. Hence he defended himself against the possible "reproach" of being orthodox:

> One will perhaps reproach the Philosophy of Revelation for being orthodox (for it is a reproach to most). However, we are not dealing here with orthodoxy —I reject that, since it would provide an entirely false standpoint for the Philosophy of Revelation. In fact, it is all the same to me what dogmatics sets out or asserts. It is not my task and it is not the task of a philosopher to agree with any of them.[55]

And even while maintaining New Testament phrases and church doctrines in name and form, he remarked quite candidly, "I shall not assert that the author of the gospel thought the same thing by an expression as we do," and then continued, "That is also entirely unnecessary."[56] Yet the same lecturer did not see this as leading to inauthentic Christian teaching. On the contrary, he thought that his philosophy would finally uncover the truth that scripture and doctrine revolved around but frequently missed.

In his return to Christianity, reason remained the standard even if he noted its limits. Only reason could articulate the true content and meaning of Christian teaching. Hence Schelling's theism required speculative reason to bring out the true, deeper meaning. The Philosophy of Revelation did not reject the esoteric interest of the *Lectures on University Studies,* but it emphasized doctrines and affirmed the history of Christianity in a way that the earlier work did not.

BIPOLAR GOD

The evolution in Schelling's God-concept revolves around not only the nature of God but the mode of experiencing him. In the early Philosophy of Identity, God was held to be the point of indifference, and intellectual intuition was the experience of the meeting point where differences vanish. It was asserted, moreover, that, if one were to raise intellectual intuition to "original" intellectual intuition, one would come to knowledge of

---

[54]SW XIV:201.
[55]SW XIV:80.
[56]SW XIV:177.

the absolute. But, if God is the point of indifference and if all being belongs to God as identity, then all differences are nothing more than ap-
pearances, as Hegel noted in his famous barb about this amounting to a
night in which all cows are black.[57] Recognizing the difficulty that Hegel
pointed to, Schelling then sought a way of allowing God to be indifference
but also of letting all that contradicts this be included in God. The solution,
which points the way to the late philosophy in which ecstasy (as well as
revelation itself) is stressed as experience of God, led Schelling to posit
God as in unity with himself at the same time as he recognized as real all
that is negative and contradictory of God's unity and to think it, furthermore, as contained within God himself. The reality of unity and of contradiction is posited in the new God-concept in *Of Human Freedom* that
describes two equally eternal beginnings in a God who has two poles: (1)
God as conscious subject and (2)the dark ground of God that is not conscious, that is inseparable from God and yet also different.

The dark ground is not only ground for the becoming of all that is not
God (namely, the world) but also for the becoming of God himself. With
this notion, Schelling sought to describe a living God who is his own creator and who is ground and creator of both that which will be apart from
him and that which he himself will become. But the condition for the possibility of a becoming, existing God is at the same time the condition for
the possibility of good and evil.[58] Furthermore, the notion of a becoming
God ultimately connects with the notion of revelation. Addressing this
point, Heidegger remarks,

> Man must be, so that God can be revealed. What is a God without men?
> The absolute form of absolute boredom. What is man without God? Pure
> madness in the shape of harmlessness.[59]

Self-revelation belongs to the essence of an existing God, of a God who
comes forward from his ground.

The bipolar God-concept revolutionized Schelling's philosophical
standpoint and contained within it an explanation of freedom, both divine
and human, and explanation of fall and the seeds of theodicy. Evil could
now be understood as real without positing some demigod as its source.
For evil proceeds from the dark ground of God. The notion included all

---

[57] In the preface to the *Phänomenologie des Geistes* (Hoffmeister edition, page 19).
[58] Cf. Heidegger, *Schellings Abhandlung*, 143.
[59] Ibid.

within God's being yet at the time allowed for difference and contradiction of God's essential goodness—even to the extent of positing evil as real and grounded in God— without thereby compromising the goodness of God or being obliged to embrace good/evil dualism. How can a good God permit evil? The age-old question of theodicy found a new response in Schelling: All that is and that has come to be proceeds from the dark ground of God— including that which ought not to be. Why is there not perfection from the beginning? Simply put: because God is a living God.[60]

The becoming of God—or theogony—was central in Schelling's new God-concept. Schelling was not the first to emphasize it, as he well knew. Fichte had already stressed God as becoming being.[61] Hegel was similarly disposed and would go on to give the epoch-making formulation to the dynamism of God's being. Schelling's notion was nonetheless distinctive. In the 1802 *Lectures on University Studies,* Fichte's influence was discernible as Schelling re-embraced a trinitarian notion of God's being and stressed that being as becoming:

> the eternal Son of God, born of the essence of the Father of all things, is the finite itself, as it exists in God's eternal intuition; this finite manifests itself as a suffering God, subject to the vicissitudes of time, who at the culmination of his career, in the person of Christ, closes the world of the finite and opens the world of the infinite, i.e., the reign of the Spirit.[62]

In 1802, the emphasis was largely speculative and the historical had not yet received its due. *Of Human Freedom* in 1809 returned to the notion of a suffering, becoming god as it pointed out that all life is subject to suffering and development and that God freely submits to this as well.[63] "All history remains incomprehensible without the concept of a humanly suffering God." In God's life, the principal moment of philosophical interest for Schelling's philosophy was that of the incarnation of the Son in whom God's suffering reaches culmination. One must note, however, that the becoming of the Son was not restricted to the life and death of Jesus of Nazareth, either in this early formulation or subsequently. Schelling stressed the incarnation of God as not taking place all at once but rather as proceeding from all eternity. Thus he wrote in 1802:

---

[60]*Of Human Freedom;* SW VII:403. This God is also implicitly a limited God, at least until he achieves perfection in his life.

[61]Cf. Fuhrmans, *Schellings letzte Philosophie,* 24.

[62]SW V:294; *On University Studies,* 91.

[63]*On Human Freedom;* SW VII: 403.

> The process of God's becoming man has been going on from all eternity. The culmination of this process is Christ's assuming visible human form, and for this reason it is also a beginning; starting with Christ, it has been going on ever since —all of his successors are members of one and the same body of which he is the head.[64]

In 1809 the teleological dimension is clearer:

> Indeed, in order to encounter personal and spiritual evil, light appears in personal and human form, and comes as mediator in order to reestablish the relationship between creation and God on the highest level. For only personality can make whole what is personal, and God must become man in order that man may be brought back to God.[65]

REVELATION

Schelling's mature philosophy began in the Philosophy of Identity's attempt to grasp the absolute as it is in itself. Access to the absolute had been thought to be the ego. But Schelling had discovered a moment in the ego that was not strictly human and was thus forced to move beyond the human ego of Fichte, first to absolute ego and then beyond the ego since the realization of God's freedom pointed to a different source of knowledge of the absolute. This new knowledge was not knowledge of the absolute ''as it is in itself'' but as it *had been* and *is, in history.* Moreover, thought had never arrived at the source of this knowledge—God's historical self-revelation. Not only could speculative logic not account for the world as it really is, as over against what abstract thought would lead one to expect, but it could also not account for decisive, actual, free-and-unexpectable happenings without recourse to simple reductionism. Access to the fact of revelation came solely through the event of God's revelation (this, of course, in contrast to Hegel) and access to its full meaning through the Philosophy of Revelation.

In the 1802 *Lectures on University Studies,* Schelling had already spoken of the reality of God's revelation as idea.[66] And because God reveals, he maintained, Christianity as the highest religion must take God's revelation as a central notion. This conviction endured even as the content of revelation changed in his thinking. In 1809 he had already advanced to the

---

[64]SW V:298; *On University Studies,* 89.
[65]*On Human Freedom;* SW VII:380.
[66]SW V:292-93; *On University Studies,* 89.

notion that ''The procession of things from God is God's self-revelation. But God can only reveal himself in creatures who resemble him, in free, self-activating beings.''[67]

PHILOSOPHY AND RELIGION

The relationship between philosophy and religion is a constant theme in Schelling's writings. It is particularly emphasized in the 1802 *Lectures on University Studies,* in the 1804 essay *Philosophy and Religion,* and in the 1809 treatise *Of Human Freedom.* It is also a theme of the Philosophy of Revelation of 1827 and following. In 1804, Schelling declared philosophy the truth of religion, in an idealist position that might equally have issued from Hegel. But Schelling never appears to have been prepared to go as far as Hegel went. For Schelling, philosophy was limited to understanding *(Verstand).* Even in his early idealist philosophy, it was not *Vernunft* or reason that had access to identity and the ideal but religion. Philosophy belongs to ''this side,'' religion to ''the beyond.'' For philosophy concerns itself with differentiation, while it is religion that finds the way to indifference. As Fuhrmans observes on this point, ''The absolute identity, however, is present only in faith, in presentiment, and thereby in the realm of religion. Religion stands essentially above philosophy on that account.''[68]

Religion brings one to the absolute of which philosophy has knowledge. But knowledge is not experience of the absolute. Schelling's placing of his ultimate faith in faith itself rather than in reason thus dates from his early career. Philosophy may aim to be an a priori science and to provide knowledge of things as they are in themselves and as they ought to be. But since things are not such, the a priori science only provides knowledge of how they were supposed to be. The ambition of arriving at indifference, or unity with the absolute, remained a goal; but Schelling recognized that philosophy was not the unifier. As a result, philosophy had to become more modest. It may illuminate factual reality and attempt to discern the deeper sense in what may appear to be non-sense. To get beyond these limits, one

---

[67]*Of Human Freedom;* SW VII:347. Despite the freedom context and emphasis in his *Of Human Freedom,* Schelling states in two places—p. 374 and p. 402—that God must *necessarily* reveal himself, that he had to reveal himself or else inwardness would have triumphed over love. Such remarks take less distance from the Hegelian necessity of God's life than he would no doubt wish.

[68]*Schellings letzte Philosophie,* 31.

has recourse to faith and religion. The Philosophy of Revelation strived to show that, once one gets beyond the limitations of a priori philosophy and of *Verstand* (without falling into the realm of Hegelian *Vernunft*), philosophy could again be of service in bringing out the full sense of the new and higher truths of God's self-revelation in the history of religions.

"NEGATIVE" AND "POSITIVE" PHILOSOPHY

Schelling's reflections on the philosophy-religion relationship culminated in the decisive refinement between "negative" and "positive" philosophy. *Of Human Freedom* proclaimed a new philosophical program based on the radical insight into the reality and implications of freedom. It rendered Schelling's own previous philosophical efforts negative and set him in search of a positive philosophy to counterbalance it. From the new standpoint, the view of "negative philosophy" was at first quite negative. Only much later did Schelling attempt to portray negative philosophy in a more favorable light, as having genuinely contributed to the establishment of positive philosophy.[69]

For Schelling, all of philosophy revolves around the possible. But negative philosophy revolves *merely* around the possible, while positive philosophy revolves around the possible that has been actualized.[70] Schelling thus called for two philosophies and their unification in a broadened definition of philosophy. His program remained incomplete. For he never completed the positive philosophy, nor did he rewrite a negative philosophy from the higher standpoint. The result is that Schelling's own "negative philosophy" comes to mean his own earlier Philosophy of Identity and "positive philosophy" the large fragments published published posthumously as his late philosophy.

The clarion call for a new philosophy had been provoked by Hegel's identification of logic and metaphysics. Schelling countered with the assertion that logic and metaphysics have fundamentally different tasks. Since both are valid, philosophy must include both, but separately, in a two-part philosophy. With this new program, Schelling abandoned the aim of achieving one all-encompassing science of philosophy,[71] although he later

---

[69]It is by no means incidental that the positive appraisal of negative philosophy comes only after the death of Hegel who, for Schelling, had become the principal proponent of negative philosophy.

[70]Schulz, *Vollendung*, 81.

[71]Cf. Kasper, *Das Absolute*, 105.

tried to articulate a unity of negative and positive philosophies. The implications for idealism were clear: it was not to be rescued or corrected internally.[72] Nothing less than a new point of departure was demanded that would redefine philosophy and reassess all previous philosophies. Schelling found precedence for the positive philosophy in Plato's *Timaeus,* while Aristotle became the prototype of negative philosophy.[73] In setting up this contrast, Schelling clearly suggested that he was playing "Plato" to Hegel's "Aristotle" and wished to proclaim the restoration and final triumph of the Platonic principle.[74]

The line between the two parts of philosophy was unclear then and remains so. But if the demarcation is imprecise, it is not imperceptible. The new positive philosophy defined itself both negatively and positively: negatively in that it sought to overcome pantheism and idealism, positively in that it professed its own new source, namely, revelation. But the relationship between negative and positive philosophies is unclear in that the end of negative philosophy is *not* the beginning of positive philosophy. For the ultimate point of the negative philosophy is a *concept* of God, not an actual and existing God. Schelling is forced beyond any claim of two *equal* parts. For the relationship between the two philosophies is hierarchical.[75]

---

[72]As in the manner of I. H. Fichte who had attempted to make it theistic. Cf. Kasper, *Das Absolute,* 105.

[73]Fuhrmans, *Schellings Philosophie der Weltalter,* 286-87.

[74]Since the call for a new philosophy was so highly personal in tone and in the perceived objects of criticism, its audience responded in kind, and frequently with excess. Jakob Salat, for example, mocked the entire affair as he suggested that "positive philosophy" was pleonasm and that "negative philosophy" was a contradiction in terms (quoted by Tilliette, *Schelling, une philosophie en devenir,* II 38). And Søren Kierkegaard expressed his growing disillusionment with Schelling's 1841 Lectures in an ironic letter back to Copenhagen in which he mused about the possibility of earning future degrees in *both* philosophies—once Professor Schelling had actually made clear what his new philosophy was supposed to be. (Letter of 14 December 1841 to Emil Boesen; *Kierkegaard's Writings* XX:104.)

Kierkegaard is being characteristically sharp in such a remark, but there is truth to his point that Schelling had not made sufficiently clear what the exact difference between the positive and negative philosophies was —except that Schelling's was to be the new, higher and positive philosophy, while Hegel represented the negative that was now superseded.

[75]Kasper (*Das Absolute,* 143) offers the following useful schematization for the negative and positive philosophies:

	Negative Philosophy	Positive Philosophy
point of departure	before experience, relative Prius	above experience, absolute Prius
mode of proceeding	necessary	free
relation to experience	confirming	demonstrating
result	concept of God	actuality of God.

PHILOSOPHY OF MYTHOLOGY

While Schelling's Philosophy of Mythology chronologically belongs to his late philosophy, it logically belongs to what Schelling termed negative philosophy.[76] It is more than negative philosophy but not positive philosophy. The concept of mythology had become important in Schelling's thinking even before revelation became so.[77] At first he called for a new mythology. Later he distinguished between mythology and revelation and cited them as opposite, if related, concepts. Mythology for Schelling was, above all, not some kind of aberration in human religious history, nor was it witness to the level to which humankind had fallen away from God prior to the saving events of Christianity, as many had previously held.[78] For Schelling, mythology is part of the larger process by which the God-idea has been restored. Mythology thus contributed to the movement that was fulfilled in Christ.[79] Schelling viewed mythology, however, as a blind and *unfree* process by which the God-idea moved back to its original condition, in a development from polytheism to monotheism. And it culminated in its very opposite: God's *free* self-revelation.[80]

The importance of the concept of mythology was emphasized by a summary of the Philosophy of Mythology in the Philosophy of Revelation. Philosophy of Mythology belongs to the orbit of the Philosophy of Revelation,[81] as religious preparation for revelation, just as negative philosophy is the philosophical preparation.[82] While many details of his philosophical reading of mythology were taken askance in the 19th century and are even more questionable today when a science of mythology has developed, Schelling's Philosophy of Mythology should be regarded as part of the cultural recovery of mythology. Moreover, many have found in it enduringly rich suggestions for grasping myths, even if they do not accept Schelling's overall viewpoint.

---

[76]Tilliette, *Schelling, une philosophie en devenir*, II:343.

[77]Cf. Hermann Zeltner, *Schelling* (Stuttgart: Fromanns Verlag, 1954) 223.

[78]For a fuller discussion of this theme, cf. Vladimir Jankélévitch, *L-Odysée de la Conscience dans la dernière Philosophie de Schelling* (Paris: Librairie Felix Alcan, 1932) 226ff.

[79]Kasper, *Das Absolute*, 354.

[80]Cf. Copleston, *A History of Philosophy*, 7:172.

[81]Cf. Tilliette. *Schelling, une philosophie en devenir*, II:300.

[82]If one takes the Philosophies of Mythology and Revelation together, one has a parallel to Hegel's philosophy of the history of religions, with the important difference (emphasized by Schelling) that historical revelation, following the necessary mythological process, is utterly free.

"POSITIVE PHILOSOPHY" AND "PHILOSOPHY OF REVELATION"

Schelling sought to distinguish between ''positive philosophy'' and ''Philosophy of Revelation.'' The latter is a part of the larger whole, but it is the sole portion that Schelling completed. From Schelling's standpoint, the Philosophy of Revelation is an application of positive philosophy to the historical fact and content of God's free revelation in Christianity. Philosophy of revelation was thus a positive ''science of reality,'' rather than a philosophy of mere possibility.

Schelling further stressed the free character of revelation in his emphasis upon its a priori inaccessibility. Thought, as reflection, can think revelation after the fact, or a posteriori, but could not, Schelling maintained, arrive at revelation by thought alone. It is, in itself, *unvordenklich* or ''unthinkable.''[83] Philosophy is a remembering of happenings that are part of the story of humankind and of its interaction with the divine and, by applying speculative reason to revelation, Schelling could reconstruct events before human history. They are recoverable because God, as the transcendent-made-immanent, has made himself to be the content of reason.[84]

Philosophy of Revelation as Philosophy of Christianity

The Philosophy of Revelation is not the whole of the positive philosophy, as has been observed above, and may more aptly be termed ''philosophy of Christianity'': a philosophy that accepts facts of Christian history as philosophical facts and is determined by Christian theological tenets, most notably confession of a metaphysical and transcendent dimension to certain facts in the life of Jesus of Nazareth. It is thus a philosophy that infuses facts with Christian faith. (For Jesus of Nazareth as Lord and Logos is not of course a matter of historical fact but of faith.) It proceeds no longer from and by reason *alone* but only by reason *subsequent* to adopting a standpoint of faith. Schelling is fully aware of his method of procedure. And in thus proceeding, he emphatically and self-consciously broke not

---

[83]Schelling's point is clear enough, but his category of the *Unvordenklich* is exaggerated. Surely the atheist who hears so many claims about historical revelations has no trouble in reducing them to vain imaginings—in short, to thoughts that are *not* facts and that, from his standpoint, the human mind has been able to manufacture. One must step inside the closed circle of faith—and of Schelling's particular faith—to accept his claim. Its point—freedom—is more important.

[84]Cf. Schulz, *Die Vollendung*, 327.

only with the idealist treatment of religion and Christianity but also with the entire Enlightenment heritage that had sought to reconcile Christianity and philosophy on the basis of philosophy. Schelling accepted Christianity as a given and sought to find a philosophy—to *found* a philosophy—that explained Christianity as given. Many of the "facts" were already a hybrid of history and speculation, for example, Jesus of Nazareth as incarnate Logos. That Schelling claimed his philosophy was *a posteriori* only made the matter more difficult. For the Philosophy of Revelation does not dwell on the philosophical truth of events in the life of Jesus of Nazareth that could reasonably be termed a posteriori but is far more concerned with pre- and post-historical phases in the life of the Logos and of God himself.

The incarnation of Christ became a central event in his philosophy. The Philosophy of Mythology traced the development of religion up to this "free event," which the Philosophy of Revelation identifies as the central event in human history and in the becoming of God, and not only for humankind but for God's own life (theogony) as well.

THEOGONY: THE BECOMING OF THE TRIUNE GOD

CONTEXT: THE 1841 LECTURES

Schelling's *Lectures on the Philosophy of Revelation* were a dramatic event. The royal summons, Hegel's partisans, Schelling's long silence— all contributed to the air of excitement. Not a few resented Schelling simply because he had agreed to be the king's philosopher and mocked him for needing a royal summons to do what he himself termed his philosophical duty.[85] Schelling was fully aware of the dramatic setting and rose, at least oratorically, to the challenge. He expected an opposition, but was overly sensitive to criticism nevertheless. In Lecture Ten, for example, he tried to silence criticism by warning that those who attack a system also attack the intention of the philosopher.[86] But even sympathetic anti-Hegelians were not won over.

Since expectations of the 1841 Lectures were unrealistic on all sides, Karl Hegel may have said it best when he remarked that less vainglory or boastfulness would have diminished the eventual failure of the enter-

---

[85]Cf. C. L. Michelet, "Schellings erste Vorlesung in Berlin," quoted in Frank, ed., *F. W. J. Schelling: Philosophie der Offenbarung*, 436.
[86]SW XIII:201.

prise.[87] The opening lectures contain oratory appropriate to the original setting. But prosaic hours follow, and the reading audience tires of repetitions perhaps allowable in a lecture setting. The manuscript might have been better prepared for publication. But this is an editorial matter rather than a philosophical one. In an editing, a thematic organization might have been made, such as is given below.

Thematic Schematization
of the *Lectures on the Philosophy of Revelation*

I. Call for a New Philosophy, in order to understand God's life in human history —the intersection of divine and human becoming (Lectures 1, 9)
   A. What the New Philosophy is (Lectures 2, 5, 6, 7, 9, 24)
   B. What the Old Philosophy is (Lectures 3, 5, 6, 8, 9, 24)
   C. Relation of Philosophy and Religion (Lecture 4)
II. God and His Life: Theogony, Potencies, Creation, Trinity (Lectures 12, 13, 14, 15, 16, 17, 32)
III. Religion and its Role in God's Life:
   A. Mythology and the Movement toward Monotheism (Lectures 18, 19, 20, 21, 22, 23)
   B. Paganism and Judaism (Lectures 27, 29)
IV. Christology and its Role in God's Life (Lectures 25, 26, 27, 28, 30, 31)
V. Christianity and the Christian Church (Lectures 33, 36, 37)
VI. Other Topics:
   A. Death and Essentification (Lecture 32)
   B. Satan (Lecture 34)
   C. Angels (Lecture 35)

The Lectures thus have a discernible order, evidence natural development and have three principal theses: (1) the trinitarian becoming of God in history, (2) the incarnation of the Logos in humanity as a moment in God's becoming, and (3) the final achievement of a positive philosophy that is able to grasp philosophically what this means and how it has occurred.

---

[87]Frank, ed., *F. W. J. Schelling: Philosophie der Offenbarung*, 447.

The standpoint of the Lectures, with its theological presupposition about the fact of God's revelation, is nowhere more important than in the philosophical Christology and Christianity of the lectures. In this, Schelling confesses a Christ of Pauline-Johannine faith, but the distance he goes beyond the Gospel of John and the Letters of Paul is fueled by pure speculation. John and Paul are only the starting points and would sometimes appear to be only oracles for Schelling: inspired writers expressing, sometimes unclearly, a higher truth that it is now up to philosophy to understand and articulate.

GOD AND HIS LIFE

Schelling's God-concept is so central to the Philosophy of Revelation that one might well say that it *is* the Philosophy of Revelation. For all its major themes are in effect an elaboration of God's life. At the same time, there is an existential ring to Schelling's speculative theism, and later existentialist formulae can be superimposed upon the God-concept. For example, while Schelling would hold that God is perfect from all eternity, God's historical becoming is held to be part of his essence, and thus it would not be incorrect to paraphrase Sartre and to say that God's existence precedes his (historical) essence. There is, in addition, an existential motive behind Schelling's philosophy of religion. Simply put, for Schelling it was *existentially* important to arrive at the correct philosophical formula to express the idea of God. Only a philosophy whose concepts were adequate to the absolute could claim for itself the title of true science or knowledge. And to know was an existential accomplishment of the highest order. Schelling shared such ambitions and values with many of his contemporaries in philosophy and theology. As a young idealist he had believed that it was within the power of reason to construct a system of the highest knowledge. From *Of Human Freedom* onwards, we know, his standpoint shifted decisively. But if reason, as a priori knowledge, was insufficient to fulfilling the ambition of a philosophy adequate to the absolute, Schelling did not on that account abandon the ambition. He merely recognized the limits of reason and sought other means. Philosophy could still be the science of the absolute if it incorporated a posteriori knowledge of God, for which God himself was the source. Reason thus limited, the philosopher had to be more modest in what he could claim he had accomplished by reason alone. But the goal of a philosophical science could still be fulfilled, Schelling believed. And his belief in philosophy—by means of faith—suffuses the Philosophy of Revelation. For philosophy to fulfill its goal, he maintained the need to incorporate revelation as the starting fact that then enables philosophy to move both forward and backward—to give an a posteriori account of God as Prius and then to trace God's life in human history. But, despite the claims to an a posteriori philosophy, much is clearly speculative at base. The late Schelling is thus not so different from the early Schelling. Moreover, because of the evident speculative content, the Philosophy of Revelation was too facilely lumped together with other contemporary speculative philosophies and its distinctive points overlooked.[88]

The theogony that is Schelling's Philosophy of Revelation fully manifests his existential interest in finding the adequate philosophical formula for expressing God's reality.[89] In his account of how the absolute manifests itself, Schelling stressed God in process, a living God who realizes himself and manifests himself in freely creating and redeeming a world. Moreover, in actualizing himself, he attains a personhood that was only potential prior to creation. In this formula, Schelling wished to avoid any notion of necessity in creation or God's life, and most emphatically any notion of emanationism. He also wished to ward off any appearance of pantheism, but at the same time to validate pantheism and polytheism as phases in the history of religion that are part of the restoration of monotheism.

Since the creation is free and unnecessary, it is in no way required of God that he become incarnate and person. He becomes so freely. But since it is unnecessary, this important event is "accidental" to God's life. Indeed, however important the event may be for God's creatures, for God himself it must be held to be inessential, and with this arises the conno-

---

[88]Schelling's treatment of Christianity in the Philosophy of Revelation can also be confused with his sketch of it in the *Lectures on University Studies,* despite important differences. In the work of 1802, Schelling had cited the empirical as the limitation in interpreting Christian doctrine and called for speculative grasp of doctrine's inner truth. In the Philosophy of Revelation, the emphasis is formally upon the empirical, and yet the Philosophy of Revelation ironically fulfills, in its elaborate speculations, the program for grasping the inner truth of Christianity as outlined in the 1802 Lectures (SW V; 297-98; *On University Studies,* 93-94).

[89]On this point, Schelling was not as different from Hegel as he would have liked. The existential interest of speculation is perceived in the youthful work of Hegel, when the two were personally and philosophically close, but also in Hegel's mature works.

tation of "unimportant" as well. Surely Schelling does not desire this, but it is the price he pays to avoid Hegelian necessity.

POTENCIES

In turning to the details of God's manifest life, we follow Schelling into the darkest teaching of the Philosophy of Revelation, namely, the doctrine of potencies. According to Schelling, potency is at the center of all that is living, including the living God. Schelling's is by no means a satisfying or even persuasive teaching, but the doctrine is fundamental to the Philosophy of Revelation. Hirsch accuses Schelling of having no more justification for it than poetic fancy[90] and others have been no kinder. But Schelling cited what he considered to be firm biblical basis for the teaching in the Sapientia of the Old Testament. Schelling is resourceful in grounding the theory in both Aristotle (dunamis) and the Old Testament (Sapientia, Hacham). Still Schelling offers no credible basis for it. In the end, the three potencies of "able to be," "must be" and "ought to be" have no more status than "might be."[91] Ironically, the doctrine thus appears to be pure speculation on the part of idealism's most eager apostate.

At base, the doctrine is tied to the root teaching of God's freedom and attempts to explain how all freedom —including divine freedom— moves from the nothingness of possibility into actuality. At least as important as the details of the theory is the role it occupies in Schelling's thought about God's life. For Schelling sought to avoid the notion of creation ex nihilo at the same time as he avoided anything resembling emanationism because the latter would make the resulting creation to some extent necessary and thus less than totally free.

Creation ex nihilo is avoided because God creates not out of pure nothingness but rather out of which-is-not-yet, that is, not out of οὐν ὄν but out of μὴ ὄν. The distinction revolves around a subtle but important difference in the use of Greek negatives. In μὴ ὄν the emphasis is on being (ὄν) and it signifies that which is not presently actual. Whatever is not presently actual *can be*, even if it as yet *is not*. And it is out of *can-be*, or

---

[90]Emanuel Hirsch, *Geschichte der neuern evangelischen Theologie*, 5 vols. (Gütersloh, 1949-1954) 5:269.

[91]The terms "able to be," "must be" and "ought to be" parallel *an-sich, für-sich* and *an-und-für-sich* in Fichte and Hegel, as Schulz (*Die Vollendung*, 190) and Tilliette (*Schelling, une philosophie en devenir*) both note.

potency, that Schelling conceives of as part of God yet apart from God, that creation is held to arise.

In developing this theory, Schelling expressed it in algebraic notation. Schelling holds that to the concept of potency belongs movement of the following type: $-A + A \pm A$. This logical, rather than chronological, progression is held to characterize God's life and to express God's indissoluble unity in triplicity. There are in addition, three potencies: A^1, A^2, and A^3. There is also God as absolute (A^4, but not mentioned in the Lectures) embracing them and containing them all within himself. Sapientia, a kind of Ur-Potency, underlines all three potencies, each of which follows the movement $-A + A \pm A$. A^1, or the first potency, is spirit in-itself, interiority, *Seynkönnendes* or the able-to-be, the subject of the secondary potency. A^2, the second potency, is spirit for-itself, exteriorization, *Seynmüssendes* or the must-be, and object of the first potency. A^3 is spirit "bei Sich" or in possession of itself, the *Seynsollendes,* ought-to-be or shall-be, subject-object. The attributes and role of each potency define a clear dialectical relationship among the triad that, when actualized in divine-human history, will become trinity.

The theory of potencies explains not only the structure of God's life but also the human predicament. For the first potency, which is able-to-be, is also that which ought-not-to-be. Yet in fact this potency has been actualized, and that which ought-not-to-be has come to be. Having done so, it must go on to resolution(the meaning of $-A + A \pm A$ for the first potency), by moving *ab actu ad potentiam:* by progression from actualization to restoration as pure potency. This happens by virtue of the second potency that, in fulfilling itself, restores the original pure potency of A^1.

Schelling's obscure mathematical notations A^1, A^2, and A^3 take on new meaning when one learns that A^1 refers to fall, A^2 to God's Logos who restores, and A^3 to the spirit. The full actualization of the potencies thus represents fall and restoration but also—and synonymously—the actualized life of God, or theogony. Ultimately, the three potencies come to stand for the trinitarian life of God and the three personalities of God's life that result from the process.

All three potencies are potencies of God's being. And God is the source of all being and of all potency. The idea of perfect spirit, according to Schelling, contains the possibility of another being different from its own eternal being, and God freely accepts this other being. When God decides to place the potencies in tension, creation results and all that follows from it. Schelling stresses that God is lord of the world *before*, that is, he is its lord to posit or not to posit. He is the lord of possibilities, actualized and/ or unactualized; and he would be fully and really God even as lord of mere potencies, had he never actualized a world. Schelling underlines this point by noting negative philosophy's misunderstanding in suggesting that God would not be God without a world and thereby reducing creation to necessity.[92]

Schelling will have creation proceed from God's being, but not by necessity or emanation. Potency is there with God at the beginning. And it is from potency—with God, part of God, but not God—that Schelling has creation arise. His basis for this position is biblical, he holds. Acts 15:18 states that God knows his works from all eternity and Schelling confirms and expands this by citing Proverbs 8:22-31 where Wisdom declares, "I am from the beginning, before the Earth."[93] He argues that what is there termed "wisdom" is really potency and is termed wisdom *per anticipationem*, that is, in advance of its achievement. But the identification of wisdom and potency is the product of very dubious etymology on Schelling's part. Schelling notes, correctly, that *Wissen* and *Können* are often synonymous in many languages. To "know" something or "know how" (both meanings contained in the German *Wissen*) is to have potency. This is true for German, for French, and several other languages. But Schelling has no basis for construing the Hebrew *Hakmah* (חָכְמָה) in this way.

TRINITY AS THEOGONY

God's essence consists of being and non-being, and his non-being encompasses three potencies that he is free to actualize or not. The threeness of his potency, of the triads of pagan religion and of the trinitarian concept of God are not regarded as accidental but as importantly related. All three reflect the reality of God: the threeness of potency describes God's being, the triads of paganism describe historical moments in restoring the God-concept in man, and trinity describes the fulfilled process of God's life. For God becomes trinity and does so in Christianity. This is to say that God was not always fully triune. But his triune life is mirrored in other religions, distorted and incomplete. His achievement of actual trinity is his

---

[92]Lecture Fourteen (SW XIII:291).
[93]Quoted, SW VIII:302.

theogony, or fulfillment as God, and is Christianity's contribution to his life.

Schelling reviews the process of God's becoming in Lecture Sixteen of the Philosophy of Revelation. Plurality begins in God as potential. It is actualized as the potencies are actualized. During the process, the plurality in God is one of *potencies, not* of personalities. Thus God as creator is several, but not several persons.[94] At the end of creation, there are for the first time three personalities (but not three gods):

> The God or the personality that was in the very beginning, in whose power it is to actualize the will that he finds in himself, viz. the potency of another being, and thereby to set the other potencies in tension, and that posits all this as actual in creation without itself entering into the process but rather remaining outside the process as first cause—this all-beginning personality has itself as another personality in the Son at the end of creation (and the same in the Spirit).[95]

The life of the Son and of the Spirit is a decisive alteration in God's life. It is God's becoming God in a new way. For the godhead produces itself as trinity of persons, and this is its theogony. Schelling cites Dionysius the Areopagite: θεογόνος θεότης—Son and Spirit are "god-produced."[96] The revealed proofs for his view are to be found, according to Schelling, in the Gospel of John. There he seizes upon the phrase of the prologue θεὸς ἦν ὁ λόγος. This he interprets to mean "The word was (a form of) God" or divine. He stresses the importance of the phrase's *not* reading ὁ λόγος ὁ θεός, which would mean "The word was God"—the present "incorrect" rendering of the prologue's first verse in some translations. Schelling holds that the definite article would be required in order to construe the Son as fully God from all eternity, and the definite article is not found in the Greek original. The Son is thus revealed, according to Schelling, as divine and a form of God and ultimately as becoming fully God, but not as having been fully God from the beginning.

Schelling forthrightly acknowledges that his interpretation contains more than is explicit in orthodox Christian trinitarian doctrine. But he deems his own the correct articulation of God's being as becoming and hence holds that his God-concept is more adequate to grasping God's life than the trin-

---

[94] SW XIII:337.
[95] SW XIII:338.
[96] SW XIII:323.

itarian theology of his day. He also recognizes that his view expands the notion of creation so that both New Testament and pagan theophanies are reconciled. His theory prides itself on its religious inclusiveness, and the Philosophy of Revelation proves itself adequate not only to Christianity but to the history of religions thereby—that is, to *all* revelation.

Schelling attaches himself in a formal sense to the theological teaching that all three persons of the trinity are active in creation. All three act in fact as creator: the creator as Father is he who goes out in exclusive being, the creator as Son is he who overcomes this exclusive being, and the creator as Spirit is he who completes or perfects arisen being. In this, the Father provides the "stuff" of creation and is its material cause; the Son gives creaturely form and is thus the formal cause; while the Spirit as the common will of both brings creation to what it should be, perfects it and is thus the final cause. Schelling finds this reading of Aristotle into the trinity supported by St. Paul himself in the Epistle to the Romans (11:36) where the Apostle spoke of all that is created "from him, through him, and in him." The revelation in Paul sanctions and completes the revelation present in Aristotle. Thus Schelling establishes the connection between demiurge and Logos that early Christian gnostics were tempted to make.

Schelling traces movement in God from (1) potential plurality to (2) plurality of actualized potencies to (3) plurality of personalities. Only at the end are there three persons in God. Meantime, stresses Schelling, the unity of God as one is eternal throughout. But at the beginning, only the Father is actual.

The second part of Schelling's Lectures outlines the place of humankind in creation and the role it plays in God's theogony. This turns out to be very significant, even if it is not part of any aboriginal divine plan. For creation has not followed its ideal course. This is not of course because of any inner necessity but because of freedom—in this instance, the freedom of the human creature. Humankind had been made the lord of causes *(Ursachen),* but only insofar as it preserved their unity. However, humankind, who would be lord of potencies in their dispersal and not just in their unity, set the potencies in opposition. In doing this, humankind made itself lord of the world—but lord of a fallen world "outside God." Alienation of the world from God is thus man's free deed. Schelling's philosophical account of fall is replete with problems. Like many such accounts or myths, it indicates in the last analysis only *that* something occurred and not *why* it occurred. The account explains the presence of evil as a misuse of freedom. God allowed the possibility of evil by having set the potencies in tension in creation. But humankind is responsible for the entrance of evil into the world by having set the potencies in opposition. The alienation or extra-divinity of the world vis-à-vis God is thus not the result of any cause independent of God, even if it proceeds originally from God. Humankind's desire or will to be like God makes it into a demonic force that plays havoc with creation. The usurper emerges as a perverse lord of being. It becomes "like God," but not God-like. Schelling's theory parallels the Christian account of fall and restoration but with its own distinct content. Most strikingly different in his conception is that the Son or Logos immediately and *freely* follows the creation into alienation or extra-divinity (*Außergöttlichkeit*).[97]

God the creator has, in a sense, "lost control" of his creation. He is still creator and sustainer of the world, but he does not set the form or manner of being. He maintains a creation that has broken with him, that has become alien or extra-divine in fall, and does so for the sake of reconciliation. As Schelling subsumes redemption into theogony and recounts the trinitarian gain that results from it, he pays a high price for freeing himself from the category of necessity. For Schelling's creation theory unintentionally revitalizes Enlightenment theodicy questions and leads one to ask if a "more perfect" creator might not have created a less imperfect world and to ask this precisely because the creator is held to be *totally* free. Or is an eternally perfect God whose being contains potency not master of potency after all? Indeed, Schelling's theory (like Hegel's) might even suggest that the absolute is, in the end, not entirely absolute. For while not subject to inner necessity (as in Hegel's concept), the creator would seem to be the unfortunate victim of caprice in his own creation. For he freely allowed actions that affect not only creation but even his own being. Schelling's God might even seem foolish for having allowed himself to be determined by others' misuse of God-given freedom, instead of serene in a freedom that transcends Hegelian necessity, as is Schelling's intention. Human freedom chooses alienation from God and brings God into self-alienation in the extra-divinity of the Logos. And humanity binds itself under the laws of necessity, until the Son's intervention frees humankind once

---

[97]This would sound Manichean except that in the Manichean teaching Primal Man (who might be construed as Logos) is taken prisoner in the creation and is thus under a *necessity*.

again. God is not required to restore creation, because he is free. Yet a living God could not be indifferent to his creation's miscarriage.

Despite God and humankind's eventual gain from fall, there is a sense in which there is no *felix culpa* motif here. The history of the world is a record of misused freedom in great part, and one must hesitate to account by-products "happy" (*felix*). Nor does it appear that one could account God's theogony desirable, no less a desirable good. For a desirable good, one might argue, must be willed necessarily by a God who wills the good. One cannot overlook the fact that the actualized trinity is the end product of that-which-ought-not-to-be. Had humankind done what it ought, God would never become actualized trinity. For Schelling does not suggest, as some speculative Christian theologians have, that the Son would have become incarnate even if humankind had not fallen. Nor does Schelling indicate how the tension posited by the begetting of the Son would otherwise have been resolved if humankind had not fallen and the Son not followed it into alienation. To be sure, one cannot construe God's becoming as an ill. But in the final analysis, it has the ring not only of the *accidental* but of the *incidental*—of being without interest, and perhaps even without importance *for God*. And if God's becoming does not matter to God (insofar as he did not will it in the way it happened but merely allowed it), one may ask with the *philosophes,* how much should it really matter to humankind?

RELIGION'S ROLE IN GOD'S LIFE

For Schelling, both paganism and Christianity belong to the moment of the Son in the life of God. Hence the Philosophy of Revelation offers a philosophical Christology that appreciates paganism's contribution to Christianity and theogony. For both Christ and Christianity build on paganism's attainment. Indeed, Christ is also present in paganism, although unincarnate. In holding this view, Schelling adapts the "Logos Spermatikos" notion of early Christianity. But there is a difference. For in Schelling's view, God does not sow the seed in paganism that then prepares the pagan world for accepting Christ. Instead, the seed was tragically scattered in humankind's fall. Paganism's role is to gather it together once again for planting in the fertile soil of restored monotheism. Pre-Christian religions have a task, therefore, in relation to God's life. The god-image must be recollected from its fragmented polytheistic forms.

Christianity is the true religion, but false religion does not equal irreligion. Paganism is religion in error, and Schelling stresses how seriously he takes it. Paganism and mythology are in fact nothing less than the *presupposition* of Christianity.

Myths reveal humankind as having fallen out of an original relationship with God and evidence the shattering of the God-image into the resulting polytheism. But paganism was not a static affair. Paganism and mythology are movement back to monotheism. As soon as this preparation stage was completed, Christianity appeared and paganism immediately disappeared.[98] But in his attempt to issue a proper evaluation of pagan religion, in the face of the recurring Western theological temptation to reject pagan, pre-Christian and non-Christian religion as aberration and abomination, Schelling made clear that his principal interest was really Greek religion, and Greek religion as amalgamated with Roman religion. Schelling inflates the Greek background of Christianity at the expense of the Jewish, which is hardly mentioned. In this Schelling followed the strong German fascination with ancient Greece and as a result his notion of Christianity is "Graeco-Christian."

However, Schelling's neglect of Judaism is more than merely cultural prejudice, since it leaves a lacuna in his history of religions and his explanation of Christian origins. And it is ironic that a philosophy that boasted of its fundamental a posteriori and historical interests should be so unconcerned with the Judaic context in which Jesus of Nazareth emerged. Instead, Schelling's philosophy is far more oriented toward the Hellenistic philosophical culture and mystery cults that are the vague background of Christ the Kyrios and Logos. The result is an exaggerated Greek Christos that overly emphasizes the writings of Paul and John, while the Synoptic Jesus of Nazareth and Jewish Messiah is largely ignored. For the true forerunners of Schelling's Christ are not the prophets and faithful of Yahweh but the gods and heroes of Greek legend and epic. On the surface, Schelling holds that both paganism and Judaism are the presuppositions of

---

[98]One need not be a historian of religions to recognize that this reading is too simple. Pagan religions did not vanish immediately or even completely. Moreover, a pagan religion that had achieved a monotheistic conception of God—Zoroastrianism—was a rival of Christianity in the ancient world, survived in Persia until the Islamic conquest, and endures to this day (even if frequently seeming on the verge of extinction). In the West itself, one cannot contest the triumph of Christianity as a fact, but paganism continued in Europe after the advent of the Gospel and certainly continues in other Christianized lands outside Europe (particularly in Latin America and Africa). In Europe itself, important pagan vestiges survive, some would hold, in the cults of angels, saints, and even the Virgin Mary.

Christianity and that paganism is not inferior to Judaism. But the details of his account indicate much more. If he starts out to revalidate paganism, he ends by relegating Judaism to an unmistakably inferior position, without any serious justification of this position and despite the occasional remark to the effect that Judaism is the fulfillment of paganism.[99] His occasional praise of Judaism thus rings hollow. Schelling always seems to strain when he seeks a role for Judaism—much like the Hegel from whom he tried to appear so different. At one point he even calls Jewish monotheism into question as de facto polytheism. At the same time, he detects a "shadow monotheism" amidst the formal polytheism of paganism and this, he finds, amounts to genuine monotheism when crystallized by Greek philosophy. Hence the Greek pagans make the real contribution toward restored monotheism, not the Jews who only appear monotheists.

In according a place to non-Christian religion, Schelling believes that his philosophy earns the title "Philosophy of Revelation." The Philosophy of Revelation is thus *Philosophie der Offenbarung*, not *Offenbarungsphilosophie*. The latter would limit itself to only one revelation, and a "philosophy of Christianity" would be such an *Offenbarungsphilosophie*. The Philosophy of Revelation aims to discern the rightful place of all revelations. Analysis of the revelations in historical religions indicates that religion has three moments or divisions: natural religion (mythology), supernatural religion (revelation) and the religion of free philosophical knowledge. Natural religion includes Graeco-Roman and Judaic. Supernatural religion includes a Petrine, Pauline, and Johannine phase, with the last being a transition to philosophical religion. However, Schelling indicates as little about Johannine Christianity, philosophical religion and the Spirit as trinitarian theologies normally do when it comes to the third element. What is clear about the religion of free philosophical knowledge is that Schelling's own Philosophy of Revelation views itself as its decisive launching.[100]

---

[99]For example, SW XIV:88.

[100]The details of the history of religion are incomplete, because the Johannine moment and philosophical religion are not yet accomplished. But the view of Judaism will simply not hold up, nor will his view of paganism withstand serious scrutiny. Anyone who knows anything of the sublime spiritual interest of Buddhism immediately recognizes the inadequacy of Schelling's view of pagan religion. His analysis of paganism will thus not hold up in face of the fact of non-polytheistic, non-Christian spiritual religion. Some might counter that Buddhism has polytheistic tendencies, as Judaism has also manifested. But so does Christianity itself, if not in the notion of trinity then in the cult of Mary and saints who in part represent "baptized" pagan powers.

CHRISTOLOGY: THE THEOGONY OF THE LOGOS

The central event in God's becoming is the Logos's full actualization as God. For due to the entrance of the eternal, preexistent Logos into human history, being becomes restored and God's own being is enhanced. The process began when the Son followed creation into alienation from God and continues during his hidden presence in paganism. It culminates in his incarnation as Christ in Christianity, although it is not completed until the Parousia.

Although the Son and Logos come to be fully God through the events of fall, pagan restoration of monotheism, and finally incarnation, Schelling has made it clear that the Son, as well as the Spirit, preexisted and were already divine and united with the Father. But he does alter the traditional Christian understanding of their anterior life. Logos and Spirit were contained in God before creation, but existed as potential and were not actual. Schelling is trying to avoid the notion that the Son was brought forth or begotten out of any *necessity* of God's nature. God's freedom remains paramount. At the same time Schelling guards against any suggestions of creaturehood for the Son that would diminish the role or standing of the Logos. He thus cites Col. 1:15, for example, where St. Paul describes the Son/Logos as "the firstborn of all creatures." Schelling stresses "the firstborn" and reads the verse to mean that he is *not* a creature but is *above* all creatures. Schelling further construes the Son as the being through whom *all* is created. He is, in a word, the demiurge.[101]

The demiurge or Son is being over against the Father, freely begotten by him. He is not the Father, nor is he God. Yet he is of the same substance as the Father. The Son, moreover, has been *eternally Son for the Father*, in an internal or implicit sense. It is only his externalized and explicit sonship that is begotten and noneternal.[102] The begetting of the Son posits a tension in creation that is destined (but not required) to be resolved in cre-

---

[101]Spirit, it should be noted, is also demiurge and personality when returned to the godhead. Schelling has the familiar theological difficulty of finding a genuine role for the Spirit in his trinitarian conception. Schelling's philosophy, like most trinitarian theologies, strains mightily on the subject. And Schelling, like many others, remains open to the charge that the role assigned the Spirit is little more than a systematic afterthought.

[102]SW VIII:321. In formulating his notion of the Son, one can almost sense Schelling feeling his way through the heresies and creedal formulations of early Christianity.

ation's fulfillment when the potency that is the Son reenters (and thus is no longer external to) the godhead, when the pure flow of the divine life is reconstituted.[103] Since this potency has become for-itself, or independent of God, it enters back into godhead as a distinct personality (as does the Spirit), so that the reconstituted godhead becomes a plurality of persons.

SON OF MAN

While remaining Son of God, the Logos becomes the Son of Man in following the world into alienation. "Son of Man" is thus a title of humiliation, according to Schelling's reading.[104] The Son of Man takes on an extra-divine personality that will remain the independent personality of the Son when he is restored to union with the Father. Schelling's reading of the fall story contains a *felix culpa* motif after all. For although the world has fallen—and fallen *freely,* it must always be emphasized— a great new good is to be achieved at least for humankind. In becoming, God may be said to gain as well, even if Schelling does not give us any reason to count God's unplanned gain as a willed good.[105] (God's life as fully actualized trinity awaits fulfillment in the moment of the Spirit at the end of time, a moment that Schelling does not speculatively elaborate.)

The history of the human world becomes the "time of the Son of Man." The Logos was present throughout all of human history and in all of its religions. Its most decisive presence is in Christianity and, before that, Greek paganism. The earthly life of the Logos has two phases. The first phase was the time in which the second personality has effect (*Wirken*) not according to its will but according to nature, and thus was under the laws of necessity. This was the period of the freely accepted suffering of the unincarnate Son of Man, and it was the time of paganism. The second phase is the appearance of the Son in Christianity, in a new time of acting (*Handeln*) according to the divine will and in *freedom.* Schelling emphatically validates pagan religion as a genuine part of God's life. At the same time

---

[103]SW XIII:317-18.

[104]SW XIII:371 n1. According to Schelling, humiliation is suggested by the melancholy content of the New Testament uses of the term.

[105]Schelling's notion of God's gain is distinctly his own. In Hegel's account of humankind's necessary fall God gains consciousness as humankind "restores" itself in attaining consciousness of divine-human unity, but in Schelling's account, God's very being is altered in becoming a trinity of persons.

he makes it clearly subordinate to Christianity as the fulfillment of God's life.[106] Paganism moved from a fragmented image of God in polytheism, through tritheism, to monotheism. The limitation of tritheism was that it failed to grasp the unity in God's life.[107] Interestingly, Schelling remarks that the tritheism of paganism is sometimes superior to the hitherto nominal trinitarianism of Christian theology.

LIFE OF THE LOGOS:
FROM DIVINE BEING TO FULL DEITY

The fundamental fact of Christology for Schelling is that Christ moves from being dependent upon the Father to actualizing being independent of him, not through the agency or intention of the Father but through the contingencies of history. In the fall, the demiurge was displaced by humankind from his original relation to the Father. Inwardly, he remained in the same divine personality but was outwardly changed. The Son submitted and followed creation into alienation from the Father as extra-divine personality in order to overcome the new principle posited by humankind's fall and thus to save humankind from itself and for God.[108] And the Son willingly paid the price of outward alienation from the Father in suffering as the Son of Man.

Although Schelling stressed the Son's free decision to follow fallen creation into alienation from God and to take upon himself God's wrath in order to restore it, he comes perilously close to Manicheanism and its depiction of Primal Man taken captive in fallen creation. But Schelling's version differs in its stress on the Son's free self-surrender and his remaining internally united to God. The scriptural basis of his interpretation is found in Philippians 2:6-8 where Christ is described as "though he was in the form of God, did not count equality with God a thing to be grasped, but emptied himself, taking the form of a servant" (RSV translation). Schelling thus made familiar kenosis theology the cornerstone of his Christology but discloses a new phase in the life of the Logos, namely, that in which he was an extra-divine personality after fall without yet being incarnate.

---

[106]Lectures Eighteeen through Twenty-Three of the *Lectures on the Philosophy of Revelation* contain a summary of the Philosophy of Mythology. For a grasp of Schelling's philosophy of Christianity, the details of the Philosophy of Mythology are not nearly as significant as the inclusion of the summary itself: mythology has a role in revelation.

[107]SW XIV:68-80.

[108]Cf. SW XIV:36.

The phrase "in the form of God" is held to indicate that, in this phase, while the Son was godlike or divine, he was not true God as such. Schelling insisted that the passage in Philippians is incomprehensible without presupposing Christ as other than God before incarnation.[109] He finds that the Gospel of Mark implies the same when it quotes Jesus saying that no one knows the day and hour of the last day—not the angels, not the Son, only the Father. For Schelling, this verse speaks not only of the external separation of Son from Father but of the ontological difference between Father and Son in their "internal" relationship in the godhead prior to the exaltation of the Son to full deity.

Schelling's exegesis of the prologue of the Gospel of John in Lecture Twenty-Eight is the high point of his "philosophical literalism" in reading Scripture. Every phrase and verse is made to disclose its hidden philosophical truth. In the prologue of John, Schelling sees revealed what he also finds in the kenosis theology of St. Paul: the Logos lowering and emptying himself, with distinct moments in his life noted. "In the beginning was the Word, and the Word was with God, and the Word was God." The Greek text is essential to his interpretation, particularly the use and non-use of the definite article. Begotten of God before all ages, the Logos is not a creature, that is, not a part of creation, but the demiurge of creation. The Logos was πρὸς τὸν θεόν ("with God") and θεός ("God"), but he was *not* ὁ θεός ("God himself"). In this, Schelling sees himself avoiding Arianism, despite his theory that the Logos did not begin as fully God. For, he remarks, the Son is still so essentially God that the Father would not be God without him.[110]

Schelling stresses that the opening verses of the prologue are not mere parallelism but an elaboration of the life of the Logos. Hence "The light shined in the darkness and the darkness grasped it not" is taken to refer to an important but hitherto neglected phase in the preincarnational life of the Logos: the light was already present in paganism but paganism did not grasp it for what it was. In Schelling's reading, the prologue of John's Gospel does not leap immediately from "the beginning" of creation to baptism by John, but in a few cryptic lines, describes the Logos's life in pre-Christian religion.

---

[109]SW XIV:45.
[110]SW XIV:112.

Schelling's incarnational philosophy cannot be construed in the strict-est sense as God becoming man.[111] For the Word—and not God himself—becomes flesh. God does not become man in Christ since the Logos is not pure God or fully God at the moment of incarnation. It is more correct to say that the divine Logos who becomes human subsequently becomes God. For what the historical Jesus manifested was the extradivine or outer-godly (*außergöttlich*) personality of the Word.[112]

Schelling's philosophy revises the doctrine of the two natures of the incarnate Logos as well. The orthodox view, he maintains, is really veiled Nestorianism. The being of Christ, he holds, is not the product of two na-tures mysteriously fused together. Christ's human nature is, moreover, not independent of his divine nature and then joined to it. Rather, his human nature is created out of his divine nature. The kenosis of incarnation, fur-thermore, is the emptying of the "false divinity" that the Logos had in his condition *extra Patrem*.

> Christ is God and man at the same time and in one person for the first time in the incarnation, just as he was God and the extra-divine in one person before the incarnation, where however the divine was concealed in the ex-tra-divine. The incarnation is the condition of the freeing of the divine in him that was previously bound in him and hidden.[113]

In sum, Christ was truly human and now possesses two eternal natures that he did not possess at incarnation. In addition, both natures are in a sense the product of the incarnation, and not the human nature alone. For the Logos loses false divinity and gains true divinity through his human life, during which he also takes on human nature. But the humanity of the Logos nowhere seems to have value in and of itself. Hence the Philosophy of Revelation seems "cryptomonophysite," since the instrumental human nature was created out of the divine nature to begin with. Only the now deified divine nature seems essential, and the instrumental human nature is a phase in the past. Formally the Logos has two natures, but essentially he has only one.[114]

---

[111]SW XIV:165.

[112]SW XIV:163.

[113]SW XIV:186.

[114]As Tilliette notes (*Schelling, une philosophie en devenir*, II:447), what is striking by its absence is any mention of the Christologies of Schleiermacher and Strauss, both of which antedated Schelling's Lectures by nine and six years respectively and were widely known.

ATONEMENT

Schelling subsumes incarnation beneath a traditional Protestant atonement theology, with a few minor variations, as he argues that Christ died in our place, that he underwent physical death to save us from spiritual death.[115] Christ was, in fact, born in order to die and thereby atoned for the sinfulness of mankind. All this is quite traditional. In addition, since Christ the Logos was the principle of paganism, it was appropriate that he die a *pagan* death.[116] But Christ's death did far more than restore humankind. It also restored the Logos himself and enhanced his own divine status. Schelling's Christology is not a "Cur Deus Homo" but, instead, a kind of "Cur Verbum Homo"—a speculative explanation of why the Logos became human. While Schelling acknowledges the redemptive aspect of the Son's human life, it can appear subordinated to theogony. The Son becomes extra-divine and then incarnate in order to restore creation and to restore the potencies that had been set in opposition. In a true sense, it is in his own interest to do so, and the gain is his as well.

CHRISTIAN RELIGION AND CHRISTIAN CHURCH

Schelling's notion of the Christian religion and Christian church are naturally derived from his Christology with its emphasis upon the Logos as Christ and its neglect of the historical Jesus. For the Philosophy of Revelation, the unique content of the Christian religion is the person of Christ. Thus it is not Christ as teacher that distinguishes Christianity (as it does for Kant) or Christ as founder, but Christ as the content itself.[117] As he specifies the content, Schelling makes it clear that Christology largely means "Logogony," or the becoming of the Logos in human history. The Christ as Jesus of Nazareth counts only as the being *extra Patrem* who is negated in death by crucifixion, with the important result that the Logos incarnated in Jesus then returns to the Father while maintaining the independent personality gained in alienation and incarnation. The human dimension of Jesus' life is virtually ignored, apart from birth and death. And this, as has been noted, is ironic in a philosophy that stresses its a posteriori or factual ground. But, from Schelling's own point of view, his Christology is not

---

[115]SW XIV:197.

[116]This attaches Christianity even more firmly to Greek paganism and detaches Christ even more from the Judaism into which he was actually born.

[117]SW XIV:35.

thereby reduced to speculation since the (a priori) "facts" about the Logos have been made known in Scripture and thus rendered a posteriori. Speculation alone, moreover, would never have come upon such "unthinkable" ideas.

Thus the Christian religion does not revolve around the public ministry or teaching of Jesus but rather around the revealed meaning of its Christ:

> The proper content of Christianity is Christ himself and his history, not merely the external history of his deeds and suffering during the time of his visible humanity, but the *higher history* in which his life as man is itself only transition and on that account only a moment.[118]

The content of Christianity is the full and hitherto unfolded special personality of the Christ. In this sense, Christianity antedates both the birth of Jesus and even the creation. And the full meaning of the Christ, that is Christianity, can be properly and adequately grasped only by thought that has made itself adequate to the free revelation that discloses the Christ's higher life. Hence, while mythology and reason have their proper role, revelation alone discloses the higher life and enables a revelation-grounded philosophy to articulate the true meaning of Christianity. And while Christianity as a process antedates creation, the attainment of philosophical Christianity has waited upon the Philosophy of Revelation.

Just as God's life is process (theogony) and that of the Logos as well (Logogony[119]), so too is the life of the assembly that revolves around the Christ. And it too is triadic in form. The life of the Christian church has three phases, symbolized by the three special apostles Peter, James and John.[120] Peter stands for primacy, not superiority. For the rock of Peter is to be the foundation, not the edifice itself. A second stage must follow. It is, however, not "Jamesian." Schelling notes the early death of James and his "replacement" by Paul.[121] Schelling calls James the "provisional representative of the future Apostle Paul." On the basis of this insertion of Paul into the original company of apostles, Schelling describes the destined second phase in the organic growth of Christianity as "Pauline."[122]

---

[118]SW XIV:227. My emphasis.

[119]The term is mine, not Schelling's.

[120]SW XIV:298ff.

[121]SW XIV:302.

[122]The organic image is important. And by equating James and Paul, Schelling is able to preserve it. Historically, there is of course no disputing the monumental impact of Paul in the development of Christianity. It is no exaggeration to call him "the second founder of Christianity."

Where Peter was the principle of stability and the setting of the foundation, Paul is the principle of movement, development and freedom.[123] Paul is in fact a principle free of Peter and thus able to rebuke and correct him.[124]

Peter stands for the Petrine Christianity of the pre-Reformation; Paul for the Pauline Christianity of the Reformation and the ascendancy of the Pauline over the Petrine principle. Schelling stops short of Protestant triumphalism, however, and observes that both movements are but part of a process destined to culminate in Johannine Christianity, when the "true church" may at last be said to exist.[125] Johannine Christianity is thus the Christianity of the future, the Christianity that begins when the Pauline moment has run its course. It is to be marked by the mild and heavenly spirit of John, characterized by freedom and destined to subsume both the Petrine and Pauline moments, but also both paganism and Judaism.[126] The dawning Johannine church is to endure until Jesus comes again, when the threefold movement of the time of the Son will have been fulfilled and the Age of the Spirit then begins.[127]

Schelling's notion of a Johannine church is a rich and striking one. And the spiritual, philosophical Johannine principle has the attraction of moving out of Reformation Christianity without regressing to the Petrine church, while at the same time remaining part of the Christian tradition. Schelling never makes it explicit but his audience is left to advance to the easy inference that the Philosophy of Revelation is the herald of the imminent Johannine period. The Johannine church can even be said to have begun, for a positive philosophy has at last appeared that can affirm and incorporate all previous moments.

ASSESSING SCHELLING'S PHILOSOPHY OF CHRISTIANITY

Schelling had long claimed that he had a system that only needed articulation. Even if one overlooks his procrastination and allows that the

---

[123]SW XIV:303.

[124]SW XIV:307. The "Protestant" nature of the Peter-Paul comparison is evident here.

[125]SW XIV:310.

[126]These are among the few dialectical, triadic movements that Schelling observes.

[127]Schelling does not assign moments to the life of the church as periods corresponding to Father, Son and Spirit, as one might expect. In Lecture Thirty-Seven (SW XIV:326-27), he does, however, call Peter "the Apostle of the Father," Paul "the Apostle of the Son" and John "the Apostle of the Spirit." He orders the gospels along these lines as well. Thus, the Gospels of Mark and Matthew are Petrine, while Luke's is Pauline and John's is of course Johannine. All three moments of the church belong to the Age of the Son. But the Gospel of John proves the transition to the Spirit.

Philosophy of Revelation is not the finished product, one cannot fail to see that his visions and revisions of a new positive philosophical system do not and cannot hold together in the way that Schelling would insist that they can and do. The "positive philosophy" is tellingly incomplete; and the Philosophy of Revelation lacks ripeness, for all its years on the vine. As one critic has observed, for all the force of its rhetoric, it lacks continuity and power of thought.[128] And in it, as another has remarked, erudition seems to have displaced the inspiration that fueled his earlier works[129] and to weigh down the huge fragment that aspires to be a system.

Yet the work is rich in suggestions and lessons all the same. Schelling surely evidences some of the excesses of speculation. In the Philosophy of Revelation, speculation, or some hybrid of speculation and history, hits upon a notion and then unfolds it. Alternatives are not seriously examined or even entertained. Argumentation is formal and shallow. The possibility of uncertainty in even quite esoteric matters seems not seriously considered. Interpretations are declared fact with full confidence and no evidence. The thinker thinks a thought and his very enthusiasm seems to constitute sufficient—even "empirical"—proof. Schelling's "eisegesis" of Scripture and the claim that such interpretation constitutes a posteriori information is the most extreme example of his license. The category of the *Unvordenklich* (the "unthinkable" apart from revelation) is ultimately hollow to any who know from the history of thought the myriad fancies that the human mind has entertained. For those who appreciate the power of human imagination, Logos and demiurge and divine incarnations are by no means "unthinkable." They have been thought. It is only a feeble theological reductionism and circular reasoning to assert that the mind thinks them because they were first revealed.

But if Schelling's "data" sometimes make for curious arguments and if his crossing from negative to positive philosophy is not possible by virtue of the theological presuppositions that he would erect as bridge, and if reason and revelation are not philosophically reconciled as the Philosophy of Revelation would have them, there are nevertheless valuable lessons to be learned from Schelling's effort and exercise. His experiment in philosophy of religion remains instructive—a warning in its stumblings as well as in its leaps, a guide in its modest but fundamental achievements.

---

[128]Cf. Furhmans, *Schellings letzte Philosophie*, 95.

[129]Tilliette, *Schelling, une philosophie en devenir*, II:16.

For there is much that is still positive in the achievement of the positive philosophy. Schelling's attempt to articulate a notion of divine freedom and to develop a theodicy on this basis has come to be increasingly esteemed. The far-reaching implications of the treatise *Of Human Freedom* have finally been acknowledged by a posterity that questions, however, their application and elaboration in the Philosophy of Revelation. Divine freedom itself is not compromised thereby but endures as a valid antithetical principle to Hegel's divine necessity. The elaborately developed theogony principle successfully hinders any attempt on the part of philosophy of religion to return to a traditional static God-idea. For God lives and has lived in the history of religions. And the Logos, his Christ, has lived in them apart from him and now with him as he traced a course from alienation to fully actualized divinization in the founding phase of Christianity. Moreover, God has continued to live in the Christian religion, as he guides it through Petrine, Pauline, and now Johannine phases of its own triadic life.

Schelling, like Hegel, places God's life in the center of philosophical theology and philosophy of religion. He demands that philosophy of religion hereafter take account of the free, living God of human-divine history. And his insight that the actual is not the ideal, precisely because of freedom, applies to both the divine and human sides in the encounter that we term religion. But this rejoins the topic of theogony and attests to its centrality. On this subject, Schelling's contribution is rich and his emphasis enduring: both divine and human freedom operate in the divine-human encounter, and human freedom substantially affects the very life of God.

Together with Hegel, Schelling's emphasis upon the entire family of human religions as having a role in God's theogony and human destiny makes it far more difficult for any philosopher of religion to return to a facile Christian triumphalism. The historical dimension of religion must be incorporated, with all its breadth and complexity. Schelling names the direction in which religiously sensitive philosophy must proceed—the Johannine church—but fails to lead the way. Despite the difficulties contemporary philosophy of religion may have in absorbing the plethora of information increasingly available about the religions of humankind, Schelling and Hegel's respective treatments of the history of religions are nonetheless a prolegomenon to any future philosophy of religion. They bury the triumphalism of earlier Christian philosophy of religion but at the same time overcome Enlightenment disparagement of the Christian religion. Their philosophies of religion are in the end, admittedly, centered on the

Christian religion and the prominence of Christianity may still strike some as unwarranted. But the significance of their achievement is attested by those theologians who warn of the danger of philosophy of religion now that it has been permanently freed from the handmaiden's role, now that it has created a permanent place for all religions as valid and important in human—and divine—history. This has not prevented some theologians from affixing Barthian blinders but it has at least deprived them of invoking philosophy to support their determination not to see.

Schelling's treatment of doctrine contributes to the growing consciousness of the historical character of Christianity's "eternal truths," even if this was not his intention. While he protests that he is not interested in Christian doctrine, his treatment of Christianity is imbued with doctrinal content, even if he does not mention creeds and councils. His own teachings occasionally strike the reader as modern variations of third and fourth century heresies, but even as such they heighten consciousness of the original hybrid of historical fact and philosophical speculation that constitute seminal dogmas of Christianity. In developing his Christology—or "Logogony"—Schelling was aware of the novel course he was charting in the philosophical interpretation of Christian doctrine. This is reflected by his preliminary discourse on the history of doctrinal formulation, where he noted that church doctrine had been highly influenced by scholastic terminology and concepts. Schelling ought to have extended this observation further to the formative doctrinal period of the early church and even to the writings of John and Paul themselves, where neo-Platonic language and concepts influence formulations. But to do so would have exposed the tangle of Greek philosophy and Christian faith that has existed since the inception of Christian theology. Schelling noted the scholastic phase in order to rescue doctrinal forms for a nineteenth-century updating. To have taken his insight back to the first and second centuries might have called the notion of revelation itself into question.

Schelling is ultimately a transitional figure, but in a sense so is every thinker. His uniqueness on this score is that he served twice in the role, and each time in an important fashion. In the first instance, he served as the decisive transition between Fichtean subjective idealism and the objective idealism that has become largely identified with Hegel. And to this extent, it is not inaccurate to say that he served as a transition to Hegel. But he also had the distinction of serving as the transition *beyond* Hegel to existentialism, most radically in the treatise *Of Human Freedom* and most dramatically in the *Lectures on the Philosophy of Revelation.*

CONCLUSION

MORAL CHRISTIANITY: ROUSSEAU AND KANT

If the publication of Rousseau's *Profession of Faith of the Savoyard Vicar* (1762) had followed Kant's *Religion within the Limits of Reason Alone* (1793) rather than preceded it by thirty-one years, and if Rousseau had read Kant to the extent that Kant did read Rousseau—in short, if ages and publication orders had been reversed, surely some critic would have found grounds for concluding that the *Profession* was highly influenced by *Religion within the Limits of Reason Alone* and would have judged the former a poetic form of the latter. That a reverse judgment—although it would be incorrect—has not occurred is almost as much a reflection of the underestimation of Rousseau's religious position as it is a perception of the important differences between the two works. The *Profession* compares very well with *Religion within the Limits of Reason Alone,* and perhaps one ought to read it once again after a study of Kant's work, not only to hear the basic core of Enlightenment religion in a very different tone and to note the distance from Savoy to Königsberg but also to hear the Vicar's flowing expression of much that both thinkers held to be of genuine importance in religion.

Remove *Religion within the Limits of Reason Alone* from the cosmic drama between good and evil and abstract the *Profession of Faith of the Savoyard Vicar* from its hillside setting and one feels that the two share much in common. Both are pioneering attempts to consider religion philosophically, tolerantly, and positively, within the acknowledged limits of reason. Both select and emphasize Christianity and its Christ somewhat arbitrarily and then seek to make a positive affirmation of both religion and Christianity in the face of *philosophes* and *Aufklärer* respectively. Both fully see the limits of Christianity as found and recognize the need of reason to pare down claims made in its name. Thus prayer and miracles are rejected as offenses to reason, and Christ is brought down to human scale where he can be the more exemplary. Morality for both is the essence of religion and religion is true to the extent that it stays true to its core. For both, atheism is associated with immorality and deism with an anti-Christianity that is impractical. Thus both come to a theistic position that is intellectually easy for neither. Both stress the active role of the individual in morality and religion, in self-recovery. Both stress the lie that divides and corrupts and counter it with emphasis on sincerity that makes one whole within oneself and that can then unite one with others.

The differences, of course, between Kant and Rousseau are not to be ignored or smoothed over. Kant is more thorough, more systematic, more politic and diplomatic—in sum, more successful philosophically and personally in his study of religion. Rousseau, along with Lessing, is tolerant of Judaism and Islam whereas Kant, proceeding as he believed analytically on the basis of his idea of religion, finds Christianity superior. Rousseau's Vicar generally dismisses church doctrine and reduces the institution to a cultural fellowship forum, while Kant finds a way to give symbolic interpretation to the former and a teleological role to the latter. Ironically here, it was Kant who personally remained outside the church doors, which were always open to him, while Rousseau yearned for the fellowship behind doors barred to him. At the same time, Rousseau believed in providence, despite his own persecutions, and attempted a theodicy, while the (finally) successful Ordinarius in Königsberg dismissed both providence and any attempts at theodicy. On the subject of religious experience, Rousseau, despite a shared fear of quietistic effects, spoke of direct intuitions of the soul, which he then quickly linked to moral stimulation, while Kant denied any faculty for such intuitions. In Christianity, Rousseau stressed only the role of Jesus, as moral teacher, while Kant saw a role both for the teaching of Jesus and for the movement that claimed to embody and preserve them.

The most decisive and fundamental issue of nonagreement between the two, with implications for the understanding of religion to be sure, is original sin. Their respective notions arise not from any idea of God, however, but rather from the respective perception of the human condition and results in Kant's well-known pessimism on the one hand and Rousseau's equally well-known optimism on the other. For Kant, the fallen individual does not seem to be able to attain moral perfection, despite his obligation and inferred capacity, and seems to require an ethical community and even a divine supplement to complete a process that ought to occur in the nature of things. For Rousseau, in contrast, society corrupts and the individual, if left alone, has the ability to reach moral perfection. Rousseau denies original sin as emphatically as Kant points out the radical evil in human nature. Where both are of one voice is in the affirmation of the moral destiny and of the continuing importance of maximal human effort in reaching it. But their disagreement—in which Rousseau stands closer to the Enlightenment than Kant does—is not without important implications in theory and praxis. For Kant, it requires postulates such as immortality (in which Rousseau also believed) and social cooperation, not merely fellowship. And in this, Kant moves in *Religion within the Limits of Reason Alone* beyond the moral individualism of Rousseau's *Profession of Faith of the Savoyard Vicar* and of his own *Critique of Practical Reason.*

At the end of the *Profession of Faith of the Savoyard Vicar,* the Vicar warned against haughty philosophy that leads to atheism and recommended sincerity and humility—in short, a recognition of the limits of reason. In addition, he recommended, ''Keep your soul in such a state that you always desire that there should be a God.''[1] His commitment to theism was firm and unwavering. Returning from the *Profession* to *Religion within the Limits of Reason Alone,* one almost feels that Kant followed Rousseau's advice personally and that his observations and consequent pessimism about human nature not only made God a necessary postulate of practical reason but kept Kant a believer as well. Without this pessimism, one might speculate about whether Kant personally might have followed the agnostic drift of his thought that seems ready to dissolve God into a symbol. Kant's God is, nonetheless, less deistic than Rousseau's. For although endowed with person-like qualities, God merely functions mechanically in Rousseau's conception. For Kant, the fulfillment of the laws of justice and justification require something more, and even if his vagueness on this is reminiscent of Rousseau, it is already beyond him.

The moral Jesus of the *Profession* and of *Religion within the Limitis of Reason Alone* is the personified ideal of each thinker's moral philosophy and the centerpiece of the religion of moral reason. Yet there are differences. Rousseau's Jesus is a suffering historical moral hero; Kant's Jesus is the powerful, timeless and guiding symbol of morally restored humanity. Rousseau's figure is theoretically dispensable yet clung to with sympathetic need; Kant's figure is practically indispensable in view of man's self-inflicted moral condition, yet he is never so much as named.

---

[1] *Émile,* 275; OC IV:631.

THE RELIGION OF GOD'S LIFE:
HEGEL AND SCHELLING

Schelling and Hegel deserve to be compared, but whenever this happens, Hegel almost invariably carries the day and must be said to do so deservedly. Unfortunately, Hegel's wicked remark about Schelling carrying on his philosophic education in public was still as true in 1841, the time of the *Lectures on Philosophy of Revelation* in Berlin, as when Hegel first uttered it. It was an education never satisfactorily completed but only abruptly terminated in bitter old age. Thus, while not the Proteus he was accused of being, Schelling did remain true to a pattern of breaking off the execution of a system of philosophy once its problems came to the fore. And this is, in its own way, a commendable stance of self-criticism. Only in the Philosophy of Revelation is the author's consciousness of the problems lacking, while the execution is once again incomplete.

But their philosophies, on balance, share a great deal in common and, in substance while not in form, would appear of relatively equal merit. Both contain moments of soaring speculative brilliance and long hours of prosaic details. Both are philosophies of religion in the grand style, in which philosophy of religion finds its place within the larger compass of a thinker's system and aims to be the culmination of the philosophical program. For both Hegel's and Schelling's philosophies of religion issued from a time when God still stood at the center of philosophy, when philosophy still held itself responsible for an adequate conception of the reality of God and extended this program to religion, both conceptually and historically. Each philosophy is suffused and propelled by the importance of the becoming of God and each, in its own fashion, identifies humankind's becoming in it or with it. In the end, Schelling's emphasis is upon theogony while Hegel's is upon anthropogony. This is to deny that the subject-object equation, or a convincing statement of divine-human unity, finally holds for either of them.

In each, Christianity is accorded a special place because it revolves around the restoring-fulfilling figure of Jesus. Both Hegel and Schelling would be able to maintain that what Jesus accomplished is equally important for God and for humankind, that Jesus is therefore truly the intermediary between God and humankind who reconciles and unites their "becomings." But in Hegel, the human gain in the end seems the greater (in Jesus' consciousness of God-human identity), whereas in Schelling the gain (full deity for the Logos, actualized trinity) really seems more God's.

Why then is Hegel's philosophy of religion frequently held to be superior, while Schelling's is passed over? It is not because there are fewer curiosities or because the human gain is more attractive. It is in part because the form, produced by Hegel's dialectic, is superior and the details are thus supported by it. The result is that, even if one cannot see with Hegel or allow his grand vision of divine-human interaction as accurate, one cannot deny its power. To the extent that one recognizes Hegel as having penetrated to something dynamic and true in all life, both divine and human, the grand form adds to the intellectual awe that his philosophy can inspire. No systematic thrust carries Schelling forward in an enterprise that in many respects is no more abitrary than Hegel's. Schelling's Philosophy of Revelation is more vulnerable than Hegel's Philosophy of Religion because Schelling never provided the full system—the promised positive philosophy—to command the allegiance of the sympathetic and to enclose, protect and serve as reserve line of defense against hostile critics.

Schelling's critique of negative philosophy is perceptive and telling. But despite his rhetoric, he fails to persuade in any significant measure those who are not ill-disposed toward Hegel from the outset. Meantime, those unprepared to heed Hegel are no more likely to harken to Schelling, even if they briefly gave him audience in Berlin. The anti-Hegelians did not and do not become Schellingians, while the Hegelians—of all schools—remain true believers. But the real reason for the eclipse of Schelling's philosophy of religion is that, both in its ambition and in its effect, it has no practical application, particularly in the social or political arena. For Hegel had the insight that the God-idea had to serve as the sufficient basis of the state. Schelling's God-idea has no such ambition and no such application.

Hegel's philosophy is sustained by the principle of identity that requires an act of philosophical faith. Schelling's begins with a principle of freedom but moves on to a notion of revelation that requires theological faith. But Schelling's faith repels the rationalist and fails to appease the "faithful," while Hegel's confidence in reason consummates the speculative rationalist faith of his age. In Schelling, theology briefly reverses roles with philosophy and becomes the *ancilla philosophiae* when it warns of the hubris of reason. But it does not, and cannot, provide an alternative principle for philosophy generally or for philosophy of religion. For Schelling's incorporation of revelation is manifestly unphilosophical. Thus, if one cannot accept Hegel's faith in *Vernunft,* one cannot on that account—or any other genuinely philosophical count—accept Schelling's theologically based alternative.

Schelling's philosophy of religion in the *Lectures on the Philosophy of Revelation* was neither a satisfying outward nor inner success. Its reception was stormy, its inherent problems not long in being exposed by critics, both sympathetic and hostile. But Schelling's failure does not discredit in advance the attempt by others to formulate a philosophy of religion that incorporates his program—while not his presuppositions—and that takes account of freedom and its unpredictable results. For Schelling's success is to persuade us not to fall under the spell of the Hegelian thought experiment. This is not to say that we are forced to take the road to Kierkegaard or Barth, nor, of course, does it mean we must travel the route of Feuerbach and Strauss.

Where Schelling's efforts do succeed, they do so theologically and in a Kierkegaardian direction. For if one denies the principle of identity, one might as well maintain the Christian world-picture, with its meaning of history revolving around the person and poetry of its Christ, and in the terms in which it is first found and confessed. Even if one regrets the Patristic period of Christianity—with its sorting out of congenial and uncongenial philosophical elaborations of the meaning of Jesus as Logos, Schelling is really not an improvement upon the past, nor a meaningful updating, but merely an odd modern variation. One might as well return then to the creedal formulations themselves, or call for a recovery of the New Testament and its Jesus. But this is to pursue orthodox theology, not unorthodox philosophy or some synthesis of the two. Schelling's unintended lesson here is that one cannot make theology—even ancient philosophical theology—appear to be adequate philosophy. The Age of Faith is in the past. While his philosophy points *theology* back towards orthodoxy, it points *philosophy* in quite different directions. In this respect at least, Schelling was clearly beyond Hegel.

One may continue philosophy in light of his critique of idealism and the lesson of his own failure. One may even attempt again a philosophy that allows for the freedom of God and humankind, but without the dubious speculative a posteriori with which Schelling burdened himself. Reason, returning to a more Kantian modesty in philosophy of religion, can restrain itself from speculative leaps and fanciful embellishments and still speak of the living God in interaction with the evolving universe. A more modest program could still include the essentials of what he called for in a new, positive philosophy and at the same time make up for the evident deficiencies in Kant's own philosophy of religion. For if Schelling's efforts suggest the validity of a new departure from Kant's *Religion within the Limits of Reason Alone,* certain Schellingian-Hegelian principles would find prominence. Firstly, the concept of God would need to be a dynamic one (unlike the static moral perfection of Kant's concept). Secondly, a full range of religious experience—and not exclusively moral intuition—would require discussion. Thirdly, Christianity would be viewed within the full context of human religions, and not merely abstractly or nominally as it is in Kant. The final element in the program suggested turns on the essential Hegel-Schelling divide: necessity vs. freedom, Hegel's strength and Schelling's greatness. Kant remarked that necessity and freedom constitute one of the antinomies of reason. The implications of the one vs. the other become soon evident in any philosophy and derived philosophy of religion. On this issue the relatively greater success of Hegelianism is not the sufficient basis for choice. And Schelling's insight into the radical freedom of the universe is still compelling. The freedom of the living God and of God's creatures constitutes a radical antithesis to Hegel's philosophy. Yet the emphasis on a living God and evolving humanity that collaborate in fulfilling themselves and each other is one that both Hegel and Schelling share and will to future philosophical attempts to grasp and articulate the meeting of the divine and the human.

END OF A QUEST

The post-Enlightenment quest for a philosophical Jesus was not a complete success and no effort was uncontested, either by philosophers or theologians. But by no means was the enterprise a failure. Each sought and found in accord with his own philosophical needs and requirements. Each set others looking. And yet the quest for a philosophical Jesus within the context of a philosophical Christianity ended almost abruptly. The vitriolic split between right- and left-wing Hegelians, the collapse of Hegelianism itself and the consequent diminishment of systematic philosophy all contributed. On the other hand, some had viewed the religious thought of Kant and Hegel as implicit atheism and the debates about Kant's *Opus Posthumum* and Hegel's *Lectures on the Philosophy of Religion* continue, although it seems clear that both Kant and Hegel were not personally atheistic.

But, for some, a philosophical Jesus was simply a human Jesus rather than an elevated or divinized humanity. Nor did they recognize Jesus as entitled to preeminence as symbol or representative of human fulfillment.

Theologians eventually rose to the challenge posed by Kant and Hegel to return to systematic theology, and the great work of Schleiermacher was in fact already underway before Hegel's tenure began in Berlin. That theologians did not find a "philosophical Jesus" to be theologically acceptable does not matter, of course, from the standpoint of philosophy. Rousseau, Kant, Hegel and Schelling were fully convinced that the philosophical meaning they ascribed to Jesus was the highest meaning possible and, since grounded in reason—God's supreme revelation, was better grounded than the supernatural meanings articulated by theology. But their ultimate failure to attain consensus among philosophers and to persuade the theologians allowed the eventual return of intellectual momentum to the camp of theology, although it has remained highly influenced by these same philosophers to this day.

Partially in response to the same Enlightenment stimulation that prompted Rousseau and post-Enlightenment philosophers and partially in response to the philosophical experiments to articulate a meaningful modern understanding of Jesus, theologians sought to return to the historical Jesus as the basis for a new modern understanding. David Friedrich Strauss's *Life of Jesus,* itself under the spell of Hegelianism, was the daring opening charge in what became a dramatic intellectual battle. But by that time the philosophical quest already seemed to have run its course, and the quest for the historical Jesus virtually eclipsed it.

This is not to suggest that philosophers no longer referred to Jesus or Christianity. But those who did so only furthered the course. The nineteenth century witnessed at least two more philosophical statements about Jesus. The chronologically later statement of Nietzsche, who generally spoke derisively of both Jesus and Christianity, was in the negative spirit of the Enlightenment that Rousseau and Kant had reacted to. On the other side was the statement of Kierkegaard, written in the spirit of theology. Through his pseudonym Johannes Climacus in *Philosophical Fragments,* the very name of which is an implicit attack upon Hegelianism, Kierkegaard set up a stark contrast: Jesus and Socrates. Socrates, he sought to persuade, was the "Christ" of reason and philosophy, not Jesus of Nazareth. Jesus of Nazareth was the Christ of faith, the stumbling block for reason.

Kierkegaard's declaration recalls the Enlightenment's own distinction between Jesus and Socrates and its daring suggestion that the wise Socrates and his tradition were a more suitable model for an age freeing itself from superstition and ignorance than a Palestinian Jesus and his morally questionable adherents. Kierkegaard-Climacus refused to accept Rousseau's philosophical divinization of the teacher of the gospel or any of the other speculative compromises suggested. Instead, while fully admiring the pagan sage, he insisted on the radical difference between Socrates and Christ and the meaning of the human fulfillment each taught. Kierkegaard's *Philosophical Fragments* was a proclamation that the quest for a philosophical Jesus was at an end. And, for better or worse, his insistent proclamation carried the day.

With that, the breach between reason and faith was declared reopened. Matters have largely remained at this mid-nineteenth-century impasse. Were the task to be taken up anew, it would now have to be a very different one. For the intellectually and culturally broadening impact of the Enlightenment means that any modern philosophy of religion will be less tied to Christian European culture. There is no cultural need for a "philosophical Jesus" since the theological Jesus has either been neutralized or become the exclusive province of faith. And the contemporary philosopher of religion, were he or she to undertake something similar, would feel compelled to fill out the philosophical pantheon with, among others, a philosophical Mohammed and a philosophical Gautama. A philosophical Jesus is not therefore impossible and, depending upon how one lines up along the reason-faith divide, one may still dare to say that philosophy— and perhaps philosophy alone—is still capable of achieving an intellectually tenable and satisfying statement on the meaning of Jesus and other teacher-models of human fulfillment. Needless to say, any such philosophical statement will not entirely conform to the norms of the theologians, any more than the efforts of Rousseau, Kant, Hegel, and Schelling did. The mistake of Hegel and Schelling was perhaps to try to create the impression that their speculative philosophies somehow represented a continuum with theology, although manifestly reformulated, and to entertain the hope that their philosophical speculations on Christianity and its Christ would somehow become normative for theology. Philosophy of religion is not theology, nor need it pretend to be. But our age which in knowing this has an intellectual freedom even greater than that known by Rousseau, Kant, Hegel, and Schelling is yet to witness a comparable effort.

SELECTED BIBLIOGRAPHY

GENERAL

Barth, Karl. *Protestant Theology in the Ninteenth Century: Its Background and History*, Trans. J. Bowden and B. Cozens. Valley Forge PA: Judson Press, 1973. German original: *Die Protestantische Theologie im 19. Jahrhundert* (1946).

Butler, Eliza Marian. *The Tyranny of Greece over Germany*. Cambridge, 1935; also Boston: Beacon Press, 1958.

Cohen, Hermann. *Religion der Vernunft aus den Quellen des Judentums (Eine Judische Religionsphilosophie)*. Weisbaden: Fourier Verglag, 1966. Reprint of 2nd edition of 1928.

Collins, James D. *The Emergence of Philosophy of Religion*. New Haven: Yale University Press, 1967.

_____.*God in Modern Philosophy*. Chicago: Regnery, 1959.

_____. *Interpreting Modern Philosophy*. Chicago: Regnery, 1959.

Copleston, Frederick. *A History of Philosophy*. Volume 6, Parts I and II. New York: Image Books, 1964.

Flügel, O. *Die Religionsphilosophie des absoluten Idealismus: Fichte, Schelling, Hegel, Schopenhauer*. Langensalza, 1905.

v. Glasenapp, Helmuth. *Image of India*. Trans. S. Ambike. New Delhi: Indian Council for Cultural Relations, 1973. German original: *Das Indienbild Deutscher Denker*.

Greene, Garrett. "Positive Religion in the Early Philosophy of the German Idealists." Ph.D. dissertation, Yale University, 1971.

Hartmann, Klaus, ed. *Die Ontologische Option*. Berlin: de Gruyter, 1976.

Hartmann, Nicolai. *Die Philosophie des deutschen Idealismus*. Berlin: de Gruyter, 1923-1929. Third edition, 1974.

Heine, Heinrich. *Religion and Philosophy in Germany*. Trans. John Snodgrass (1882). Boston: Beacon Press, 1959. German original: "Zur Geschichte der Relgion und Philosophie in Deutschland" (1833/34).

Hirsch, Emanuel. *Geschichte der neuern evangelischen Theologie*. Five volumes. Gütersloh, 1949-1954.

_____. *Die idealistische Philosophie und das Christentum: Gesammelte Aufsätze*. Gütersloh, 1926.

Jüngel, Eberhard. *Gott als Geheimnis der Welt*. Tübingen: Mohr, 1977.

Kroner, Richard. *Von Kant bis Hegel*. Two volumes. Tübingen: Mohr, 1977. First edition 1921.

Löwith, Karl. *Weltgeschichte und Heilsgeschichte. Die theologischen Voraussetzungen der Geschichtsphilosophie.* Fourth edition. Stuttgart, 1953.

Massey, Marilyn Chapin. *Christ Unmasked: The Meaning of "The Life of Jesus" in German Politics.* Chapel Hill: University of North Carolina Press, 1983.

Nauen, F. G. *Revolution, Idealism and Human Freedom.* The Hague: Martinus Nijhoff, 1977.

Proudfoot, Wayne. *God and the Self: Three Types of Philosophy of Religion.* Lewisburg PA: Bucknell University Press, 1976.

Rorty, Richard. *Philosophy and the Mirror of Nature.* Princeton: Princeton University Press, 1979.

Schulz, Walter. *Der Gott der Neuzeitlichen Metaphysik.* Pfullingen: Neske, 1957. Fifth Edition in 1974.

Schweitzer, Albert. *The Quest of the Historical Jesus.* Trans. W. Montgomery. New York: Macmillan, 1961. German original: *Von Reimarus zu Wrede,* 1906.

Smart, Ninian, John Clayton, Patrick Sherry, and Steven T. Katz, eds. *Nineteenth Century Religious Thought in the West.* Three volumes. Cambridge: Cambridge University Press, 1985.

Weischedel, Wilhelm. *Der Gott der Philosophen.* Two volumes. Darmstadt: WBG, 1971-1972.

Welch, Claude, ed. and trans. *God and Incarnation in Mid-19th Century German Theology.* New York, 1965.

Wessel, Leonard P. *G. E. Lessing's Theology: A Reinterpretation. A Study of the Problematic Nature of the Enlightenment.* The Hague, 1977.

I. ROUSSEAU

WORKS OF ROUSSEAU: FRENCH

Corréspondence Complète de Jean-Jacques Rousseau. Critical Edition. Ed. and annotated by R. A. Leigh. Geneve: Institut et Musée Voltaire, 1965-.

Oeuvres Complètes de Jean-Jacques Rousseau. Ed. Bernard Gagnebin and Marcel Raymond. Paris: Bibliotèque de la Pléiade, 1959-.

La "Profession de Foi du Vicaire Savoyard" de Jean-Jacques Rousseau. Ed. Pierre-Maurice Masson. Fribourg/Paris, 1914.

Rousseau's Religious Writings. Ed. Ronald Grimsley. Oxford: Oxford University Press, 1970.

WORKS OF ROUSSEAU: ENGLISH

The Confessions of Jean-Jacques Rousseau. Trans. J. M. Cohen. Baltimore: Penguin Books, 1954.

Émile. Everyman's Library. New York: Dutton, 1974. Originally published 1911.

Émile or On Education. Trans. with introduction and notes by Allan Bloom. New York: Basic Books, 1979.

Julie, or the New Eloise. Trans. and abridged by Judith H. McDowell. University Park PA, 1968.

The Social Contract. Trans. with introduction by Maurice Cranston. Baltimore: Penguin Books, 1968.

SELECTED SECONDARY SOURCES

Burgelin, Pierre. *La Philosophie de l'Existence de Jean-Jacques Rousseau.* Paris: Presses Universitaires de France, 1952.

_____. *Jean-Jacques Rousseau et la religion de Genève.* Genève, 1962.

Cassirer, Ernst. *The Question of Jean-Jacques Rousseau.* Trans. and ed. Peter Gay. Bloomington: Indiana University Press, 1963. German original: *Das Problem Jean-Jacques Rousseau,* 1932.

_____. *Rousseau, Kant, Goethe: Two Essays.* Trans. James Gutman, P. O. Kristeller, and J. H. Randall, Jr. Princeton: Princeton University Press, 1945. Introduction (1963) by Peter Gay.

Derathé, Robert. *Le Rationalisme de Jean-Jacques Rousseau.* Paris: Presses Universitaires de France, 1948.

Derrida, Jacques. *De la grammatologie.* Paris: Editions de Minuit, 1967.

Green, F. C. *Jean-Jacques Rousseau: A Critical Study of his Life and Writings.* Cambridge: Cambridge University Press, 1955.

Grimsley, Ronald. *Jean-Jacques Rousseau: A Study in Self-Awareness.* Cardiff: University of Wales Press, 1961.

_____. *Rousseau and the Religious Quest.* Oxford: Clarendon Press, 1968.

Hendel, Charles W. *Jean-Jacques Rousseau: Moralist.* Library of Liberal Arts. New York: Bobbs Merrill, 1962. Originally published: Oxford University Press, 1934.

Jacquet, Christian. *La Pensée Religieuse de Jean-Jacques Rousseau.* Louvain and Leiden, 1975.

Masson, Pierre-Maurice. *La Religion de Jean-Jacques Rousseau.* Three volumes. Paris: Librairie Hachette, 1916. Reprinted 1970.

Moreau, Joseph. *Jean-Jacques Rousseau.* Paris: Presses Universitaires de France, 1973.

Payot, Roger. *Jean-Jacques Rousseau ou la gnose tronquée.* Grenoble: Presses Universitaires de Grenoble, 1978.

Starobinski, Jean. *Jean-Jacques Rousseau: La Transparence et L'Obstacle.* With seven essays. Paris: Gallimard, 1971. Originally published: Paris: Librairie Plon, 1957.

II: KANT

WORKS OF KANT: GERMAN

Kants gesammelte Schriften. Akademie Ausgabe. Berlin, 1910-1972. twenty-eight volumes. Part I: Works (Vols. I-IX). Part II: Letters (Vols. X-XIII). Part III: Nachlass (Vols. XIV-XXIII). Part IV: Lectures (Vols. XXIV-XXVIII).

WORKS OF KANT: ENGLISH

Critique of Judgement. Trans. with introduction by J. H. Bernard. New York: Hafner Press, 1951.

Critique of Practical Reason. Trans. with introduction by Lewis White Beck. Library of Liberal Arts. Indianapolis: Bobbs-Merrill Co., 1956.

Critique of Pure Reason. Trans. F. Max. Müller. Garden City: Doubleday Anchor, 1966. First published 1881.

Dreams of a Spirit Seer. Trans. Emanuel Goerwitz. Ed. with introduction and notes by Frank Sewall. London and New York: Macmillan, 1900.

Foundations of the Metaphysics of Morals. Trans. Lewis White Beck, Ed., with critical essays, by Robert Paul Wolff. Library of Liberal Arts. Indianapolis: Bobbs-Merrill Co., 1969.

Kant on History. Trans. Lewis White Beck, Robert E. Anchor, and Emil L. Fackenheim. Library of Liberal Arts. Indianapolis: Bobbs-Merrill Co., 1963.

Lectures on Ethics. Trans. Louis Infield. Indianapolis: Hackett Publishing Co., n.d. Originally published 1930.

Lectures on Philosophical Theology. Trans. Allen W. Wood and Gertrude M. Clark. Introduction and notes by Allen W. Wood. Ithaca NY: Cornell University Press, 1978.

The Metaphysical Principles of Justice. Trans. John Ladd. Library of Liberal Arts. Indianapolis: Bobbs-Merrill Co., 1965.

The Metaphysical Principles of Virtue. Trans. James Ellington. Library of Liberal Arts. Indianapolis: Bobbs-Merrill Co., 1964.

Observation on the Feeling of the Beautiful and Sublime. Trans. John T. Goldthwait. Berkeley and Los Angeles: University of California Press, 1965.

On the Old Saw: That May Be Right in Theory But It Won't Work in Practice. Trans. E. B. Ashton. Introduction by George Miller. Philadelphia: University of Pennsylvania Press, 1974.

Political Writings. Trans. H. Reiss. Cambridge: Cambridge University Press, 1970.

Prolegomena to Any Future Metaphysics. A revision by Lewis White Beck of the Carus translation of 1902. Indianapolis: Bobbs-Merrill Co., 1950.

Religion within the Limits of Reason Alone. Trans. with introduction and notes by Theodore M. Greene and Hoyt H. Hudson. New York: Harper Torchbooks, 1960. Originally published: LaSalle IL: Open Court Publishing Co., 1934.

SELECTED SECONDARY SOUURCES

Beck, Lewis White. *Early German Philosophy.* Cambridge: Harvard University Press, 1969.

_____. *A Commentary on Kant's Critique of Practical Reason.* Chicago: University of Chicago Press, 1960.

Beyers, K. *Kants Vorlesungen über die philosophische Religionslehre.* Halle, 1937.

Bohatec, Josef. *Die Religionsphilosophie Kants in der "Religion innerhalb der Grenzen der bloßen Vernunft."* Hamburg, 1938. Reprinted: Hildesheim: Georg Olms, 1966.

Bruck, Jean-Louis. *La Philosophie Religieuse de Kant.* Paris: Aubier, 1968.

Cassirer, H. W. *A Commentary on Kant's Critique of Judgment.* New York: Barnes and Noble, 1970. Originally published 1938.

Copleston, Frederick. *Kant* in: *A History of Philosophy.* Volume 6, Part II. Garden City: Doubleday Anchor Books, 1960.

Despland, Michael. *Kant on History and Religion*. Montreal: McGill-Queen's University Press, 1973.

Eisler, Rudolph. *Kant-Lexicon*. Hildesheim/New York: G. Olms, 1977. Originally published: Berlin, 1930.

England, F. E. *Kant's Conception of God*. London: Allen and Unwin, 1925.

Fackenheim, Emil. "Kant and Radical Evil," *University of Toronto Quarterly* 23 (1954): 339-53.

_____. "Kant's Concept of History," *Kant-Studien* 48 (1956-1957): 391-98.

Greene, Theodore M. "The Historical Context and Significance of Kant's Religion." In *Religion within the Limits of Reason Alone*, trans. Theodore M. Greene and Hoyt H. Hudson. New York: Harper and Row, 1960.

Heidegger, Martin. *Kant und das Problem der Metaphysik*. Bonn, 1929. *Kant and the Problem of Metaphysics*, trans. James S. Churchill. Bloomington: Indiana University Press, 1962.

Herrero, Francisco Javier. *Religion y Historia en Kant*. Madrid: Gredos, 1975.

Herring, H. *Das Problem der Affektation bei Kant*. Kölin, 1953.

Jones, W. T. *Morality and Freedom in the Philosophy of Immanuel Kant*, Oxford, 1940.

Körner, W. S. *Kant*. Baltimore: Penguin Books, 1955.

Laberge, Pierre. *La Theologie Kantienne précritique*. Ottawa: Ed. de l'Universite de Ottawa, 1973.

Leisegang, H. "Kant und die Mystik." In *Philosophische Studien* (Berlin, 1949) 4-28.

Loetzsch, Frieder. *Vernunft und Religion im Denken Kants. Luthers Erbe bei Immanuel Kant*. Köln/Wien, 1976.

Malter, Rudolf. "Zeitgenössische Reaktionen auf Kants Religionsphilosophie. Eine Skizze zur Wirkungsgeschichte des Kantischen und des reformatorischen Denkens" in *Bewusst Sein: Gerhard Funke zu eigen*, ed. A. J. Bucher, H. Drüse, and Th. M. Seebohm (Bonn: Bouvier Verlag H. Grundmann, 1975) 145-67.

McCarthy, Vincent A. "Christus as Chrestus in Rousseau and Kant," *Kant-Studien* 73:2 (1982):191-207.

Michaelson, Gordon, E., Jr. "The Historical Dimensions of a Rational Faith: The Relation between History and Religion in Kant's Philosophy." Ph.D. dissertation, Princeton University, 1976.

Noack, Hermann. "Die Religionsphilosophie im Gesamtwerk Kants" Introduction to Immanuel Kant, *Die Religion innerhalb der Grenzen der bloßen Vernunft*, ed. Karl Vorländer, 7 Auflage (Hamburg: Felix Meiner Verlag, 1961) xi-lxxiv.

Paton, H. J. *The Categorical Imperative*. New York: Harper and Row, 1965.

Paulsen, Friedrich. *I. Kant: Life and Doctrine*. New York: Frederick Ugar, 1963. German original: *Immanuel Kant: Sein Leben und Seine Lehre*, 1898.

_____. *Kant: Philosoph des Protestantismus*. Berlin, 1899.

Reich, Klaus. *Rousseau und Kant*. Tübingen, 1936.

Schmalenback, H. *Kant's Religion*. Berlin, 1929.

Schultz, Uwe. *Immanuel Kant im Selbstzeugnissen und Bilddokumenten*. Reinbek bei Hamburg: Rowohlt, 1965.

Schultz, Werner. *Kant als Philosoph des Protestantismus.* Hamburg: H. Reich Evan. Verlag. 1960. Of particular interest is chapter 3: "Das Heilige bei Kant und Goethe."

Schweitzer, Albert. *Die Religionsphilosphie Kants von der Kritik der reinen Vernunft bis zur Religion innerhalb der Grenzen der blossen Vernunft.* Tübingen, 1899.

Stavenhagen, Kurt. *Kant und Königsberg.* Göttingen, 1949.

Strawson, Peter. *The Bounds of Sense.* London: Methuen, 1966.

Tonelli, Giorgio. "Conditions in Königsberg and the Making of Kant's Philosophy" In *Bewusst Sein: Gerhard Funke zu eigen,* ed. A. J. Bucher, H. Drüse, and Th. M. Seebohm (Bonn: Bouvier Verlag H. Grundmann, 1975) 126-44.

Vorländer, Karl. *Immanuel Kant: Der Mann und Das Werk.* Second, enlarged edition, with an essay—"Kants Opus Posthumum"—by Wolfgang Ritzel. Ed. Rudolf Malter. Hamburg: Felix Meiner Verlag, 1977. First edition: Leipzig, 1924.

Walsh, W. H. "Kant's Moral Theology" In *Proceedings of the British Academy* XLIX (1963) (London, 1964) 262-89.

Webb, C. C. J. *Kant's Philosophy of Religion.* Oxford: Clarendon Press, 1926.

Wolf, Robert Paul. *Kant: A Collection of Critical Essays.* Garden City: Doubleday, 1967.

Wood, Allen W. *Kant's Moral Religion.* Ithaca: Cornell University Press, 1970.

——————. *Kant's Rational Theology.* Ithaca: Cornell University Press, 1978.

III. HEGEL

WORKS OF HEGEL: GERMAN

Sämtliche Werke. Jubiläumsausgabe. Twenty-six volumes Ed. Hermann Glockner. Stuttgart: Fr. Frommmanns Verlag, 1927-1939

Werke in zwanzig Bänden. Ed. Eva Moldenhauer and Karl Markus Michel. Frankfurt am Main: Suhrkamp Verlag, 1971

Religionsphilosophie: Die Vorlesung von 1821. Ed. Karl-Heintz Ilting. Naples: Bibliopolis, 1978.

Vorlesungen über die Philosophie der Religion. Two volumes. Ed. Georg Lasson. Hamburg: Felix Meiner Verlag, 1925.

Vorlesungen über die Philosophie der Religion. Three volumes Ed. Walter Jaeschke. Hamburg: Felix Meiner Verlag, 1983–1985.

WORKS OF HEGEL: ENGLISH

On Art, Religion, Philosophy. Ed. J. Glenn Gray. New York: Harper and Row, 1970.

The Difference between Fichte and Schelling. Trans. H. S. Harris and W. Cerf. Albany: SUNY Press, 1977.

Early Theological Writings. Trans. T. M. Knox. Intro. and Fragments trans. Richard Kroner. Philadelphia: University of Pennsylvania Press, 1971. Originally published: University of Chicago Press, 1948.

Faith and Knowledge. Trans. Walter Cerf and H. S. Harris. Albany: SUNY Press, 1977.

Hegel: The Letters. Trans. Clark Butler and Christiane Seiler. Bloomington: Indiana University Press, 1984.

Lectures on the History of Philosophy. Trans. E. S. Haldane and F. H. Simson (1892). Three volumes. London: Routledge and Kegan Paul, 1955.

Lectures on the Philosophy of Religion. Three Volumes. Ed. Peter C. Hodgson. Berkeley: University of California Press, 1984-.

Lectures on the Philosophy of Religion. Three Volumes. Trans. E. B. Speirs and J. B. Sanderson (1895). London: Routledge and Kegan Paul, 1962.

The Phenomenology of Mind. Trans. of *Die Phänomenlogie des Geistes,* with intro. and notes, by J. B. Baillie. New York: Harper and Row, 1967. Originally published: Macmillan, 1910.

The Phenomenology of Spirit. Trans. of *Die Phänomenologie des Geistes* by A. V. Miller. Foreword by John N. Findlay. Oxford: Clarendon Press, 1977.

The Philosophy of History. Trans. J. Sibree. New York: Dover, 1956.

Three Essays, 1793-1795: The Tübingen Essay, Berne Fragments, The Life of Jesus. Ed. and trans. Peter Fuss and John Dobbins. Notre Dame IN: University of Notre Dame Press, 1984.

SELECTED SECONDARY SOURCES

Bloch, Ernst. *Subjekt-Objekt: Erläuterung zu Hegel.* Frankfurt: Suhrkamp, 1977. Original: 1927.

Bourgeois, B. *Hegel à Frankfort, ou Judaisme, Christianisme, Hegelianisme.* Paris: Vrin, 1970.

Bruaire, Claude. *Logique et religion chrétienne dans la philosophie de Hegel.* Paris: Editions de Sueil, 1964.

Chapelle, Albert. *Hegel et la religion.* Three volumes and annex. Paris: Ed. universitaires, 1964-1971.

Christensen, Darrell E., ed. *Hegel and the Philosophy of Religion: The Wofford Symposium.* The Hague, 1970.

Crites, Stephen D. *In the Twilight of Christendom.* Chambersburg PA, 1972. AAR Monographs, no. 2.

Dilthey, Wilhelm. *Gesammelte Schriften,* Band IV: *Die Jugendgeschichte Hegels und andere Abhandlungen zur Geschichte des deutschen Idealismus.* Berlin: Teubner, 1921.

Dupré, Louis. "The Despair of Religion," *Owl of Minerva* 16:1 (Fall 1984):21-30.

Fackenheim, Emil. *The Religious Dimension in Hegel's Thought.* Boston: Beacon Press, 1970. Original: Indiana University Press, 1967.

Findlay, John Neimeyer. *Hegel: A Re-examination.* London and New York: Allen and Unwin, 1958.

Fischer, Kuno. *Hegels Leben, Werke und Lehre.* Two volumes. Heidelberg, 1911.

Gadamer, Hans Georg. *Hegel's Dialectic.* Trans. P. Christopher Smith. New Haven: Yale University Press, 1976.

Garaudy, Roger. *Dieu est mort. Étude sur Hegel.* Paris, 1962.

Gray, J. Glenn. *Hegel and Greek Thought.* New York: Harper, 1968.

Greene, Murray. *Hegel on the Soul.* The Hague: Martinus Nijhoff, 1972.

Häring, T. *Hegel, sein Wollen und sein Werk.* Two volumes. Leipzig, 1929-1938.

Harris, H. S. *Hegel's Development I: Toward the Sunlight (1770-1801)*. Oxford: Clarendon Press, 1972.

_____. *Hegel's Development: Night Thoughts (Jena 1801-1806)*. Oxford: Clarendon Press, 1983.

Hartmann, Klaus. "Hegel: A Non-Metaphysical View" In A. MacIntyre, *Hegel: A Collection of Critical Essays* (Garden City: Doubleday, 1972) 101-24.

Haym, Rudolf. *Hegel und sein Zeit. Vorlesungen über Enstehung und Entwicklung, Wesen und Wert der Hegel'schen Philosophie*. Berlin, 1857.

Heede, Reinhard. "Hegel-Bilanz: Hegels Religionsphilosophie als Aufgabe und Problem der Forschung." In *Hegel-Bilanz: Zur Aktualität und Inakutalität der Philosophie Hegels,* ed. Reinhard Heede and Joachim Ritter (Frankfurt: Klostermann, 1973) 41-89.

_____. "Die göttliche Ide ihre Erscheinung in der Religion—Untersuchungen zum Verhältnis von Logik und Religionsphilosophie bei Hegel." Doctoral dissertation, Münster, 1972.

Hyppolite, Jean. *Genèse et structure de la Phénoménologie de l'esprit de Hegel*. Paris, 1946.

Hodgson, Peter. C. "Hegel's Christology: Shifting Nuances in the Berlin Lectures," *Journal of the American Academy of Religion* 53:1 (March 1985): 23-40.

Ilyin, Iwan. *Die Philosophie Hegels als Kontemplative Gotteslehre*. Bern: Francke Verlag, 1946.

Jaeschke, Walter. *Die Religionsphilosophie Hegels*. Darmstadt, 1983.

Kaufmann, Walter. *Hegel: A Reinterpretation*. New York: Doubleday, 1965.

Kojève, Alexander. *Introduction à la lecture de Hegel. Leçons sur la Phénoménologie de l'esprit*. Paris, 1947. English translation: *Introduction to the Reading of Hegel* (New York: Basic Books, 1969).

Kroner, Richard. "Kierkegaards Hegelverständnis," *Kant-Studien* 46:1 (1954-1955): 19-27.

Küng, Hans. *Menschwerdung Gottes*. Freiburg: Herder, 1970.

Lasson, Georg. *Einführung in Hegels Religionsphilosophie*. Leipzig, 1930.

_____. *Hegels Vorlesungen über die Philosophie der Religion*. Kritische Ausgabe. Leipzig: Meiner, 1925-1930.

Lauer, Quentin. "Hegel on Proofs for God's Existence," *Kant-Studien* 55 (1964): 443-65.

_____. *Hegel's Concept of God*. Albany: SUNY Press, 1982.

_____. *Hegel's Idea of Philosophy*. New York: Fordham University Press, 1971.

_____. *A Reading of Hegel's Phenomenology of Spirit*. New York: Fordham University Press, 1976.

Leonard, André. *La Foi chez Hegel*. Pars: Desclee, 1970.

Leuze, Reinhard. *Die außerchristlichen Religionen bei Hegel*. Göttingen: Vandenhoeck u. Ruprecht, 1975.

Löwith, Karl. "Hegels Aufhebung der christlichen Religion," *Hegel-Studien* 1 (1964): 193-236.

_____. *Von Hegel zu Nietzsche: Der revolutionäre Bruch im Denken des neunzehnten Jahrhunderts*. Fourth edition, Stuttgart: Kohlhammer, 1956. English translation: *From Hegel to Nietzshce*, trans. David E. Green (New York: 1964).

Lukács, Georg. *The Young Hegel*. Trans. Rodney Livingstone. Cambridge: MIT Press, 1976.

MacIntyre, Alasdair, ed. *Hegel: A Collection of Critical Essays*. Garden City: Doubleday, 1972.

Marcuse, Herbert. *Reason and Revolution: Hegel and the Rise of Social Theory*. New York: Oxford University Press, 1942.

Marx, Werner. *Hegel's Phenomenology of Spirit*. Trans. Peter Heath. New York: Harper and Row, 1975.

Perkins, Robert L. "Hegel and the Secularization of Religion," *International Journal for Philosophy of Religion* 1 (1970): 130-46.

Reardon, Bernard M. G. *Hegel's Philosophy of Religion*. London: Macmillan, 1977.

Ringleben, Joachim. *Hegels Theorie der Sünde. Die Subjectivitäts-Logische Konstruktion eines Theologischen Begriffs*. Berlin. de Gruyter, 1977.

Renz, Horst. *Geschichtsgedanke und Christusfrage. Zur Christusanschauung Kants und deren Fortbildung durch Hegel*. Göttingen, 1977.

Ritter, Joachim. *Hegel and the French Revolution*. Trans. R. D. Winfield. Cambridge: MIT Press, 1982.

Rosen, Stanley. *G. W. F. Hegel*. New Haven: Yale University Press, 1974.

Schlitt, Dale M. *Hegel's Trinitarian Claim*. Leiden: Brill, 1983.

_____. "The Whole Truth: Hegel's Reconceptualization of the Trinity," *The Owl of Minerva* 15 (1984): 169-82.

Schmidt, Erik. *Hegels Lehre vom Gott*. Gütersloh, 1952.

_____. *Hegels System der Theologie*. Berlin: de Gruyter, 1974.

Schönfelder, W. *Die Philosophen und Jesus Christus*. Hamburg: Meiner Verlag, 1949.

Taylor, Charles. *Hegel*. Cambridge: Cambridge University Press, 1975.

Theunissen, Michael. "Die Dialektik der Offenbarung," *Philosophisches Jahrbuch* 72:1 (1964): 134-60.

_____. *Hegels Lehre vom absoluten Geist als theologisch-politisches Traktat*. Berlin: de Gruyter, 1970.

_____. *Sein und Schein*. Frankfurt: Suhrkamp. 1978.

Toews, John E. *Hegelianism: The Path Toward Dialectical Humanism 1805-1841*. Cambridge, 1981.

Vancourt, Raymond. *La pensée religieuse de Hegel*. Paris: Presses Universitaires de France, 1965.

Wagner, Falk. *Der Gedanke der Persönlichkeit Gottes bei Fichte und Hegel*. Gütersloh: Mohn, 1971.

Wahl. Jean. *Le malheur de la conscience dans la philosophie de Hegel*. Second edition. Paris, 1951.

Weidmann, Franz. *Georg Wilhelm Fridrich Hegel im Selbstzeugnissen und Bilddokumenten*. Reinbek bei Hamburg: Rowolt, 1965.

Westphal, Merold E. *History and Truth in Hegel's Phenomenology*. Atlantic Highlands NJ: Humanities Press, 1979.

Williamson, Richard K. *Hegel's Philosophy of Religion*. Albany: SUNY Press, 1984.

Yerkes, James. *The Christology of Hegel*. Albany: SUNY Press, 1982.

IV. SCHELLING

WORKS OF SCHELLING: GERMAN

Friedrich Wilhelm Joseph von Schellings sämmtliche Werke. Stuttgart and Augsburg: J. G. Cotta'scher Verlag, 1856-1857. Reprinted Darmstadt: WBG, 1975.

Grundlegung der positiven Philosophie: München Vorlesung WS 1832/3 und SS 1833, ed. Horst Fuhrmans. In *Schelling: Grundlegung der positiven Philosophie.* Torino, 1972.

WORKS OF SCHELLING: ENGLISH

The Ages of the World. In Frederick de Wolfe Bolman, Jr., ed., *Schelling: The Ages of the World.* New York: Columbia University Press, 1942.

Bruno, or On the Natural Principle of Things. Ed. and trans. Michael G. Vater. Albany: SUNY Press, 1984.

On "The Deities of Samothrace." Trans. Robert F. Brown. Missoula MT: Scholars Press, 1977.

Of Human Freedom. Trans. James Gutman. Chicago: Open Court, 1936.

——————. "System of Transcendental Idealism" (Selections). Trans. Albert Hofstadter. In *Philosophies of Art and Beauty: Selected Readings in Aesthetics from Plato to Heidegger,* ed. A. Hofstadter and R. Kuhns (New York: Modern Liberary, 1964).

On University Studies. In *Schelling: On University Studies.* Trans. E. S. Morgan. Athens: Ohio University Press, 1966.

SELECTED SECONDARY SOURCES

Benz, Ernst. *Theogony and the Transformation of Man in F. W. J. Schelling.* Eranos Yearbook V. New York: Pantheon, 1964.

Baumgartner, Michael, ed. *Schelling.* Freiburg/München, 1975.

Bréheier, Émile. *Schelling.* Paris, 1912.

Bruaire, Claude. *Schelling.* Paris, 1970.

Dempf, Alois. "Kierkegaard hört Schelling," *Philosophisches Jahrbuch* 65 (1957): 141-61.

Fackenheim, Emil. "Schelling's Conception of Postive Philosophy," *Review of Metaphysics* 7 (1954): 563-82.

——————. "Schelling's Philosophy of Religion," *University of Toronto Quarterly* 22 (1952): 1-17.

Fischer, Kuno. *Schellings Leben, Werke und Lehre.* Second edition. Heidelberg, 1923.

Fuhrmans, Horst. "Der Ausgangspunkt der Schellingschen Spätphilosophie," *Kant-Studien* 48:2 (1956-1957): 302ff.

——————. "Der Gottesbegriff in Schellingschen positiven Philosophie." In Anton Mirko Koktanek, ed., *Schelling-Studien: Festgabe für Manfred Schröter zum 85. Gerburtstag* (München/Wien: Oldenbourg, 1965) 9-47.

——————. *Schellings letzte Philosophie.* Berlin, 1940.

——————. *Schellings Philosophie der Weltalter.* Düsseldorf: Schwann, 1954.

Gray-Smith, Rowland. *God in the Philosophy of Schelling.* Philadelphia, 1933.

Habermas, Jürgen. *Das Absolute und die Geschichte. Von der Zwiespältigkeit in Schellings Denken.* Bonn, 1954.

Hayes, Victor C. "Myth, Reason and Revelation: Perspective on and a Summary Translation of Three Books from Schelling's Philosophy of Mythology and Revelation." Ph.D. dissertation, Columbia University, 1970.

_____. "Schelling: Persistent Legends, Improving Image," *Southwestern Journal of Philosophy* 3 (1972): 63-73.

Heidegger, Martin. *Schellings Abhandlung über Das Wesen der Menschlichen Freiheit (1809).* Ed. Hildegard Feick. Tübingen: Niemeyer, 1971.

Jankélévitch, Vladimir. *L'odysée de la conscience dans la dernière philosophie de Schelling.* Paris, 1933.

Kasper, Walter. *Das Absolute in der Geschichte. Philosophie und Theologie der Geschichte in der Spätphilosophie Schellings.* Mainz: Matthias-Grünewald Verlag, 1965.

_____. "Krise und Neuanfang der Christologie im Denken Schellings," *Evangelische Theologie* 33 (1973): 366ff.

Koktanke, Anton Mirko, ed. *Schelling-Studien: Festgabe für Manfred Schröter zum 85. Gerburtstag.* München/Wien: Oldenbourg, 1965.

_____. *Schellings Seinslehre und Kierkegaard.* Oldenbourg Verlag, 1962.

Jaspers, Karl. *Schelling.* 1955.

Marcel, Gabriel. *Coleridge et Schelling.* Paris: Aubier-Montaigne, 1971.

Marheineke, Philipp. *Zur Kritik der Schellingschen Offenbarungsphilosophie.* Berlin, 1843.

Marquet, Francois. *Liberte et existence: Étude sur la formation de la philosophie de Schelling.* Paris: Gallimard, 1973.

Ogierman, H. "Zur christlichen Philosophie der späten Schelling," *Theologie und Philosophie* 50 (1975): 321-46.

O'Meara, Thomas. *Romantic Idealism and Roman Catholicism: Schelling and the Theologians.* South Bend: University of Notre Dame Press, 1982.

Pölcher, Helmut. "Schellings Auftreten in Berlin (1841) nach Hörerberichten," *Zeitschrift für Religions- und Geistesgeschichte* 3 (1954):193-215.

Schlutter, Karl. "Schelling und die Christologie." Ph.D. dissertation, University of Göttingen, 1915.

Schulz, Walter. *Die Vollengung des Deutschen Idealismus in der Spätphilosophie Schellings.* Second edition. Pfullingen: Neske, 1975. First edition: Stuttgart: Kohlhammer, 1955.

Staiger, Emil. "Schellings Schwermut," *Studia Philosophica* 14 (1954): 112-45.

Theunissen, Michael. "Die Aufhebung des Idealismus in der Spätphilosophie Schellings," *Philosophisches Jahrbuch* 83 (1976): 1-29.

_____. "Die Dialektik der Offenbarung: Zur Auseinandersetzung Schellings und Kierkegaards mit der Religionsphilosophie Hegels," *Philosophisches Jahrbuch* (1964-1965):134-60.

Tillich, Paul. *The Construction of the History of Religion in Schelling's Positive Philosophy: Its Presuppositions and Principles.* Trans. Victor Nuovo. Lewisburg PA: Bucknell University Press, 1974.

_____. *Mysticism and Guilt-Consciousness in Schelling's Philosophical Development.* Trans. Victor Nuovo. Lewisburg PA: Bucknell University Press, 1974. Original: *Mystik und Schuldbetwußtsein in Schellings philosophischer Entwicklung,* volume 1 of *Paul Tillichs Gesammelte Werke* (Stuttgart, 1959) 11-108.

Tilliette, Xavier. "Schelling: Le conflit des Interpretations," *Etudes Philosophiques* 2 (1974):211-20.

_____. "Schelling Critique de Hegel," *Hegel-Studien* 4 (1969):193-203.

_____. *Schelling im Spiegel seiner Zeitgenossen.* Torino, 1974.

_____. *Schelling, une philosphie en devenir.* Two volumes. Paris: Vrin, 1970.

Weischedel, Wilhelm. *Jakobi und Schelling: Eine philosophisch-theologische Konfrontation.* Darmstadt: WBG, 1969.

White, Alan. *Schelling: An Introduction to the System of Freedom.* New Haven: Yale University Press, 1983.

Zeltner, Hermann. *Schelling.* Fromanns: Stuttgart, 1954.

_____. *Schelling Forschung seit 1954.* Darmstadt: WBG, 1975.

INDEX

DATE DUE
